Information and Human Values

Synthesis Lectures on Information Concepts, Retrieval, and Services

Editor

Gary Marchionini, *University of North Carolina, Chapel Hill*

Search-Based Applications: At the Confluence of Search and Database Technologies
Gregory Grefenstette, Laura Wilber
2010

Information Concepts: From Books to Cyberspace Identities
Gary Marchionini
2010

Estimating the Query Difficulty for Information Retrieval
David Carmel, Elad Yom-Tov
2010

iRODS Primer: Integrated Rule-Oriented Data System
Arcot Rajasekar, Reagan Moore, Chien-Yi Hou, Christopher A. Lee, Richard Marciano, Antoine de Torcy, Michael Wan, Wayne Schroeder, Sheau-Yen Chen, Lucas Gilbert, Paul Tooby, Bing Zhu
2010

Collaborative Web Search: Who, What, Where, When, and Why
Meredith Ringel Morris, Jaime Teevan
2009

Multimedia Information Retrieval
Stefan Rüger
2009

Online Multiplayer Games
William Sims Bainbridge
2009

Information Architecture: The Design and Integration of Information Spaces
Wei Ding, Xia Lin
2009

Automated Metadata in Multimedia Information Systems: Creation, Refinement, Use in Surrogates, and Evaluation

Michael G. Christel

2009

© Springer Nature Switzerland AG 2022
Reprint of original edition © Morgan & Claypool 2014

Information and Human Values
Kenneth R. Fleischmann

ISBN: 978-3-031-01204-4 print
ISBN: 978-3-031-02332-3 ebook

DOI 10.1007/978-3-031-02332-3

A Publication in the Springer series
SYNTHESIS LECTURES ON INFORMATION CONCEPTS, RETRIEVAL, AND SERVICES #31
Series Editor: Gary Marchionini, University of North Carolina, Chapel Hill

Series ISSN   1947-945X Print   1947-9468 Electronic

Information and Human Values

Kenneth R. Fleischmann

University of Texas at Austin

SYNTHESIS LECTURES ON INFORMATION CONCEPTS, RETRIEVAL, AND SERVICES #31

ABSTRACT

This book seeks to advance our understanding of the relationship between information and human values by synthesizing the complementary but typically disconnected threads in the literature, reflecting on my 15 years of research on the relationship between information and human values, advancing our intellectual understanding of the key facets of this topic, and encouraging further research to continue exploring this important and timely research topic.

The book begins with an explanation of what human values are and why they are important. Next, three distinct literatures on values, information, and technology are analyzed and synthesized, including the social psychology literature on human values, the information studies literature on the core values of librarianship, and the human-computer interaction literature on value-sensitive design. After that, three detailed case studies are presented based on reflections on a wide range of research studies. The first case study focuses on the role of human values in the design and use of educational simulations. The second case study focuses on the role of human values in the design and use of computational models. The final case study explores human values in communication via, about, or using information technology. The book concludes by laying out a values and design cycle for studying values in information and presenting an agenda for further research.

KEYWORDS

human values, value-sensitive design, core values of librarianship, social psychology, science and technology studies, information studies

Contents

List of Figures

Acknowledgments

This material was based in part upon work supported by the National Science Foundation under grant numbers SES-0217996, SES-0521117, SES-0646392, IIS-0729459, and IIS-0734894. Any opinions, findings, and conclusions or recommendations expressed in this material are those of the author and do not necessarily reflect the views of the National Science Foundation.

Many thanks to Gary Marchionini for encouraging me to write and submit this book, and for providing wise and helpful advice throughout the writing and editing process. Many thanks to Gary, Barbara Wildemuth, and Cory Knobel for their constructive and insightful feedback on an earlier draft of this book. Many thanks also to Diane Cerra and Deb Gabriel at Morgan & Claypool for their help in making the publication of this book possible.

This book has benefited from conversations and collaborations with a list of individuals too long to name here. Most notably, I would like to thank my current and former doctoral students An-Shou Cheng, Clay Templeton, and Jes Koepfler, as well as other collaborators in previous projects, most notably including Jordan Boyd-Graber, Emi Ishita, Doug Oard, Russ Robbins, Katie Shilton, and Al Wallace, as well as Justin Grimes, Paul Jaeger, Kari Kelton, Yasuhiro Takayama, Yoichi Tomiura, Ping Wang, Zheng Wang, and Yingjie Zhou. It is important to note that although the research projects described in previous publications were collaborative in nature, this summary and analysis of these projects and their implications is my own, and I bear full responsibility for any errors therein.

Many thanks to my colleagues at the School of Information at the University of Texas at Austin for providing such a warm (emotionally, as well as climatologically) environment for facilitating scholarship. It is truly a pleasure and honor to be able to work with such talented and personable colleagues.

Many thanks to those who have helped me along the way, including my late mother, Chris Fleischmann, my father, Bob Fleischmann, my grandmother, Meredith Goetz, my late grandfather, Burton Goetz, and my great aunts, Anne Goetz and Dorothy Theller; also, my doctoral advisor, David Hess, as well as the many other great teachers I encountered in my undergraduate and graduate studies, particularly Woody Gaines, Cynthia Beall, Randy Beer, Langdon Winner, Ron Eglash, Kim Fortun, Mike Fortun, Atsushi Akera, Nancy Campbell, and Ray Fouché.

Finally, my greatest thanks go to the love of my life, Bo Xie, and to our incredible son, Austin Burton Fleischmann, for their patience and love as I wrote and edited this book. Every day is something new to look forward to thanks to them. Austin was born eight months ago today, and at the same time, it feels like he was born yesterday and that he's always been a part of our family.

CHAPTER 1

Why Human Values?

Is all information equally valuable to all individuals? Clearly, the answer to this question is no. Sometimes, this is due to situational factors. For example, knowing if a pitch is a fastball or a slider is less valuable ten seconds after it is thrown than ten seconds before. It is also more valuable to the batter than to the on-deck hitter. However, in some cases, there are trans-situational factors at play, referred to as human values (Hitlin and Piliavin, 2004). For example, a wine review might have less value to a teetotaler than to a wine connoisseur, and a review of a nearby Brazilian steakhouse might have more value to a steak aficionado than to vegetarian. In these cases, the value of the information (or the lack thereof) is tied to what these individuals value in life. To understand if and to what extent information will be valuable to a particular audience, it is important to understand what they value.

Why values instead of value? Economics, like other social science disciplines, is sometimes portrayed as reducing human behavior to a single variable, the financial/value/capital dimension. In this sense, an economist tends to see the world in terms of monetary value much as an anthropologist tends to see culture or a sociologist tends to see institutions. While each of these dimensions do carry significant explanatory power, no single dimension can explain all human behavior. While monetary value is an important value, there are many others that are much harder to quantify financially. In ethics, the two are often confounded. For example, Quinn (2013), in explaining act utilitarianism, first defines it in terms of maximizing happiness, and then quickly goes into a cost-benefit analysis scenario where everything is monetized (including the value of wildlife habitat, purely in human financial terms). However, reducing the world to this one dimension is quite limiting and problematic, especially when considering other cultures that may not have the same capitalist system as the contemporary U.S., such as animal social groups, many indigenous tribal cultures, and the fictional needs-based economy within Star Trek. Focusing on values allows us to consider a broad range of motivating factors that drive human behavior, including but not limited to monetary value.

The value of information to an individual is unavoidably tied to that individual's core values. We value different things, to different degrees, and those values tend to be formed early in our lives and to remain relatively static for most of our lives (Hitlin and Piliavin, 2004). Those values are influenced by family, community, and, increasingly, media. It is important to consider both how values are formed early in life and the effects that they then have throughout one's life.

Values serve as bridges between the individual and the social. Individuals hold values, but others influence the formation of those values. Families, groups, and societies tend to share common values, although not necessarily universally. It is possible to use values to differentiate among individuals within and across societies (Schwartz, 2007). Further increasing the extent to which values are fixed and enduring, people embed their values in both information and technology (Johnson, 1997). Values provide an important window for understanding the relationship between people, information, and technology.

In the information age, it is vitally important to understand human values. For example, targeted marketing typically seeks to predict individual behaviors and preferences through demographics. While demographics are an important piece of the puzzle, they do not explain the full range of human diversity, and are not always directly correlated with decision-making. Including consideration of human values provides a more complete picture of an individual, and has significant predictive power in anticipating behaviors and preferences, as well as attitudes (Schwartz, 2007).

Understanding human values has clear commercial implications, but it is also important for any aspect of life that involves decision-making. For example, in public health interventions, values can affect how a message is perceived, and should be factored into the delivery of the message. Similarly, in politics, the crafting of rhetoric can appeal to particular values that may be widely held. Information professionals need to consider the role of human values in their work, as the systems and services that they develop and maintain should be sensitive to the values of their users.

Ethical decision-making is a critical competency in contemporary society. Often, ethical decision-making is viewed as stemming partly or completely from morality, which conveys a sense of good versus evil and right versus wrong. But we need to ask right or wrong for whom, in what situations, and in what ways? Morality is a false binary that seeks to universalize yet always comes with slightly different caveats. Killing is wrong, right? Well, not in self-defense. And certainly not in defense of one's country, provided you serve in your nation's armed forces (note that the victim, perhaps increasingly over time, does not need to serve in the armed forces of the other nation) and your two countries are officially at war. Also, not animals, if one is planning to eat them (cruelty is another matter, but killing animals for consumption is typically not considered cruelty, whereas killing a human for consumption is typically considered the most appalling and cruel taboo). It seems that morality is very limiting in its explanatory power in helping us to understand ethical decision-making.

Why focus on values instead of morality? Morality involves doing the right thing, and the emphasis is on ensuring that everyone does the right thing. However, not everyone agrees on what the right thing is. It is reasonable to presume that many, perhaps even most (but unfortunately likely not all) politicians want the best for their country, they just want different bests. The main difference between politicians is not that, for example, one party acts morally while the other acts immorally, but rather, that they have legitimate differences in their values, which in turn guide their decision-making. For example, both the George W. Bush and Obama administrations have employed controversial tactics in the name of protecting homeland security in a post-911 world. However, critics have criticized both administrations as infringing on privacy in the process. This ongoing conflict between security and privacy is one of the major value conflicts within our current political discourse, and, interestingly, it cuts across the political spectrum, uniting hawkish Democrats and neo-conservative Republicans in favor as well as libertarian Republicans and civil liberties–oriented Democrats in opposition. Thus, the critical piece to understand is the underlying value conflict that drives these different but genuine positions on critical issues.

Similarly, while there is always the potential that a few information professionals and information technology developers have malicious intentions, by and large the vast majority are again well intentioned. However, they are not necessarily always completely aware of the role that values play in the design and use of information services and technologies, and may unwittingly act against the values of their users. They may do things the way they were taught without thinking, which Langdon Winner (1987) terms technological somnambulism, or sleepwalking through technology design. My goal is not to improve the morality of these professionals, as the vast majority have the best of intentions, and such an orientation is typically formed very early in life, long before the start of their college education let alone their careers. Rather, my goal is to highlight value conflicts and illustrate where their values might differ from those of their users, so that they can make more conscious and informed ethical decisions about design to ensure that they work to support rather than undermine the values of their users.

In this book, I seek to build a unified framework of the relationship between the values of people, information, and technology. These three dimensions of values are represented by three distinct literatures, with few significant overlaps or bridges between them to date. The primary literature on the values of people comes from social psychology, although sociologists and anthropologists, among others, have also done work on this topic. The main literature on values in information is found within the field of library and information science, although it is also relevant in communication and media studies. Finally, the dominant literature on values in technology is contained within the field of human-computer interaction, although there is also salient work within science and technology studies and the philosophy of technology. Chapter 2 will explore each of these literatures in turn and then bridge these literatures.

In Chapter 3, I will consider the role of human values in the design and use of educational simulations, and what it can teach us about values and information more broadly. It will include three sections. The first two sections include the role of frog dissection simulation in secondary biology education and the role of gross anatomy simulation in graduate medical education. The third section will discuss efforts to develop and evaluate an educational simulation for information ethics education.

Chapter 4 will consider the role of human values in the design and use of computational models, again exploring what it can teach us about values and information more broadly. The first section will tackle the topics of trust, transparency, and accountability. The second section will examine the importance of value conflicts in design. The final section will discuss the roles of professionalism and codes of ethics.

Chapter 5 will explore human values in communication via information technology, about information technology, or using information technology. The first section discusses manual content analysis of values contained within texts. The second section considers how crowdsourcing can be used to scale up this content analysis. The third section explores efforts to further scale up this content analysis of human values through automation using techniques from computational linguistics and natural language processing.

Chapter 6 will develop a values and design cycle that illustrates how to detect and resolve value conflicts through design. Finally, Chapter 7 will lay out an agenda for further research, encouraging the field to undertake new projects to expand our understanding of the relationship between information and human values.

My goals for this book are to shed further light on an important topic, to connect literatures that have to this point developed fairly independent of each other, to reflect on my fifteen years of research on the relationship between information and human values, to advance our intellectual understanding of the key facets of this topic, and to encourage further research to continue exploring this important and timely research topic.

CHAPTER 2

Approaches to Understanding Values

Various strands of literature in different fields have explored the importance of human values, but for the most part, these strands have remained distinct and disconnected. The goal of this chapter is to weave these strands together into a tapestry that we will employ throughout the remainder of the book. First, we will explore the values held by people, primarily through the literature on the social psychology of human values. Next, we will examine how human values influence information, focusing particularly on the core values of librarianship within the field of library and information science. After that, we will consider how human values are embedded in technology, relying predominantly on the values and information technology design literature from human-computer interaction. Finally, we will explore the interaction and synergy among these diverse literatures, and determine how they can potentially be unified to develop a theoretical understanding of the relationship between information and human values.

2.1   SOCIAL PSYCHOLOGY OF HUMAN VALUES

How can we understand, explain, and predict human behavior? Each of the social sciences, in its own way, seeks to answer this question. Sociology focuses on human behavior at a societal level, predominantly using macro-level quantitative analysis. Anthropology instead looks at the level of groups, with ethnography serving as a way to develop a deep understanding and a thick description of constructs such as culture and power. Much of psychology focuses on the level of the individual, with more interest in the internal workings of the human psyche rather that consideration of interpersonal factors. Economics cuts across all of these levels, through both macroeconomic and microeconomic approaches, but with a particular focus on capital that restricts inquiry. Similarly, communication science and political science focus predominantly on communication and politics, respectively. While each of these lenses has merit, history has shown that no one of these approaches can definitively explain human behavior.

Rather than restrict ourselves to any one disciplinary perspective, instead it is useful to consider how we might usefully unify these intellectually diverse threads. While psychology often focuses on personality, which is understood largely as an internal and intrinsic property of individuals, anthropology focuses on culture, a construct that spans large groups of people and that is greater than any one individual. Are there any concepts that span these and other intellectual spaces?

What motivates human behavior? Is it internal forces or external? Are we a product of nature or nurture? Clearly, these are false dichotomies of the type that Haraway (1988) so eloquently argues against. Instead, these are processes of mutual constitution. The collective shapes the individual. The individual shapes the collective. Personality is not transferrable enough to explain this type or process. Culture does not take into sufficient consideration individual variation. We need a different concept to unify the opposite ends of the false dichotomy.

Are there factors that influence or determine the behavior of individuals, and which are transmitted among individuals within a group or society? Each person has a different set of principles that help to govern their behavior, which are influenced by and in turn influence others. Sociologists, anthropologists, psychologists, and others refer to these principles as human values. Human values intermediate between the individual and the group. In some ways, they are universal in nature, illustrating commonalities among societies (Schwartz, 1994). In other ways, they illustrate the diversity of individuals and societies (Parsons, 1935).

A wide range of definitions of values have been developed over time. For example, the sociologist Parsons defines values as, "the creative element in action in general, that element which is causally independent of the positivistic factors of heredity and environment" (1935: 306). Building on Parsons, sociologist Spates defines values as, "those moral beliefs to which people appealed for the ultimate rationales of action" (1983: 28). Hitlin and Piliavin (2004) summarize a number of definitions of values, including anthropologist Kluckhohn's definition of a value as "a conception, explicit or implicit, distinctive of an individual or characteristic of a groups, of the *desirable*, which influences the selection from available modes, means, and ends of action" (1951: 395, cited in Hitlin and Piliavin, 2004). They also provide a definition by psychologist Rokeach that values are "enduring beliefs that a specific mode of conduct is personally or socially preferable to an opposite or converse mode of conduct or end-state of existence" (1973: 5, cited in Hitlin and Piliavin, 2004). Finally, they provide a definition from sociologist Marini, that values are "evaluative beliefs that synthesize affective and cognitive elements to orient people to the world in which they live" (2000: 2828, cited in Hitlin and Piliavin, 2004).

Perhaps the most widely used definition is provided by Schwartz: "A value is a belief pertaining to desirable end states or modes of conduct, that transcends specific situations, guides selection or evaluation of behavior, people, and events, and is ordered by importance relative to other values to form a system of value priorities" (1994: 20). Hofstede reviewed existing value inventories and "found three types of values: those dealing with our relationships with (1) other people, (2) things (our nonhuman environment), and (3) our own inner selves and God" (2001: 8). Similarly, Cheng and Fleischmann review many of these as well as other definitions of values and summarize them as follows: "values serve as guiding principles of what people consider important in life" (2010: 2).

Values have far-reaching impacts. For example, Rokeach states: "Values are determinants of virtually all kinds of behavior that could be called social behavior or social action, attitudes, and ideology, evaluations, moral judgments and justifications of self to others, and attempts to influence others" (1973: 5). Similarly, Schwartz writes that value priorities can play a key role in "explaining socially significant attitudes and behaviour at both the individual and the country level" (2007: 197). Understanding values provides tremendous explanatory power for understanding human behavior at the individual, group, and societal levels.

Rokeach (1973) separates values into two categories, instrumental values and terminal values. Instrumental values focus on the intentions behind human behavior, while terminal values focus on its consequences. Schwartz incorporates both types of values in his work, resulting in a hybrid set of values that mix intentions and consequences, introducing grammatical inconsistencies.

The Holy Grail in social science research on human values is the development of a universally applicable inventory of human values. Schwartz (1994), building on Rokeach and others, is widely recognized as having best achieved this goal, through surveys conducted in 44 countries. Schwartz's value hierarchy includes three levels. At the top level, he identifies two dimensions of values, conservation vs. openness to change and self-enhancement vs. self-transcendence. From these, he derives ten value types (universalism, benevolence, conformity, tradition, security, power, achievement, hedonism, stimulation, and self-direction) and 56 basic human values.

Universalism is found in the self-transcendence quadrant of Schwartz's (1994) value dimensions. Universalism includes the values of *protecting the environment, a world of beauty, unity with nature, broad-minded, social justice, wisdom, equality, a world at peace,* and *inner harmony.* Basically, universalism represents the instinct to seek harmony among people, between people and both animals and the environment, and within oneself. The values contained within it are quite diverse; for example, while *social justice* and *equality* might seem synonymous at first blush, recent debates about affirmative action revolve about arguments about whether or not the undeniably socially just approach of giving preference to individuals from underrepresented ethnic groups in the interest of making, for example, college student bodies more diverse and more representative of their communities and the nation, are denounced by some as unequal. Similarly, being *broad-minded* about people who do not share other values such as *protecting the environment* or *a world at peace* creates a potential paradox. Universalism is one of Schwartz's most complex value types.

Benevolence is also found in the self-transcendence quadrant of Schwartz's (1994) value dimensions. Benevolence includes the values of *helpful, honest, forgiving, loyal, responsible, true friendship, a spiritual life, mature love,* and *meaning in life.* Benevolence is about being good, in a moral sense. There is also the potential for value conflicts among these values; for example, friendship and love can often come into conflict, as, in some cases, can being honest and being loyal (if, for example, a friend asks you to lie).

Conformity is found in the conservation quadrant of Schwartz's (1994) value dimensions. Conformity includes the values of *politeness, honoring of parents and elders, obedient,* and *self-discipline.* Conformity involves maintaining social norms in treatment of others, particularly elders and superiors. It is interesting to note that there are broad differences, both cross-culturally and cross-temporally, between perceptions of these values; for example, behaviors that might seem polite in one culture or time period may be offensive in others, sometimes with disastrous consequences.

Tradition is also found in the conservation quadrant of Schwartz's (1994) value dimensions. Tradition includes the values of *devout, accepting my portion in life, humble, moderate, respect for tradition,* and *detachment.* Tradition involves playing one's role within the time-honored boundaries of a society. It is important to note that these values can be portrayed and perceived differently across different cultures and individuals. For example, while *detachment* often has negative connotations within many Western cultures, it shares a kinship with the process of attaining nirvana, the final goal of Buddhism (Obeyesekere, 1985). Similarly, perceptions of *respect for tradition* might vary widely depending on if the tradition is a traditional dance or a traditional ritual human sacrifice.

Security is also found in the conservation quadrant of Schwartz's (1994) value dimensions. Security includes the values of *clean, national security, social order, family security, reciprocation of favors, healthy,* and *sense of belonging.* Securing involves looking out for the well being of oneself and others, particularly family and friends. Many of the biggest political debates today center on security values, such as debates about the Iraq War and drone strikes, which are defended on the basis of *national security,* and arguments against gun control that are often predicated on *family security.* The gift exchange economy fostered by *reciprocation of favors* has positive implications in Chinese culture (*guanxi*) while a fairly negative one in U.S. political discourse (influence peddling).

Power is found in the self-enhancement quadrant of Schwartz's (1994) value dimensions. Power includes the values of *social power*, *authority*, *wealth*, *preserving my public image*, and *social recognition*. Power involves one's control and influence in society, as well as worth from an economic perspective. As noted above, values are often reduced to a single dimension of value in a monetary sense, which matches the value of *wealth*, which includes currency as well as material possessions. Like the other values in Schwartz's inventory, these are not universally coded as positive or negative, but rather their meaning is highly contextual depending on the individual, culture, and situation.

Achievement is also found in the self-enhancement quadrant of Schwartz's (1994) value dimensions. Achievement includes the values of *successful*, *capable*, *ambitious*, *influential*, *intelligent*, and *self-respect*. Achievement relates to the success one achieves, largely in a more positive light than power. In a sense, social power and authority are also achievements, but the values within the achievement value type, by contrast, do not necessarily come at the expense of others. Like the other value types, Schwartz's achievement mixes what Rokeach (1973) terms instrumental values and terminal values. Instrumental values, such as *capable* or *ambitious*, refer to the means, while terminal values, such as *successful*, refer to the ends. Interestingly, Schwartz's value hierarchy can be seen as encompassing both ethical approaches that focus on intentions, such as deontology and virtue ethics, as well as ethical approaches that focus on outcomes, such as consequentialism. However, it is important to note that Schwartz takes a descriptive rather than normative tact; it is not his intent to pass value judgments but rather to accurately study and explain the values of different individuals and cultures.

Hedonism is the one value-type that does not fit squarely into one quadrant of Schwartz's (1994) hierarchy; rather, it spans the quadrants of self-enhancement and openness to change. Hedonism includes the values *pleasure* and *enjoying life*. Hedonism reflects the gratification of a wide range of desires. It is self-enhancement in the sense that it is inward-looking rather than outward-looking; and it is openness to change in the sense that it may involve trying new things or seeking particular experiences.

Stimulation is found in the openness to change quadrant of Schwartz's (1994) value dimensions. Stimulation includes the values of *daring*, a *varied life*, and *an exciting life*. Stimulation focuses on seeking new experiences. Stimulation reflects a larger generational divide typically found between conservation and openness to change. Typically, the perception is that most people seek stimulation early in life and security later in life. However, there are certainly exceptions to this rule, such as President George H.W. Bush's longstanding predilection for skydiving, which is how he celebrated his 75th, 80th, and 85th birthdays.

Finally, self-direction is also found in the openness to change quadrant of Schwartz's (1994) value dimensions. Self-direction includes the values of *creativity*, *curious*, *freedom*, *choosing own goals*, and *independent*. Self-direction focuses on the ability to determine one's own fate. Self-direction is inward-looking while power is outward-looking. Interestingly, while *freedom* and *independent* might lead one to go against conservation values, they might also in some cases cause one to follow conservation values. The self-direction values are particularly salient in academia, where intellectual freedom and the ability to choose one's research direction and projects are typically held in high regard, although in some cases there are conflicts where a need for wealth to successfully complete projects (particularly in the hard sciences and engineering) leads to the tailoring of one's research to suit the desires of funding agencies.

The Schwartz (1994) Value Inventory is a highly nuanced and sophisticated tool for viewing the social world in terms of human values. It has been widely used and has great influence. Later in this chapter, we will discuss other value inventories from the library and information science and human-computer interaction literatures, and consider the commonalities and contrasts among these different perspectives. To recap, Figure 2.1 illustrates the value types situated in the four quadrants of the Schwartz Value Inventory.

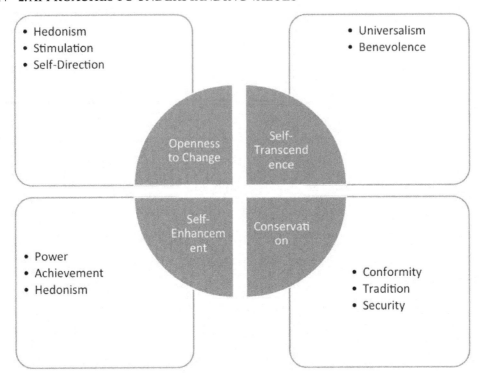

Figure 2.1: The Schwartz Value Inventory.

Most value inventories, including the Schwartz (1994) Value Inventory, were developed through and applied to survey research. Surveys, as self-report data, are subject to several types of bias, including participation bias (since participants can choose to participate or not, and there may be some systematic bias in why some people choose to participate while others choose not to) and response bias (since participants may consciously or subconsciously alter their responses to match their perception of the social expectations or desire of the researcher). In contrast, observational methods, such as content analysis, provide the opportunity to observe human behavior in the wild, without self-selection and social desirability. Thus, there may be some advantages to employing content analysis rather than just surveys (Fleischmann et al., 2009a).

Research on human values, primarily within social psychology but also scattered across the social sciences, provides a strong foundation for research on values beyond just people. Information and technology are created by humans with values, and used by humans with values. Herein lies the potential for significant value conflicts between the values embedded in information and technology by their designers and the values experienced by users. The remainder of this chapter focuses on the role of values in information and technology design and use.

2.2   VALUES AND INFORMATION USE

Of course, people don't exist in a vacuum, and in particular, they don't exist without information. To understand the values of people, it is important to understand how those values shape and are shaped by the information that they produce and consume. Scholars in the field of library and information science have been studying the production and consumption of information since the inception of the field, and have often paid particular attention to the role of human values.

The role of human values in information is embodied most directly by the American Library Association (ALA), the leading organization for librarians, particularly public librarians. Librarianship is a service-oriented profession, devoted to serving the needs of users (Fleischmann, 2010a). The ALA has played a prominent advocacy role, particularly in recent years, in public debates such as that surrounding the USA Patriot Act (Phenix and McCook, 2005). This is not to say, of course, that librarianship has been perfect in this regard; in particular, a bias toward so-called high culture, which tends to be biased in terms of particular socio-economic and demographic factors, has historically impaired the field's diversity and openness to different perspectives (Wiegand, 1999). While the field still has a long way to go, overall it is a fairly pioneering and inclusive profession in terms of its emphasis on human rights and how information can serve a diverse range of users (Phenix and McCook, 2005).

Over the years, ALA released many documents that described the values advocated by the organization, such as the "ALA Code of Ethics" (ALA, 1939/2008), the "Library Bill of Rights" (ALA, 1939/1996), the "Freedom to Read" statement (ALA, 1953/2004), and "Libraries: An American Value" (ALA, 1999). In 2004, ALA further codified its values by releasing the "Core Values of Librarianship", which includes 11 human values. The Core Values of Librarianship include: *Ac-*

cess, Confidentiality/Privacy, Democracy, Diversity, Education and Lifelong Learning, Intellectual Freedom, The Public Good, Preservation, Professionalism, Service, and *Social Responsibility.*

Access includes ensuring equal access to all materials by all people (ALA, 2004). Access can be seen as an application of equality, and is certainly motivated by a social justice perspective. As a very universalistic value, in terms of Schwartz's (1994) dimensions, access best fits within the self-transcendence quadrant. Access is technically nontrivial, in the sense that it requires providing materials in a way that is as broadly usable as possible, such as providing audio or braille versions of books and closed captioning for videocassettes. Truly universal access seems like a very high bar to pass; indeed, everyone's reading or viewing experience is different, regardless of differences in eyesight, hearing, literacy, etc. However, it is certainly an admirable goal and one that libraries have worked long and hard to achieve, which has certainly provided many more people access to many more materials.

Confidentiality/privacy focuses on restricting access to users' records (ALA, 2004). Interestingly, while libraries strive to make their materials as accessible as possible, they resist similar efforts to gain access to the private records of users. Indeed, the ALA and many individual librarians have fought directly against the provisions of the USA Patriot Act that seek to give law enforcement access to library records. In some cases, librarians have used creative means to accomplish this goal, such as failing to keep records, as it is hard to seize records that are not kept. In terms of Schwartz's (1994) dimensions, confidentiality/privacy likely fits best within the self-enhancement quadrant, as it is highly related to power, and specifically to the value of *preserving my public* image, as one's "face" is highly interconnected with the information available about someone these days.

Democracy focuses on libraries' contributions to ensuring and maintaining an informed citizenry, an essential component of any successful democracy (ALA, 2004). Democracy is also related to self-direction and can be situated within Schwartz's (1994) openness to change quadrant. Providing access to information is a critical component of informing the electorate. Democracy as ALA defines it also includes free expression, which again relates to self-direction.

Diversity emphasizes the importance of serving a wide range of users (ALA, 2004). As a universalistic value, this fits within the self-transcendence quadrant of Schwartz's (1994) value inventory. Diversity overlaps with access, but has less emphasis on equity and more emphasis on being broad-minded. Diversity includes both serving a diverse range of individuals and also catering to and providing a diverse range of perspectives. The emphasis on diversity found at ALA is compatible with Haraway's (1991) notions of situated knowledges and the view from below which emphasize the importance of considering a broad range of perspectives and further arguing that the perspectives of the disempowered may be more useful than those of the empowered because they may have a better vantage point on how that power was achieved and enacted.

Education and lifelong learning emphasizes the role that libraries play in educating the public from young to old age (ALA, 2004). This value fits into Schwartz's (1994) value type of achievement, and is situated in his self-enhancement quadrant. Many library programs are specifically geared toward educational goals, and public libraries are a key site for informal learning among youth, preschool aged, school-aged, and beyond. School libraries play an important role in formal education, as do academic libraries, law libraries, and medical libraries.

Intellectual freedom focuses on the importance of free expression and resistance of censorship (ALA, 2004). As a self-direction value, intellectual freedom can be found in Schwartz's (1994) openness to change quadrant. Indeed, all of the values within self-direction apply to intellectual freedom; most obviously, it is a subtype of *freedom*, but it also involves protecting creativity and curiosity, as well as individuals' ability to choose their own goals and remain independent. The ALA regularly organizes events such as Banned Books Week that documents the historical challenges to intellectual freedom and reinforces its importance. Perhaps the most creative invocation of this value was the "book burning" campaign waged by Troy Public Library in Michigan, where the library successfully avoided a steep budget cut by indirectly (through satire) connecting a reduction of library services to facilitating Nazi-style book burning (Edwards et al., 2013).

The public good stresses the positive role that libraries play in society (ALA, 2004). Indeed, public libraries historically have been one of the most trusted public institutions, and are looked to and depended on during times of crisis (Jaeger and Fleischmann, 2007). The public good, as a benevolence value, fits into Schwartz's (1994) self-transcendence quadrant. Libraries act toward the public good in many ways, including by upholding the values listed in the Core Values of Librarianship. In this way, libraries uphold the values of *helpful* and *responsible*.

Preservation emphasizes the need to maintain access to information over time, combatting forces such as the potential decay of physical materials and the degree to which virtual materials become obsolete due to hardware and software changes (e.g., decline of floppy drives; legacy file formats) (ALA, 2004). Preservation clearly fits within the conservation quadrant of Schwartz's (1994) value inventory, and is most closely connected to the value type of tradition. Indeed, one of the key roles of public libraries is to preserve the traditions of the past as embedded in physical and digital materials.

Professionalism involves meeting the public expectations for information professionals (ALA, 2004). Part of this emphasis is rooted in education, in the sense that professional education can help imbue this value, but ultimately it gets down to values such as honesty. As such, it fits into Schwartz's (1994) benevolence value type, within his self-transcendence quadrant.

Service is perhaps the foremost value of librarians, who strive to serve the needs of their users (ALA, 2004). As Fleischmann (2010a) argues, librarians were the original user-centered designers, in designing library services and resources to meet the needs of users. Service also fits into Schwartz's (1994) benevolence value type within his self-transcendence quadrant. In particular, it focuses on the values of *helpful* and *responsible*.

The final core value of librarianship is *social responsibility*, which involves the responsibilities of libraries toward their communities and society at large (ALA, 2004). Libraries have a social responsibility to improve society and to make it a better place for everyone, even those who are not direct users of library services and resources. As above, social responsibility can be identified with the value of *responsible*, and fits into the benevolence value type of Schwartz's (1994) self-transcendence quadrant.

To summarize, Figure 2.2 depicts how the Core Values of Librarianship would be situated within the four quadrants of the Schwartz Value Inventory. We can observe several patterns that emerge. There is at least one value from the Core Values of Librarianship within each of the quadrants of the Schwartz Value Inventory. There is an uneven weighting, with self-transcendence being the dominant quadrant for this set of values. The juxtaposition of the two inventories reveals key value conflicts between the values within the Core Values of Librarianship. For example, *access* and *confidentiality/privacy* are found on opposite sides of the Schwartz Value Inventory, and they often come into conflict, as access focuses on giving everyone access to everything, and confidentiality/privacy involves giving some people less access to some information. Similarly, there is a potential conflict between *service* and *education and lifelong learning*, as service might involve giving users what they want when and how they want it, while education and lifelong learning is about giving them the tools to be self-sufficient, similar to the difference between giving a person a fish (to eat for a day) and teaching that person to fish (to eat forever). Finally, there is a potential value conflict across the opposite diagonal, between *intellectual freedom* and *preservation*, in cases where the author's intent is to avoid, rather than facilitate, preservation, such as William Gibson's "Agrippa," an electronic poem that was designed to self-erase after playing (Marshall and Golovchinsky, 2004). In such cases, the act of preservation might violate the creator's intent and, potentially, their intellectual freedom to either facilitate or avoid preservation. These value conflicts underline the challenge of following any specific prescription of behavior based on values; even the core values of this one professional association can come into conflict with each other, let alone with other such lists of values. Codes of ethics and lists of human values rarely provide any guidance about what to do when difference principles come into conflict with each other. It is particularly interesting to examine these value conflicts that arise at the intersection of values and information use.

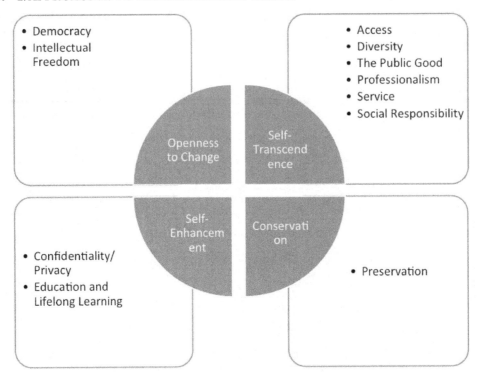

Figure 2.2: The Schwartz Value Inventory and the Core Values of Librarianship.

2.3   VALUES AND TECHNOLOGY DESIGN

Finally, values not only shape and are shaped by information, but also shape and are shaped by computing and information technology. The designers of information technologies need to ensure that their innovations take into consideration the values of users and other stakeholders. The two main strands in this literature are the value sensitive design (Friedman, 1996) and values in design (Knobel and Bowker, 2011; Nissenbaum, 2005) literatures, and other related literatures that fit into the broad umbrella of user-centered design, include culture-centered computing (Hakken, 1991), worth-centered development (Cockton, 2006), participatory design (Schuler and Namioka, 1993), experience-centered design (Wright & McCarthy, 2010), contextual design (Beyer and Holtzblatt, 1998), usability engineering (Rosson and Carroll, 2002), reflective design (Sengers et al., 2005), and interaction design (Rogers et al., 2011).

User-centered design primarily focuses on the needs of users, which in software engineering is referred to as requirements analysis or requirements engineering (Pohl, 2010). While needs are certainly important, needs are highly contextual and situational. Further, they do not fully encompass the user as a human being; people working in various parts of an enterprise are not merely components in an assembly line, but rather, are real, breathing human beings with distinct personalities, perspectives, and values. By designing for users' values, along with their needs and other aspects, information technology designers can help ensure that their products will be used and successful in the marketplace.

In their formulation of value sensitive design, Friedman, Kahn, and Borning (2006) explicitly focus on human values with ethical import. They argue that it is particularly important for designers to be aware of and sensitive to these values. Specifically, based on the expansive literature within value sensitive design and beyond, they identify a set of 13 Human Values with Ethical Import. Those values include *human welfare, ownership and property, privacy, freedom from bias, universal usability, trust, autonomy, informed consent, accountability, courtesy, identity, calmness,* and *environmental sustainability.*

Human welfare involves the physical, psychological, and material well-being of people (Friedman et al., 2006). Friedman and Kahn (2008) discuss several examples of technologies that can have life-and-death consequences, such as the infamous Therac-25 laser surgery tool that injured and killed cancer patients, as well as information technologies implicated in nuclear disasters such as Chernobyl. Human welfare is situated within the self-transcendence quadrant of Schwartz's (1994) value inventory, within the value type of benevolence. Specifically, Schwartz's value of *helpful* involves working for others' welfare. Information technology designers should work to ensure that their creations can be used to contribute to, rather than detract from, human welfare.

Ownership and property involves property rights such as the right to own an object (or information), manage it, use it, profit from it, and give it to others (Friedman et al., 2006). Ownership and property fits in the power value type within the self-enhancement quadrant of Schwartz's (1994) value inventory.

Specifically, it most clearly invokes Schwartz's value of *wealth*, which involves material possessions as well as money, but also potentially invokes the values of *social recognition* (people respecting the property rights of others) and *preserving my public image* (which particularly involves owning information about oneself, an important issue in the social media age). Indeed, this leads to issues such as who owns photographs taken by one person of other people, in public or private spaces. Further, ownership and property is a particularly salient point in the digital age, where it has become so easy to duplicate information using DVD-R drives or the cloud rather than monks.

Privacy refers to self-determination about what information about oneself an individual can communicate to others (Friedman et al., 2006). As noted above in the discussion of confidentiality/privacy within the core values of librarianship (ALA, 2004), privacy fits in the power value type of the self-enhancement quadrant of Schwartz's (1994) value inventory. As Nissenbaum (1999) explains, privacy has, over an extended period of time, been one of the most contentious aspects of computing. Privacy often conflicts with the trend toward personalization, since personalizing software to particular individuals, such as advanced recommender systems, is facilitated through data collection about the user, which may or may not involve informed consent, which will be discussed in more detail below. Threats to privacy are one of the primary factors motivating the ongoing emphasis on personal information management. Information technology has radically transformed the prior divide between public and private spaces, with significant implications for privacy.

Freedom from bias involves avoiding systematic inequalities and unfairness directed toward individuals or groups (Friedman et al., 2006). Many forms of bias predate computing, but can be perpetuated through new technologies. Other new forms of bias can be created by computers themselves, depending on their design and its alignment with the needs and abilities of their users. Finally, computers can also be used to create new social biases. Freedom from bias fits into the universalism value type of the self-transcendence quadrant of Schwartz's (1994) value inventory. Specifically, it invokes the values of *equality*, where equal treatment without bias or prejudice is emphasized; *social justice*, wherein such bias can be seen as unjust; and *broad-minded*, in the sense that bias is typically manifested at least in part by narrow-mindedness.

Universal usability involves ensuring that all people are able to use information technologies (Friedman et al., 2006). Specifically, according to Shneiderman (2000), universal usability confronts three main challenges: technology variety, user diversity, and gaps in user knowledge. Technology variety is related to the properties of the technology itself, in terms of how it interfaces with other technologies. User diversity reflects the properties of the user, and considers that users have different needs, abilities, and values. Gaps in user knowledge represent the interface between people and technology, interestingly putting the onus on the user to gain knowledge rather than on designers to develop technologies that are as intuitive and user-friendly as possible. Like access within the core values of librarianship (ALA, 2004), *universal usability* is situated within the universalism value type of the self-transcendence quadrant of Schwartz's (1994) value inventory. However, it is interesting to note that *universal usability* puts more emphasis on the technology and how it is designed, while (universal) access puts more emphasis on the use of the technology in and of itself. Advocates of *universal usability* argue that it is not enough for a person to have physical access to a technology, they must also be able to use it. However, even a perfectly useful technology is not helpful to someone who cannot afford to use it or who otherwise does not have access to it.

Trust involves maintaining confidence from others, and acting in ways to uphold that confidence (Friedman et al., 2006). *Trust* is vitally important for the success of both information (Kelton et al., 2008) and information technology (Nissenbaum, 1999). If people do not trust information or information technology, they will not use them; for example, if people read health information and do not trust the source, they are less likely to employ the advice in their everyday lives; similarly, if people do not trust online encryption of information such as credit card numbers, they are less likely to order products online. *Trust* is critical for maintaining both a successful society and a successful economy, as if people do not trust others, they will not trust the civic organizations and businesses essential for keeping both running. Within Schwartz's (1994) value inventory, *trust* is located within the benevolence value type of the self-transcendence quadrant.

Autonomy involves people's ability to maintain their own independence, autonomy, and agency (Friedman et al., 2006). Schwartz's (1994) value inventory would identify *autonomy* as part of the self-direction value type within the openness to change quadrant. Specifically, self-direction includes the values of *freedom*, *choosing own goals*, and *independent*. To be truly autonomous, one has to have the freedom to choose their own goals and to act independently. This emphasis on human autonomy can be seen, at least in part, as a reaction against the potential for increased autonomy and agency by non-human actors, most notably, by technology (Fleischmann, 2007a). Winner (1977) provides a careful analysis of both the perception and reality of the prospect of technology infringing on human autonomy and agency. It is important to situate such concerns about technological agency usurping human agency within the broader historical context, where throughout the history of human society, there has been the perception of an inherent conflict between structure and agency, originally realized as a confrontation between social structure and individual agency (Giddens, 1979). Technology merely makes these structures more rigid and visible—for example, the ability with most graphic design programs to easily make an organizational chart that makes static and visible an existing but perhaps previously unspoken hierarchy. *Autonomy* involves maintaining one's independence and agency in the face not only of increasingly complex technologies but also increasingly complex social structures and forms of governance.

Closely related to the notion of autonomy is the notion of *informed consent* (Friedman et al., 2006). To be autonomous, one must not only have the power to choose but also the power to know, and informed consent safeguards this ability. *Informed consent* is the notion that people should be informed of the conditions and implications of their participation in something, and given the ability to choose whether or not to consent. *Informed consent* is a hallmark of human subjects research, and according to the Belmont Report (Department of Health, Education, and Welfare, 1979), it is an application of the three basic ethical principles of respect for persons, beneficence, and justice. *Informed consent* is an interesting value to situate within the Schwartz (1994) Value Inventory, as the "informed" aspect is most similar to *honest*, *helpful*, and *responsible* within the value type of benevolence, while the "consent" refers most directly to the self-direction value type, particularly values such as *freedom*, *independent*, and *choosing own goals*. Further, there is an implicit emphasis on *social justice* involved in the process and goals of *informed consent*. *Informed consent* fits within both the self-transcendence and openness-to-change quadrants of Schwartz's Value Inventory.

Accountability refers to the notion that people are responsible for the consequences of their actions and that people should be held responsible if things go badly (Friedman et al., 2006). *Accountability* fits within the benevolence value type of the self-transcendence quadrant of the Schwartz (1994) Value Inventory, which is where Schwartz situates the value responsible. Another Schwartz value within that value type is *honest*, which is clearly related to *accountability*, because it requires people to be honest, open, and transparent about what they have done so that they can be held accountable if necessary. It is important to note that *accountability* is not identical to responsibility; for example, with the notion that "The Buck Stops Here" on President Truman's desk, the president is accountable for anything that happens in his administration, even if he is not directly responsible; for example, if a government official lies, cheats, or steals, while the action was not taken by the president, the president hired and supervises that individual (or hired the person that hired the individual, etc.) and is accountable for any actions that individual takes. Similarly, if hardware and/or software errors occur, in the case of Therac-25 or the massive Toyota vehicle recalls due to issues with brakes, the individuals in charge of the organizations are accountable, even if they did not write the deficient line of code or design the defective parts.

Courtesy involves treating people with consideration and politeness (Friedman et al., 2006). Schwartz (1994) situates the value of *politeness*, along with other potentially courteous behaviors such as *obedient* and *honoring of parents and elders* within the conformity value type of the conservation quadrant. *Courtesy* is typically considered a uniquely human concept, but information technologies can also use politeness, from a sign or a book to a robot or an intelligent agent. Within information technology design, it is possible to see *courtesy* on at least two levels, including the degree of courtesy that designers show to users and the degree to which they design software to be courteous. Specifically within the case of intelligent agents, there may be differences in how positive and negative feedback is received—referring to the user by name is fine for positive feedback ("good job, Lisa"), but may appear discourteous and condescending when done in negative feedback ("incorrect, try again, Lisa").

Identity invokes how people feel about themselves (Friedman et al., 2006). Identities are both static and dynamic, in that in some ways one's identity tends to persist over time, such as, for example, one's name or ethnicity, while other aspects of one's identity change over time, for example, becoming a professional or parent. Much like informed consent, *identity* is a sufficiently nuanced value that it is difficult to locate within a single Schwartz (1994) value type or even quadrant. One aspect of *identity* is *meaning in life*, which is found within the benevolence value type of the self-transcendence quadrant of the Schwartz Value Inventory. There is also an element of *inner harmony*, which is also within the self-transcendence quadrant, but in the universalism value type. Finally, there is a degree of *self-respect* and *choosing own goals* that also positions identity in the self-direction value type of the openness-to-change quadrant. There are also values within other value types, at the opposite end of Schwartz's spectra, that also seem potentially relevant at first glance, such as *preserving public image*, *social recognition*, *sense of belonging*, and *accepting my portion in life*, but those are all more closely tied to outside perceptions rather than one's internal self-identity.

Calmness is an indication of a composed and peaceful state of mind (Friedman et al., 2006). Perhaps the Schwartz (1994) value most closely related is *inner harmony*, which is found, along with *world at peace*, in the universalism value type of the self-transcendence quadrant of the Schwartz Value Inventory. The idea here is that technologies should facilitate calmness and tranquility. Perhaps the most salient example here is a study by Kahn et al. (2008) to compare three treatments: an office with no window, an office with a traditional window, and an office with a large-screen plasma display showing images of the outside world. The simple technology of providing a window did improve calmness, measured through biometric factors such as heart rate. However, the high-tech displays did not appear to have any effect on calmness relative to the blank wall. It is important to note that the importance of this value is highly contextual depending on the user, the activity or tasks, and the environment. For example, while calmness is a reasonable value to emphasize for office workers, it may be problematic if taken to extremes with, for example, truckers doing long overnight cross-country drives.

Finally, *environmental sustainability* involves building technologies that are sustainable in the long run and do not endanger the natural world (Friedman et al., 2006). Environmental sustainability aligns with several values within the universalism value type of the self-transcendence quadrant of the Schwartz (1994) Value Inventory. The strongest connections are with *unity with nature* and *protect environment*, although there is also a potential connection to *a world of beauty*, insofar as it denotes natural beauty; beauty is, notoriously, in the eye of the beholder. Notions of environmental sustainability invoke the more cyclical views of many Native American groups rather than the traditional linear progress narrative of the dominant modern European and North American societies. While making technology environmentally sustainable is a very positive goal, it is important to note that, like many things, it can be taken to extremes. A satirical example is a mock news story by the *Onion* about a new electric car that guarantees to reduce the driver's carbon footprint to zero; by killing her/him and converting their body into a biodegradable fertilizer. There are real life examples as well; Westerners often lament the destruction of rainforests and other habitats of endangered animals in places like Madagascar; however, if one is faced with the choice of eating an endangered animal or starving to death, turning one's back on environmental sustainability in favor of personal survival is quite understandable. Interestingly, Fleischmann (2003, 2004) found that simulation designers were able to latch onto the environmental sustainability message of animal advocacy groups, which document the hazards not only to animals but also to the environment and humans as a result of the widespread removal of animals from their natural habitats to be put to use as educational tools in middle-school biology classrooms; indeed, Digital Frog 2 was marketed as "Frog-Friendly Software" denoting a mild degree of animal advocacy as well as a broader message of environmental sustainability.

Figure 2.3 depicts how the Human Values with Ethical Import (Friedman et al., 2006) relate to the Schwartz (1994) Value Inventor. Again, most of the values are clustered within the self-transcendence quadrant, although again all four quadrants are represented. As in the case of the Core Values of Librarianship (ALA, 2004), the Schwartz Value Inventory reveals several key value conflicts within the Human Values with Ethical Import. For example, the value of *autonomy* emphasizes allowing people as much self-control and self-determination as possible, which might in turn conflict with the value of *politeness*, which is about conforming to societal norms. Interestingly, this reveals a contrast between the values ascribed to designers and those ascribed to users. Friedman and her colleagues are more concerned about users' *autonomy*, and also with *politeness* on the part of designers in ensuring that their technologies are not insulting to users. Another value conflict is between *human welfare* and *ownership and property*, as one can imagine cases where ownership can lead to negative effects in terms of human welfare, such as someone in a third world country dying of a disease that can be cured by a very expensive medicine that they cannot afford. This scenario is much more complex in real life, as advocates of patents argue that they are necessary to ensure that companies will invest money to develop these life-saving cures in the first place, and also many pharmaceuticals have charitable programs that give medicines for free or reduced cost to those in need; however, the point still stands that there are likely individuals who have died or otherwise been adversely affected by the inability to afford expensive medications. Finally, there is also a potential conflict between *accountability* and *privacy*, as holding people accountable involves knowing who did what, which in some cases might violate privacy. Again, though, Friedman and colleagues are focused on ensuring the privacy of users, and in holding designers accountable. It is important to also consider, though, cases where the privacy of designers is in question, and where users need to be held accountable. However, the Human Values with Ethical Import were developed in light of the power dynamic between technology designers and users, whereby users have much less power than designers. As such, it can be seen as an effort to level the playing field between designers and users, by ensuring that designers are sensitive to users'

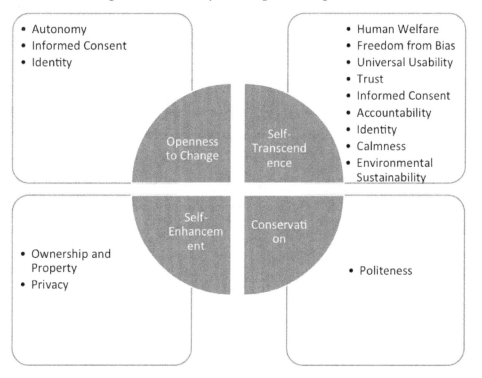

values.

Figure 2.3: The Schwartz Value Inventory and Human Values with Ethical Import.

2.4   VALUE CONFLICTS IN INFORMATION TECHNOLOGY DESIGN AND USE

Based on this analysis, we can now look more carefully both within and across the Core Values of Librarianship (ALA, 2004) and Human Values with Ethical Import (Friedman et al., 2006) by contextualizing them within the framework of the Schwartz (1994) Value Inventory.

In addition to conflicts within the Core Values of Librarianship (ALA, 2004) and the Human Values with Ethical Import (Friedman et al., 2006), there are also conflicts between the two value inventories. The biggest value conflict at the intersection of information and technology is the conflict between *access* from the Core Values of Librarianship and *ownership and property* from the Human Values with Ethical Import. This conflict reveals a larger divide between these two inventories and communities; librarians typically focus on and promote universal access, emphasizing cases where users should have the right to various forms of information and information technology; whereas designers have a vested interest in ensuring that their ownership and property in the form of patents and copyright are respected. There is a clear divide between producers and consumers, reflective of a larger divide between, for example, the ALA and the Association for Computing Machinery (ACM), which is reflected in differences in their respective codes of ethics, with ALA more focused on users and society, and ACM more focused on designers and corporations.

CHAPTER 3

Education and Human Values

Information is embedded within other human activities. In particular, information is frequently embedded within communication, education, and technology. This chapter explores case studies within each of these three areas. First, in the realm of education, we will consider three cases, including biology education, medical education, and information ethics education, focusing in particular on the use of simulations within each of these areas. Next, for technology, we will look at computational modeling, including value conflicts; issues of trust, transparency, and accountability; and professionalism and codes of ethics. Finally, we will explore values in communication, focusing on values in communication about IT, in communication through IT, and using IT to study values in communication.

This section explores the role of human values in educational simulations within three domains: biology education, medical education, and information ethics education. In each of these domains, information is embedded in and conveyed through these educational technologies, and values are in turn embedded within that information, including which information to provide and how to provision that information.

3.1 BIOLOGY EDUCATION AND HUMAN VALUES

Biology education has traditionally relied heavily on dissection as the hands-on laboratory element and as the way to educate students about human anatomy and physiology, usually by using lower animals to serve as substitutes for the human body, given the many complications of human dissection which will be discussed in more detail below, and which are further amplified for K–12 biology education, particularly at the middle school and high school levels. Frogs are the most classic animal used for K–12 biology dissection labs, but other animals used include earthworms, crayfish, fetal pigs, and cats (Fleischmann, 2004).

The use of animals in K–12 dissection has attracted some controversy and opposition. First, there are safety considerations, including concerns about the safety of the preservatives used to embalm the animal specimens. In an attempt to diffuse such concerns, dissection supply companies such as Carolina Biological Supply developed newer and supposedly safer alternatives to the traditional formaldehyde (which is now known to be a carcinogen), and markets these products under names such as Carosafe to emphasize the safety of the preservative. Further, even the implements used to conduct the dissection can be, in the wrong hands, potentially deadly weapons. As a consequence, many educational institutions, particularly alternative schools or night schools for students with documented disciplinary issues, tend to avoid incorporating dissection into their curriculums, due to concerns for the safety of the students and teachers from intentional (in particular) or accidental misuse of the dissection tools by students (Fleischmann, 2004).

Beyond concerns for the safety of students and teachers conducting and observing the dissections, there are also concerns about the sourcing of dissection specimens. In some cases, these concerns are motivated from an animal advocacy perspective, with some individuals and organizations making the case that animals should have rights and should not be used as means to an end in biology education or, in some cases, even in biomedical research. Further, others are concerned about the message that animal dissection sends about animal cruelty and the value of animals within society. Beyond just animal rights, others are concerned about the removal of these animals from their habitats, and the impact this has on ecosystems and the environment (Fleischmann, 2004).

Animal advocacy covers a broad range of organizations with widely varying values and tactics. Perhaps the best known (and also in many cases widely hated) animal advocacy organization is People for the Ethical Treatment of Animals (PETA). PETA argues for a strong form of animal rights, and urges a vegan lifestyle and the avoidance of using animals in education and research. PETA is perhaps best known for its shock advertising, frequently featuring partially nude celebrities to make the case against wearing fur in particular or for a vegan lifestyle more generally. PETA is not the most extreme animal advocacy organization; that dubious distinction most likely belongs to the Animal Liberation Front (ALF), which has employed tactics that have been criticized as terroristic in nature. The ALF website prominently features images of people wearing black ski masks (presumably for disguise) holding animals, and has an extensive discussion of terrorism, including quotes from many notable individuals to support the idea that animal mistreatment is the real terrorism. ALF is famous for breaking into medical research facilities, releasing lab animals, and vandalizing or destroying laboratory equipment. This tactic is not always effective; for example, in releasing lab rats from cages, half of them may run out into the street and get run over, while the other half may cower in their cage, afraid to go out because it is the only home they've ever known. Even if one agrees with the animal advocacy position of PETA or ALF, their tactics can be distasteful to many, and overall they have a problematic impact on the perception of animal advocacy organizations more broadly, especially the idea that they are anti-science, and, as a consequence, anti-progress (Fleischmann, 2004).

The animal advocacy movement also includes more moderate voices. Chief among these is the Humane Society of the United States (HSUS). The HSUS focuses most of its energy on correcting mistreatment of animals; unlike PETA and especially ALF, they do not see pet ownership in and of itself as a moral problem, only cases where pets are abused or neglected. HSUS also provides resources for parents and educators, and problematizes the use of animals in research and education. Similarly, several anti-vivisection societies fight not only vivisection (which is used, for example, in medical education, where living dogs are killed to demonstrate the beating of their heart) but also dissection, particularly in K–12 education. Specifically, such organizations include the National Anti-Vivisection Society (NAVS), the American Anti-Vivisection Society (AAVS), and the New England Anti-Vivisection Society (NEAVS) (Fleischmann, 2004).

Interestingly, animal advocates have been able to use the issue of dissection to shift public perception. Again, due to the tactics of ALF and PETA, as well as the concerns about (potentially life-saving) medical research voiced by HSUS and the anti-vivisection societies, there is a general perception of animal advocates as anti-science and thus anti-progress. However, with the dissection debate, animal advocates have capitalized on the opportunity to emphasize that they are advocating a high-tech approach which is backed up by educational research, and that they are the pro-science, pro-technology, and pro-progress side in the debate, whereas biology teachers using traditional dissection are the sticks-in-the-mud teaching biology through dissections simply because that was how they had learned about biology (Fleischmann, 2004).

Animal advocacy organizations did not just happen upon this approach; it was a very systematic and intentional shift. This shift is evident in the new education wings that many of these organizations created specifically to engage in the dissection debate, with names such as the Ethical Science Education Campaign (NEAVS), the Biology Education Advancement Program (BioLEAP) (NAVS), and Animalearn (AAVS). Who doesn't want to be ethical about science education, or advance biology education? In so doing, these organizations took advantage of the same public sentiments in favor of science, technology, and progress in general that had previously acted against them (Fleischmann, 2003, 2004).

Importantly, this shift was both motivated and mediated by human values. Specifically, these animal advocacy organizations were able to form informal partnerships with the companies producing the dissection simulations. These partnerships were based upon and built through a convergence of peripheral values. The core value of animal advocacy organizations is to protect animal rights, a position strong enough to be problematic for some simulation designers. Similarly, simulation design companies, first and foremost, as companies, need to make money. The profit motive is not appealing to not-for-profits such as animal advocacy organizations; indeed, it might often be perceived as distasteful. Thus, the two groups maintained distinct sets of core values (Fleischmann, 2003, 2004).

Peripheral values are often the place where organizations can explore partnerships and synergies. It is hard to shift the core value of an organization such as an animal advocacy organization or a simulation design company. However, peripheral values can more easily be latched onto and added. Specifically, in this case, while simulation design companies did not adopt the strong animal rights approach of many animal advocacy organizations, they did begin to incorporate less controversial values of animal advocacy organizations, such as reduction of animal suffering and environmental protection. Similarly, while animal advocacy organizations did not adopt the profit motive, they did latch onto the development of new technologies and the promotion of science education (Fleischmann, 2003, 2004).

This value alignment can be seen through a number of specific examples. For example, animal advocacy organizations created science wings with names oriented toward science, technology, and education. In the other direction, simulation designers used animal advocacy values to market their software, such as the tagline for Digital Frog 2: Frog-Friendly Software or the promotional packaging of the same product, which features a live frog jumping from one lily pad to another (rather than a dead frog with its guts splayed open for all to see). These values seeped not only into the marketing and packaging of the dissection simulations but even into the interfaces of the simulations themselves; indeed, many of these products took the concept of dissection simulation very loosely, such as Schneider & Morse Group's Prodissector, which allows the user to make the layers of the frog transparent, providing a Superman-like X-ray vision into the inner workings of the frog visible; and Lawrence Berkeley Laboratory's Build a Frog Game which involves building, rather than dissecting, a frog. These approaches deviate significantly from the traditional dissection simulation experience of cutting into a frog using tools such as a scalpel (Fleischmann, 2003, 2004).

As an interesting postscript to this case: today both dissection and dissection simulation appear to be on the decline, victims of the No Child Left Behind (NCLB) standardized testing regime, which has extended to science education, and which focuses on factual, textual questions rather than the lab practical approach often used to evaluate knowledge of anatomy following a dissection. Although animal advocates often promote the cost advantages of dissection simulation as an advantage of simulation, the reality is that both approaches are expensive and require large amounts of equipment and time. For better or for worse, standardized testing tends to encourage and, potentially, reward teaching-to-the-test, and lab activities are becoming the victims of this top-down standardization (to the least common denominator, raw textual facts, unfortunately), including both physical and virtual lab activities in biology, chemistry, and physics (Fleischmann, 2007b).

Biology education provides a compelling example of the potential intersection of values related to animal advocacy and educational technology, demonstrating that values can serve as a tool for connecting divergent communities for mutual benefit. The next section explores a similar technology applied in a very different context: human anatomy simulation deployed within graduate medical education.

3.2   MEDICAL EDUCATION AND HUMAN VALUES

Human dissection has a long and controversial history. Western biomedical knowledge is rooted in the dissection of dead bodies, a practice which was at one time controversial and even illegal in countries such as England due to concerns about grave robbing, which was a common means of acquiring bodies for research and education. The origins of biomedicine differ significantly from other medical traditions, such as Traditional Chinese Medicine, which is based on a notion of chi or life force that is not found in dead bodies. Even acquiring human skeletons for displays has proven highly problematic, and lifelike models are far more common today (Fleischmann, 2004).

Perhaps the most interesting value-related issue in medical education is the relationship between the goals of educational activities and how they are evaluated. Typically, one would expect that assessments would be aligned with the goals of an activity, but this is more challenging when the goals include more tacit, intangible elements. As in the biology education case discussed above, there is often a tendency in evaluation to go to the least common denominator and focus on the most surface level and easiest to assess dimensions, without digging deeper into the goals that motivate the educational activity or technology in the first place (Fleischmann, 2004, 2007b).

Historically, gross anatomy served as the entry point and obligatory passage point (Callon, 1986) for medical education, and human dissection served as the chief activity in gross anatomy lab. Gross anatomy was not only the place where medical students learned to identify body parts, but also the chief activity in establishing a tactile understanding of the structures of the human body, socialization into medicine, establishing the medical gaze (Foucault, 1973), and dealing with death and the disgusting. As a hands-on activity, human dissection has a clear tacit dimension. Also, since students go through gross anatomy lab together, the highly emotionally charged and stressful experience serves as a bonding experience and socializes them into the community of doctors. Students learn to see the human body in parts, instead of merely focusing on the humanity of a person, a skill which, when taken to the extreme, can cause depersonalization of medical interaction and poor bedside manner (but is still necessary, to a degree, to achieve the objectivity and professionalism that are so highly valued in medicine). Finally, doctors will need to spend significant portions of their careers dealing with death, particularly in specialties such as oncology, cardiology, surgery, and emergency medicine, and they may commonly encounter diseases or conditions that make many people uncomfortable, but must still, again, maintain objectivity and professionalism. Overall, it is clear that the gross anatomy lab experience serves many important roles in medical education (Fleischmann, 2004).

Today, human dissection carries fewer ethical controversies than animal dissection. Individuals who died of other causes donate their bodies to science through willed body programs. However, scarcity and cost of specimens, as well as the cost and space required for the dissection labs, are major issues raised in relation to both K–12 animal dissection and human dissection as part of the gross anatomy lab experience. As a result, there has been increased emphasis on identifying alternatives to the gross anatomy lab dissection experience (Fleischmann, 2004).

As in the case of animal dissection, while there were previously lower-tech approaches to replacing the experience such as physical models, the first technology to be widely viewed as a viable alternative to the gross anatomy lab dissection experience were computer simulations. One of the earliest such efforts was the Visible Human Project, which set out to digitize a human body. The Visible Human Male was a death row inmate who was killed by lethal injection and then his body was set in a rubbery substance to keep it in place. The body was then sliced at such tiny intervals that at the end of the process, all that was left of the body was a pile of shavings. After each slice, photographs were taken, and these photographs were then put together to build early computer simulations of human anatomy such as Animated Dissection of Anatomy for Medicine (A.D.A.M.) (Fleischmann, 2004).

Many sophisticated simulations of human anatomy followed, such as Anatomy Revealed, the precursor to and human version of ProDissector, wherein students learn anatomy by making the layers of the body transparent. It is interesting to note, though, that the social, tacit, and emotional elements of the dissection lab experience did not seem to have a major impact either on the design of these simulations or in the evaluations used to compare their effectiveness to the gross anatomy lab. Instead of looking at the rich range of knowledges produced through the traditional gross anatomy lab dissection experience, these simulations have typically been evaluated in terms of their ability to aid in identification and recall of parts of the body, certainly an important element in gross anatomy but hardly the only goal, based on the medical education literature (Fleischmann, 2004).

Medical education provides an example of the need to align the design and evaluation of educational technologies to match the goals of users, not just those of the designers. In this case, users include the instructors and students of gross anatomy. Completing these two case studies led me to pursue the value-sensitive design of simulations for information ethics education.

3.3   INFORMATION ETHICS EDUCATION AND HUMAN VALUES

One area where educational simulations were not already in widespread use was information ethics education. Ethics education for information professionals tends to be fairly haphazard, as some schools have stand-alone courses in information ethics; other schools incorporate information ethics into other courses, such as core courses; and even some schools do not directly address the ethical responsibilities of information professionals. Based on my belief that information professionals have important ethical responsibilities, and that they should be given a safe environment to explore these responsibilities, I developed stand-alone information ethics courses at both the University of Maryland and the University of Texas at Austin, and they were, to the best of my knowledge, the first graduate-level information ethics courses offered at either institution.

In teaching ethics, it was important to me to make the topic timely and relevant. Ethics is often thought of as dry and dusty, something where all of the important thought occurred hundreds or thousands of years ago—of limited contemporary relevance. One measure that I have taken to address this concern is to broaden the range of ethical theories covered. Most information ethics textbooks use the same few ethical theories from "dead white men." In my information ethics course, we cover a wide range of ethical theories, including non-Western (Buddhist, Confucian, Hindu, Islamic, and Ubuntu) ethics and feminist (Ethics of Care and Standpoint Epistemology) ethics, in addition to the traditional ethical theories covered in the textbook (Quinn, 2013, which actually has a broad range relative to other information ethics textbooks, including, in recent editions, ethical egoism).

In my research, I approach ethics descriptively, in terms of wanting to understand ethical decision-making and the factors that inform and influence it, rather than prescriptively, where the purpose might be to argue that one ethical theory is superior to others and illustrate how it should be employed in different circumstances. Similarly, in my teaching, instead of trying to teach one specific ethical theory as the "right" theory, alongside teaching a wide range of ethical theories, I also think of myself as teaching ethical decision-making, in terms of helping students to understand what it is, when to do it, and how to do it, in a broad sense. My foremost concern is the danger of technological somnambulism (Winner, 1987)—that students will sleepwalk through their ethical decision-making as information professionals, failing to consider the ethical implications of the actions that they take. My goal is to prepare students for the ethical decisions that they will face as information professionals.

One way to both bring ethics to life and to confront students with realistic information ethics dilemmas is to use case-based learning. This is a time-consuming educational approach that requires great skill and organization on the part of the instructor. To broaden the potential impact of this approach, we decided to develop and evaluate an educational simulation for information ethics. We employed approaches from user-centered design and value sensitive design to develop the simulation. First, we developed a paper prototype of the cases, which I used in successive offerings of the course. Then, we used this experience to develop the simulation, a tool that simplifies the typically complex process of case-based learning by leading users through a particular ethical dilemma (Fleischmann et al., 2009b, 2011a, 2011b).

The cases within the simulation differ in important ways from traditional case-based learning. While traditional cases typically present the scenario from the perspective of a single actor, the cases we developed for the simulation are multi-role cases—specifically, each case involves three students, who each make ethical decisions in sequence. The model for our cases is a tree, so each successive ethical decision is informed and shaped by those that came before. Thus, there are a total of four different ethical dilemmas that the third student might face, depending on the binary choices made by the first two students. Our cases were also intended to be forward, rather than backward looking, and to allow for both open-ended ethical decision-making (identifying alternatives) and closed-ended ethical decision-making (choosing from among alternatives) (Fleischmann et al., 2009b). The technology behind this case-based simulation was not particularly sophisticated, as the simulation is text-based, but it does assist instructors in employing case-based learning in their courses, potentially for topics beyond information ethics.

Once we had designed the simulation, we also evaluated what students learned from it as well as from the course as a whole. Specifically, we identified five themes that capture the main points that students drew from the simulation. First, we found that students learned how to apply a wide range of ethical theories to contemporary information ethics issues. Second, students learned how ethical theories connect to culture and values, in the sense that they could situate specific ethical theories within their cultural context and identify value differences among the ethical theories. Third, students learned how multicultural and international dimensions shape student self-understanding, in the sense that they were able to situate their own beliefs within this broader framework. Fourth, students applied their understanding of multicultural and international dimensions to improve their understanding of others, such that other cultures stopped being mysterious "others" and became different rationalities that had their own internal logic and practical applications. Finally, students learned about how culture and ethics shape both the design and use of information systems, since people, who have their own cultural backgrounds and ethical systems, develop them. These results illustrate that the simulation and the course were effective in teaching many of the important information ethics lessons that motivated the course (Fleischmann et al., 2011a).

Finally, we not only developed and evaluated a simulation to deliver the cases, but we also developed and evaluated a graphical user interface (GUI)-based tool to allow students (or instructors or anyone else) to develop their own cases for use within the simulation. Thus, anyone with basic computer literacy could design cases to be used in the simulation, having the effect of ensuring that the simulation would be sustainable, in that users could continue to add new cases to keep the simulation current, and also allowing for the potential for the simulation to be used to teach topics beyond information ethics, including ethics within other fields or potentially anything that can be effectively taught through case-based learning (Fleischmann et al., 2011c).

These three case studies of educational simulations in biology education, medical education, and information ethics education reveal the extent to which such simulations are value laden, and that effective consideration of human values can positively impact the uptake and success of these technologies. They also demonstrate that education itself is a value-laden activity, as instructors choose which facets of a topic to cover based at least in part on their values. In the next chapter, we will consider how values shape the design and use of another, related technology, computational models.

CHAPTER 4

Technology and Human Values

The research on educational simulations focused on both designers and users of technologies, and specifically within fairly small teams or organizations. A logical next step was to consider larger organizations that develop new technologies. Specifically, I collaborated with William A. Wallace to study the role of human values in computational modeling, which involves using computational techniques to simulate various natural and social phenomena. My collaborator for this study was himself a modeler, so he had both a deep understanding of the issues faced by computational modelers and extensive connections that allowed for access to high profile field sites.

The remainder of this chapter describes key themes from this research. First, I will discuss some of the key values involved in modeling, including trust, transparency, and accountability. Next, I will discuss the importance of value conflicts in computational modeling. Finally, I will discuss the role of codes of ethics and professionalization in computational modeling.

4.1 TRUST, TRANSPARENCY, AND ACCOUNTABILITY

To use information effectively, users must trust it. Trustworthiness is composed of several elements, including accuracy, objectivity, validity, and stability (Kelton et al., 2008). How are users to ascertain these, particularly in the case of computational models, which often serve as black boxes to their users (Fleischmann and Wallace, 2005)?

Like other digital information, users must trust the output of computational models to put it to good use. Richard O. Mason (1994) asserts that modelers must uphold two covenants: a covenant with reality and a covenant with values. That is, models must faithfully represent reality, and also must represent users' values. However, how would the typical user ascertain whether or not modelers have adhered to these covenants?

To address this limitation, we proposed a third covenant for computational modelers: a covenant with transparency. That is, modelers must ensure that the inner workings of their models are clear enough that a user can check to see how well the model aligns with reality and their values. Otherwise, without transparency, users must place blind trust in models (Fleischmann and Wallace, 2005). Transparency is more than just open source, as the importance is to empower users who may lack programming expertise to understand how models work.

Transparency is often a requirement for computational models. Transparency is needed to ensure the accountability of modelers. Motivations for transparency in computational models include political, economic, and legal factors. Politically, transparent models can help empower, rather than disempower, users. Economically, transparent models can help detect fraud and graft, and ensure that everyone is working toward the best fiscal interests of the company. Transparency is often legally required as well. There are various factors that work to support the importance of transparency in computational modeling (Fleischmann and Wallace, 2009).

Making models transparent can potentially involve rethinking the entire modeling process. First, transparency needs to be an explicit goal of the modeling process up front, which means that transparency can be what Shilton (2013) describes as a value lever, in that careful consideration of transparency up front as a requirement makes the need for transparency a feature rather than a bug in the eyes of modelers. Transparency also must shape how a model is conceptually developed and practically implemented. For example, in machine learning, there are cases where transparency is a trade-off relative to accuracy. This scenario led to one of the cases used in our educational simulation for information ethics described in the previous chapter; an engineer must decide, in designing the emergency systems for a spacecraft, whether to make them 99% accurate and opaque or 95% accurate and transparent. The answer depends in large part in one's trust in technology versus humans; would you rather only have it be wrong 1% of the time, but be completely helpless when it is, or be wrong 5% of the time, but have more control over realizing that there is a problem and hopefully correcting and accounting for it?

Finally, transparency must be evaluated and demonstrated during the deployment of the model. Making a covenant with transparency requires careful consideration throughout the entire modeling process, but it is the best and perhaps only way to empower users to make their own judgments about whether or not a model upholds the covenants with reality and values (Fleischmann and Wallace, 2009).

Transparency is critical for establishing both trust in and accountability of models and modelers. One could reasonably consider transparency to be a professional and ethical responsibility. The next chapter goes into more detail about professionalization and codes of ethics within the field of computational modeling.

4.2   VALUE CONFLICTS

Value-laden decisions are often a result of conflicts between different values. Typically, modelers were not struggling with whether or not they valued privacy, but rather how they prioritized privacy versus national security. We identified three particularly salient value conflicts both within the modeling process and also embedded in models themselves (Fleischmann and Wallace, 2010).

First, during the modeling process, there was a salient conflict between obedience and honesty. Basically, this boils down to whether to tell people the truth or what they want to hear. There is often pressure to provide results that lean in one direction or another, and in those cases, reality does not always line up with expectations and desires. Obedience was complex because modelers were, at various stages of their work, accountable to their bosses within their own organizations as well as customers and users who often, although not always, belonged to different organizations. To an extent, we can see that this might relate, at least in part, to whether computational modeling is a science, focused on seeking the truth, or engineering, focused on making things that work. This value conflict was most salient within the corporate and government labs (Fleischmann and Wallace, 2010).

Also, during the modeling process, we found a salient conflict between innovation and reliability. Often, the most efficient solution to a problem is to take a time-tested approach and adapt it to a new situation; however, doing things in a radically different way has the potential to revolutionize how the activity is done and also how future models can be built, but can also be slower and messier. This value conflict boils down to a conflict between whether computational modeling should be seen as basic or applied research; either as basic research to make new discoveries regardless of the messiness and uncertainty of applications, or as applied research that seeks to take existing knowledge and adapt it to solve specific problems. This value conflict was most salient in the academic and corporate labs (Fleischmann and Wallace, 2010).

Finally, we also found a value conflict between completeness and timeliness during the modeling process. Modelers are expected to do potentially innovative work up to a deadline, which is not always possible as both research and development can take long amounts of time. When faced with a time pressure, modelers needed to make decisions such as whether to prioritize timeliness or reliability. This value conflict was most salient in the government and corporate labs (Fleischmann and Wallace, 2010).

We also found three major value conflicts in terms of the success of models as products, which typically involved the relationships among the different stakeholder groups, such as the modelers, their bosses, their organizations, their customers, and their users. One such value conflict arose between the goals of the organization and the goals of the product. Modelers often felt conflicted between meeting the goals of their home organizations versus the customers and users of the models. This conflict arose most frequently in the corporate and government labs (Fleischmann and Wallace, 2010).

Next, we also found that the pressure to publish came into conflict with the customer's needs. This value conflict is related to the conflict above between innovation and reliability, but also includes an element of time, as there can be a time conflict between spending time on publishing versus completing a model, and such issues can be exacerbated by uncertainty about when a project is both for a customer and breaks new research ground, how much of that effort should be charged to the customer, if, for example, a specific test or step is of limited use for the specific purpose of the customer, but has significant impact for publishing. This conflict most frequently arose in the academic and corporate labs (Fleischmann and Wallace, 2010).

Finally, we found a conflict between listening to customers and listening to users. The individual or unit that orders a model is not always the same as the direct user of the model. Typically, the customer is higher up in the organization, while the user is of lower status, exacerbating the value conflict between listening to customers and users. One particularly compelling example of this value conflict is when the customer is ordering a model to achieve efficiencies that can lead to a reduction of workforce; in essence, the modeler is helping the customer to put the user out of a job (Fleischmann et al., 2011c). This conflict occurred most frequently at the government and corporate labs (Fleischmann and Wallace, 2010).

Now that we understand some of the value conflicts that can arise during the modeling process, particularly between different stakeholders, how can we address those problems to reduce conflicts during the modeling process and in the success of models as products? In the survey, we asked modelers whether or not the values of their organization had conflicted with the values of other stakeholder groups, including customers, users, and those affected by the model. At the same time, we also asked participants to complete the Schwartz (1994) Value Survey, so we also had data on the values of these individuals. We then compared the distributions of value scores between those who had acknowledged or had not acknowledged conflicts. We identified a total of 16 statistically significant value differences for 11 different values, including *a spiritual life*, *a world at peace*, *devout*, *equality*, *forgiving*, *honoring of parents and elders*, *humble*, *politeness*, *responsible*, *self-discipline*, and *true friendship*, which in turn correspond with the value types of universalism, benevolence, and conformity; however, interestingly, in all of these cases, people who reported no value conflicts more highly valued the value. Our analysis revealed that while there are values that are positively correlated with a lack of value conflicts, none of the values were correlated with increased value conflicts (Fleischmann et al., 2011d).

Interestingly, *equality* was correlated with a lack of value conflicts, indicating that people who highly valued equality were less likely to perceive and/or experience value conflicts. Perhaps the degree to which they value *equality* allowed them to avoid value conflicts, as they were able to treat all stakeholder groups equally (Fleischmann et al., 2011d). However, further research would be necessary to determine causality and the exact impact of *equality* on the modeling process and on models as products.

Value conflicts played an important role for modelers in these labs, and some values were correlated with a reduction of such value conflicts, indicating that there might be ways to screen the likelihood of individuals to experience value conflicts based on completion of a value survey, especially when tailoring to a specific organization. The following section will go into more detail about some of the most salient values that shape the modeling process and models as products.

4.3   PROFESSIONALIZATION AND CODES OF ETHICS

Modelers typically work within the context of one organization while also belonging or having affiliation to one or more professional associations, such as the Association for Computing Machinery (ACM) or the Institute of Electrical and Electronics Engineers Computer Society (IEEE-CS). Their organizational and professional ethics can come into conflict, as in the case of librarians employed within corporations whose explicit or implicit values may conflict with the ALA Code of Ethics and the ALA Core Values of Librarianship discussed above. This section explores both these organizational and professional codes of ethics and values.

Based on our survey data, we identified differences between the values of modelers at the three different organizations based on modelers' responses to the Schwartz (1994) Value Survey. For example, modelers in the academic lab rated *curious* more highly but *obedient*, *loyal*, and *honoring of parents and elders* lower, in keeping with academics' reputations for being intellectually curious and highly self-directed. Based on our coding of the interview data, we also found statistically significant differences between the frequencies of occurrence of specific values within the interview transcripts of modelers at the three sites. For example, *wealth*, *responsible*, and *accepting my portion in life* were shown to be more salient values in the corporate lab than in the other two labs. There were clear differences among modelers within the three organizations, although additional field sites would be needed to draw conclusions about whether those differences are representative of their organization types or due to idiosyncratic factors (Fleischmann et al., 2011c).

To understand modelers' experiences with and attitudes toward professional associations and their codes of ethics, we asked modelers if they were aware of the codes of ethics of any professional associations. We found that those who said yes statistically significantly more highly valued *a spiritual life*, *authority*, *helpful*, *influential*, *preserving my public image*, *respect for tradition*, *successful*, and *true friendship*. The only value that was higher among those who said no was *freedom*. This result matched our qualitative interview data findings, as there are many benefits to codes of ethics, which is why they exist, however the biggest concern about them is that they infringe on the freedom, independence, and judgment of professionals (Fleischmann et al., 2010).

We also asked modelers if they had ever read a code of ethics of a professional association, and the results followed a similar pattern. Those who said yes more highly valued (with repeated values underlined) *a spiritual life*, *authority*, *devout*, *equality*, *helpful*, *influential*, *preserving my public image*, *successful*, and *true friendship*. Again, the only value that was higher among those who said no was *freedom*. Overall, having read codes of ethics was positively correlated with a wide range of values and negatively correlated with freedom (Fleischmann et al., 2010).

Finally, we asked modelers if they thought that computational modelers should follow a code of ethics. There were positive relationships with ten values, including (with repeated values underlined) *a spiritual life*, *a world at peace*, *devout*, *equality*, *forgiving*, *helpful*, *inner harmony*, *politeness*, *sense of belonging*, and *social justice*. We did not find any negative relationships for this question. In all, a total of sixteen values were correlated with yes answers to one or more questions, with *a spiritual life* and *helpful* appearing in all three lists, with only *freedom* correlated with two of the no answers. Overall, it seems that increased familiarity with and adherence to codes of ethics is correlated with many values, with only *freedom* standing out as an outlier (Fleischmann et al., 2010).

This study demonstrated that value conflicts play an important role in the modeling process, that transparency is a key value for empowering users to ensure that models are consistent with reality and their values, and values are related to experiences with and attitudes toward professional associations and their codes of ethics. Value conflicts can emerge within or among modelers, other stakeholders, technologies, organizations, and professional associations.

CHAPTER 5

Communication and Human Values

The approach to coding values within texts employed in the above studies, particularly the systematic approach developed for and used in the computational modeling study, indicated an interesting direction for this research: to study how values are expressed in communication, and correlate those values with attitudes or behaviors. Specifically, this chapter details three methods for detecting values in communication: manual content analysis, crowdsourced content analysis, and automatic content analysis.

5.1 MANUAL CONTENT ANALYSIS OF HUMAN VALUES IN COMMUNICATION

Content analysis is typically performed by a small team of rigorously trained human coders. Typically, the first step is open coding, where grounded theory or thematic analysis is used to identify trends in the data. Next, this qualitative content analysis is used to develop a coding frame that can be used to systematically analyze the data. In some cases, this qualitative content analysis can be bootstrapped by or replaced with an existing inventory of categories developed through other means, such as surveys. Once the coding frame is established, data can be coded such that counts can be performed and statistical analysis can be applied to analyze those counts.

The holy grail of content analysis is inter-coder agreement. To ensure reliability, it is important to demonstrate that independent coders, given the same coding frame and the same data, would reach the same conclusions. The typical approach to achieve this is to train multiple coders through use of a coding manual, training examples, collaborative coding, and/or comparison of independent coding. In all cases, these examples should be from the same corpus or at least the same type of data, but they should not be directly from the subset of the corpus used to measure inter-coder agreement, as they are meant to provide guidelines, not an exact match between an example and a code.

Traditionally, researchers have studied human values using interrogative methods, most notably surveys but also interviews and focus groups. Content analysis of existing textual corpora has several advantages over these methods. The first is access. Following the guidelines of Institutions Review Boards, participation of human subjects in research must be voluntary, and acquired through a process of informed consent. Many individuals may not choose to participate in research projects involving interrogative methods, and those choices may be systematic rather than purely random, resulting in participation bias in the sense that the subset of individuals who agreed to participate in the research may not accurately represent the entire sample or population selected for study. Further, interrogative methods rely on the human subject to accurately and faithfully answer questions, while in reality this is no small task, and potentially prone to issues such as forgetfulness (particularly retrospective bias, the phenomenon that explains why many people are more aware of bad things that happen during a full moon than of bad things that happen during other moon cycles), self-deception, and social desirability bias (telling the questioners the answers that you expect they want to know) (Fleischmann et al., 2009a).

Content analysis can potentially overcome both of these limitations of surveys and other interrogative methods. Unlike surveys, universal participation in content analysis is possible, provided that the data is publicly available, such as, for example, posted online in a web archive or via social media. Further, since content was not necessarily written for coders to read, there is less potential for social desirability bias. Thus, content analysis is a worthwhile method to apply to this problem, although it is important to note that it does have its own shortcomings, most notably the amount of time and effort required by a small team of human coders; the following sections will discuss the development and application of novel approaches such as crowdsourcing and automation that have the potential to overcome this limitation (Fleischmann et al., 2009a).

We first applied this approach to studying the Net neutrality debate. Specifically, the corpus for this study included 102 prepared testimonies from ten hearings held by the U.S. Senate, House, and Federal Communications Commission (FCC). We originally started with the Schwartz (1994) Value Inventory as our coding scheme, but coders found it too challenging to code for 56 basic human values. We modified the inventory to simplify it and select the most salient values (as some values were nearly or completely absent from this discourse), and we achieved better agreement, but we felt that there still remained room for improvement. So, we next conducted a meta-analysis of human values, including reviewing and synthesizing twelve existing value inventories, including the Schwartz (1994) Value Inventory and human values with ethical import (Friedman et al., 2006) discussed above, as well as ten others. From these existing value inventories, we identified sixteen cross-cutting values found in at least five of the twelve inventories, which constituted the first version of the Meta-Inventory of Human Values (Cheng and Fleischmann, 2010). We then applied this inventory across a subset of the corpus and iteratively modified the inventory to adapt it to the corpus and our research design, including omitting values not salient in the Net neutrality debate and combining categories that were frequently confused (Cheng, 2012). In addition to coding sentences for values, we also coded testimonies as pro, con, or neutral relative to Net neutrality. Based on analysis of a subset of the corpus, we identified an interesting contrast between the pros and cons, in that the cons statistically significantly more frequently invoked the value of *wealth*, while the pros more frequently invoked the value of *innovation*. Given that the Net neutrality debate is largely driven by corporate actors, this was an interesting finding, as innovation represented to the content providers who supported Net neutrality a form of long-term wealth, whereas the service providers who opposed Net neutrality were more interested in profiting in the short run, while their oligopoly was still relatively unchallenged (Cheng et al., 2012).

Another study of values in communication was a study of the use of Twitter by the homeless, building on prior value sensitive design research on the homeless, values, and information technology (Le Dantec and Edwards, 2008; Woelfer et al.,

2011). Specifically, we were interested in studying differences between the use of Twitter by individuals who self-identified as homeless and those who did not. The first step that we took was to begin with the Meta-Inventory of Human Values (MIHV) (Cheng and Fleischmann, 2010). Specifically, we used the original 16 value formulation of the MIHV. We also conducted a thematic analysis to identify additional values found in our corpus of tweets by homeless and non-homeless individuals, and we identified two additional values that we used in our study, connectedness and comfort (Koepfler and Fleischmann, 2011).

We started with a corpus of 5,313 tweets. Our first analysis step was to throw out all non-original tweets, such as retweets, at-replies, and automatically generated tweets, resulting in a corpus of 1,717 original tweets. We then applied the extended MIHV to this corpus. Of the 18 values within the extended MIHV, we found statistically significant value differences for nine of the values: *broad-mindedness, equality, freedom, helpfulness, identity, justice, responsibility, spirituality,* and *wealth*. Interestingly, in each of these cases, the value was evoked more frequently by homeless Twitter users than by our control group. This result illustrates that homeless individuals were more likely to write value-laden tweets than the general population of Twitter users (Koepfler and Fleischmann, 2012).

These studies illustrate both the promise of manual content analysis for human values and also the extensive human cost of devoting many, many hours to coding data. In the next section, we will explore a different approach to studying human values in communication: crowdsourced content analysis.

5.2   CROWDSOURCED CONTENT ANALYSIS OF HUMAN VALUES IN COMMUNICATION

To scale up content analysis, the next step was to explore crowdsourced content analysis. Crowdsourcing involves asking people to complete relatively simple (but often tedious) tasks, typically for money (often as little as $0.05/task or less, depending on the nature of the work performed). As such, it is an effective way to take a task that might have required a great amount of time from a small number of people and reconfigure it so that it takes much less time for a larger number of people. While there are many commercial crowdsourcing platforms, perhaps the best known is Amazon's Mechanical Turk, which carries the tagline of "artificial artificial intelligence."

The key insight here is that crowdsourcing allows for a radically different approach to content analysis as it is typically employed in the social sciences as well as, particularly, the similar annotation practices involved in computational linguistics. These approaches share the idea that text should be broken down into such a simple form that anyone should be able to agree on how that text is coded. However, when different people read, they have different understandings based on a wide range of factors, including their values. Instead of treating this diversity of perspectives as a bug in content analysis and computational linguistics, it is more enriching to consider it as a feature to be exploited. That is, how people react to texts can tell us something about the person doing the reacting (Fleischmann et al., 2011e). This approach also has implications for automatic content analysis, which I will explore in the following chapter.

We first constructed a pilot study around the Park51/Ground Zero Mosque controversy, which involved public outcry about building an Islamic community center near the previous location of the World Trade Center in New York City. The controversy was a frequent topic of national news coverage from 2009–2011. In the pilot study, we used 48 opinionated paragraphs about the Ground Zero Mosque taken from online news sites, and hand coded them as either pro or con. Next, we asked turkers to first complete the Portrait Values Questionnaire (PVQ) (Schwartz, 2007) and then read the 48 paragraphs to signal their agreement or disagreement. We found five statistically significant differences among the ten value types within the instrument, including significantly higher degrees of universalism and stimulation in terms of both agreement with pro-Park51 paragraphs and disagreement with anti-Park51 paragraphs, while an opposite pattern was found for security, conformity, and tradition. The largest differences were for universalism and stimulation. These results are consistent with the Schwartz (1994) Value Inventory, as security, conformity, and tradition are all located within the conservation quadrant, while stimulation is in the openness to change quadrant and universalism is in the self-transcendence quadrant (Templeton et al., 2011a).

Building on this pilot study, we constructed a more elaborate and tightly controlled experiment. First, in the study described above, after the first group of turkers read the opinionated news paragraphs, they were asked to write a paragraph summarizing their own view on this issue. Their paragraphs were of remarkably high quality, so we decided to use them as the corpus for the next study. We recruited a second group of turkers to first take the PVQ and then register their agreement or disagreement with 55 paragraphs written by the first group of turkers. In parallel, a third group of turkers was asked to take the PVQ and then rate the sentiment contained within the paragraphs. We had three sets of turkers, all of whose values were known to us via the PVQ, representing the authors of the paragraphs, the readers of/reactors to the paragraphs, and the evaluators of (the sentiment of) the paragraphs. This study successfully replicated the major finding of the pilot study, showing a clear positive relationship between support for Park51 by those who valued universalism and a negative relationship between support for Park51 by those who valued security. We were able to use crowdsourcing to identify a strong correlation between values and attitudes within this one issue domain (Templeton and Fleischmann, 2011).

We also conducted a third experiment on a different issue, the nuclear power controversy. Nuclear power has been controversial for decades, and flared up again following the Fukushima nuclear disaster that followed the Japanese tsunami in 2011. Interestingly, for the nuclear power controversy, we were not able to identify any clear relationships between specific values and sentiment toward nuclear power. Based on careful review of the opinionated paragraphs, it was clear that these paragraphs used more sophisticated and varied arguments than the paragraphs about the Park51 controversy. We tentatively concluded that because this controversy had a much longer lifespan, it had evolved to feature several different framings of arguments, whereby one could, for example, make a safety argument either against nuclear power (by referencing nuclear disasters that have happened over time) or for nuclear power (relative to other energy sources, such as coal or petroleum, which also both have their own environmental and safety hazards (Templeton and Fleischmann, 2011).

To further explore the relationship between framing and values in communication, we looked at another controversy, this time the controversy surrounding the Homeless Hotspots at South by Southwest (SXSW) in Austin, TX, in 2012. We looked at 30 opinionated news stories and blog posts, and identified three separate frames within this debate. There is promise in exploring the relationship between values and framing in communication, although further research needs to be conducted before we can draw any firm conclusions (Koepfler et al., 2012).

Crowdsourcing represents an interesting and promising approach for studying the role of values in communication. However, crowdsourcing still requires significant human effort, although that effort is spread more thinly across a larger group of people. The most efficient, and challenging, approach to studying values in communication is automatic content analysis, the focus of the next section.

5.3   AUTOMATIC CONTENT ANALYSIS OF HUMAN VALUES IN COMMUNICATION

Can computers learn to identify human values? And can they act upon them? Recent progress in sentiment analysis, in automating the identification of positive and negative sentiment in texts, makes a compelling case for the potential for automating the detection of values (Pang and Lee, 2008). Like sentiment, values are a private state, typically revealed indirectly through expression rather than directly observed (Wiebe, 1994). This section traces a series of efforts to automate detection and classification of human values using a wide range of approaches.

Our first effort to automate detection of human values was quite primitive, failing to take advantage of the many recent advances in computational linguistics and natural language processing. Instead, we used a very simplistic thesaurus-based approach. For our corpus, we used the Enron e-mail dataset, specifically a cleaned version that included 19,063 original e-mails (Zhou et al., 2007). We used the Schwartz (1994) Value Inventory as our coding frame, and for each value, looked for the single word that best represented the value within its name plus all synonyms of the value that most frequently referred to that value. Because we did not have ground truth, it was not possible to evaluate the reliability of this approach; needless to say, it was far from perfect. However, it did serve as a preliminary example of how an approach to detect human values could be automated (Zhou et al., 2010).

Next, through collaboration with experts in computational linguistics, natural language processing, and information retrieval, we tried to develop and evaluate more sophisticated approaches to detecting and classifying human values (Cheng et al., 2008; Fleischmann et al., 2009a). Specifically, we used a subset of the Net neutrality corpus, and sought to replicate the human findings. In this case, we did have ground truth provided by the human coder (which had also been validated by a second, independent coder). Our value inventory was the Schwartz (1994) Value Inventory. We first treated this as a multiple-category classification problem, asking the computer to identify which value or values were contained within a sentence. As a result, we had most success using a k-nearest neighbor (k-NN) approach. However, one challenge in achieving success with this approach was that a sentence could contain multiple human values, so the classifier would, in reality, need to detect the number of human values contained in a sentence before it could classify them. While our results were promising, we were confident that we could further improve our approach (Ishita et al., 2010).

Since the goal was to imitate human value coding, we realized that humans do not choose from among alternatives for this task as much as they make a series of binary decisions. So, we recast the task as a series of binary decisions, either the sentence did contain a particular value or it did not. We also updated the coding frame to the Meta-Inventory of Human Values (Cheng and Fleischmann, 2010) and expanded the corpus to all 102 testimonies. As a result of these changes, support vector machines (SVM) yielded the best results, and the results achieved rivaled the degree of agreement among humans. This research represents a highly promising step in the direction of automatically classifying human values (Takayama et al., 2013).

Finally, we turned to automating the crowdsourced annotation. Here, the core insight was that people are different at least in part because of their different values, and perhaps rather than automating humans to follow rigorous coding guides through an extensive training process, instead we could benefit from understanding and seeking to automate their perspectives. Instead of seeking to boil down all human intelligence to a single point, instead we could allow for multiple points of view—and as a preliminary entry point, we started with two, although clearly the diversity of human perspectives is as diverse as humanity. Instead of training a single classifier on a set of data and using the results that it generated, instead we decided to train two separate classifiers on separate sets of data that represented different value perspectives (Fleischmann et al., 2011e).

Using the Park51 data, we did just that; we trained multiple classifiers on different segments of the data. Specifically, for the different values, we divided individuals into three categories: high, middle, and low. We threw out the middle and trained two classifiers on the high data and the low data, respectively. Applying this approach to the values of universalism and security, we were able to replicate the pattern found with human coders; the high-universalism classifier agreed with pro-Park51 paragraphs and disagreed with anti-Park51 paragraphs, while the low-universalism classifier disagreed with pro-Park51 paragraphs and agreed with anti-Park51 paragraphs. Instead of training automatic classifiers to identify human values in texts, we had, in effect, trained them to express human values in a manner similar to how humans naturally react to texts (Templeton et al., 2011b).

Together, the research described in this chapter led to the development of the Content Analysis for Values Elicitation framework. Using this approach, it is possible to use a research question to drive an analysis which may use any of a variety of value inventories, and which may employ manual, crowdsourced, or automatic content analysis. Through these projects, we have been able to explore a wide range of application areas, although there is still much more work to be done (Fleischmann et al., 2012).

CHAPTER 6

Synthesis: Reconsidering Information and Human Values

Values are properties of people, but they can also be properties of information and of technology. Information and technology are enduring forms constructed by humans to contain values that can be transmitted across individuals and stored over time. As their construction is value laden, information and technology reflect the values incorporated by their designers. People's values shape the values embedded in the information that they produce and transmit. People's values are in turn also shaped by the values embedded in information from others. Similarly, people's values also shape and are shaped by technologies. Finally, the values of information are shaped by the technology used to deliver it, such as the same information delivered via either a relational database or on a sheepskin, while the values of technology are shaped by the information contained within it, such as a website for a radically liberal or conservative political group. Figure 6.1 depicts the relationship between values, people, information, and technology.

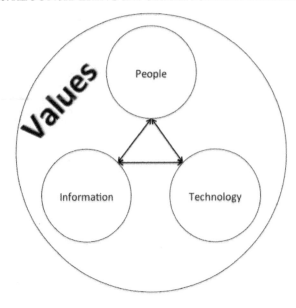

Figure 6.1: Values are properties of people, information, and technologies.

Values transmitted in information can be embedded in education, technology, or communication. Values shape how the next generation is educated, such as choices about using frog dissection or dissection simulations, or the balance between teaching evolution and creation science. Values shape the structures of new technologies, such as computational models that apply different weightings to various societal and environmental phenomena. Values also mediate communication, such as political discourse surrounding a hot button issue, or movies that can shape our views toward different historical figures and periods.

Based on the case studies presented above, a pattern begins to emerge, in terms of best practices for information technology, system, and service designers and users. The first step in the process is to identify all relevant stakeholders. In the case of computational modeling, this includes the modelers themselves, their bosses, their colleagues, their support staff, their customers, their users, and those affected by the models. It is important to include those affected, as an individual does not need to see or use a model to be affected by it, as in the case of the use of models in our financial system, whereby investors' money may be in the hands of a model that they cannot directly use and may not even realize exists (Fleischmann and Wallace, 2005). Similarly, in the case of dissection simulation, stakeholders include not only teachers and students but also administrators and animal advocates. Finally, in communication, stakeholders include the individual composing the message and the individual interpreting the message, as well as others who may be influenced by the message and its properties.

The next step is to identify value conflicts. Individuals can have internal value conflicts. Members of stakeholder groups can also have value conflicts with other members of the same group. Finally, different stakeholder groups can have value conflicts. In the case of computational models, modelers experienced different degrees of conflicts with customers, users, and those affected. In dissection simulations, there was a fundamental conflict between biology teachers and animal advocates, which simulation designers were able to exploit. In the Net neutrality and Park51 controversies, there were clear value conflicts between supporters and opponents. Understanding these value conflicts is essential for achieving a solution that aligns with the values of all stakeholders.

After that, it is important to consider the ethical implications. Many value conflicts have inherent ethical implications that must be explored. For example, the covenant with transparency within computational modeling is an ethical responsibility to empower users to evaluate performance on the covenants with reality and values. The dissection simulation debate has clear ethical implications, especially from the perspective of animal advocates. Finally, controversies such as homeless hotspots have obvious and compelling ethical implications in terms of the potential to treat homeless individuals as a means to an end rather than ends in themselves.

The following step is to consider contextual factors. While values are enduring, their expression and implications may vary depending on the circumstances. For example, organizational culture serves as an important mediating variable in computational modeling, as each lab has its own culture that is more than just the sum of its parts. For human anatomy simulation, it is important to consider the overall environment of educational reform and increasing emphasis on evidence-based medicine and how it shapes the discourse around gross anatomy lab, given the increasing tendency to teach the basic sciences in an integrated, rather than discipline-specific, manner. Finally, in the case of Park51, an understanding of the 9/11 terrorist attacks and the larger history of terrorist acts that have shaped many Americans' perspectives on Islam serves as an essential context for understanding the degree of public opposition (by many) to the Park51 project, insofar as it is unlikely that a Jewish, Christian, or even Hindu or Buddhist community center in the same location would have drawn so much attention; as further context, is important to understand how the controversy was framed radically differently by major media outlets, such as Fox News and MSNBC. Clearly, context is critical to understanding and resolving value conflicts.

Overall, it is important to resolve value conflicts through design. This approach is similar to value sensitive design (Friedman et al., 2006), but with further emphasis on the inherent conflicts among stakeholders and the goal of resolving them in mutually agreeable ways. The Holy Grail in political communication is to frame a message in such a way that it garners support from conservatives, moderates, and liberals. The design of dissection simulations, especially where animal advocacy perspectives were taken into consideration, helped to lessen the value conflict between animal advocates and biology teachers, who now had a viable alternative to dissection. Finally, modelers must consider and intermediate between the various value conflicts within and among stakeholder groups, to ensure the success of the modeling process and of models as products. Figure 6.2 summarizes this recommended values and design cycle.

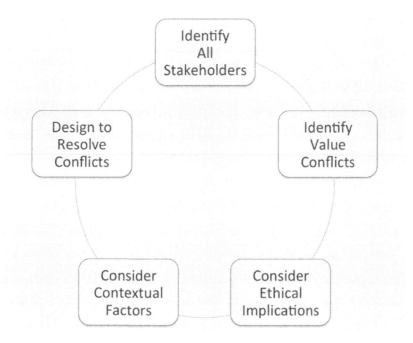

Figure 6.2: Values and design cycle.

The first step is to identify all stakeholders. This step is complex and nuanced, as stakeholders do not only include end users, but also include others who are affected by the information technology. For example, people may not be aware of the existence of a particular information technology, but if that information technology is responsible for the pricing of a product that they purchase, then they are stakeholders. It may not be possible to identify all stakeholders in advance, as it may not always be clear who will buy or use an information technology, or how they will use it, but an effort should be made to at least identify individuals who can represent likely stakeholders for the information technology.

Next, it is important to identify any value conflicts between these groups. It is important to note that information technologies may become entangled in existing value conflicts between stakeholder groups, potentially either reducing or increasing these pre-existing value conflicts. Further, information technologies may introduce new value conflicts, either by helping to reveal value conflicts that had existed previously but that had not yet been detected, or by introducing entirely new value conflicts due to a new factor introduced by the information and/ or technology.

The following step is to consider the ethical implications of these value conflicts. Here, one can imagine a wide gulf between how such value conflicts might be perceived by, for example, John Rawls or Ayn Rand. However, ideally, this step can involve a wide range of ethical perspectives that encompass the stakeholder groups represented. What will be changed by this value conflict, what steps can be taken to reduce such value conflicts, and what unintended consequences or new value conflicts might be introduced by efforts to reduce existing value conflicts?

The fourth step is to consider contextual factors. Information technology design and use does not occur within a vacuum, but rather always has a social and cultural context. How might a particular value conflict be a result of cultural differences? (of course, not strictly limited to national culture but also including the cultures of subgroups, such as professional and organizational cultures). Like the other relationships discussed above, this relationship with social and cultural context is also bi-directional, as the context may shape or be shaped by these value conflicts.

Finally, it is important to design to resolve value conflicts. Value conflicts endanger the success of an information technology, as they may prevent or problematize its use. Designers should seek to reduce existing value conflicts, while also not introducing new value conflicts. Information technologies should bring people and communities together, rather than tear them apart.

CHAPTER 7

A Research Agenda for Information and Human Values

Much important work has already been done in areas such as value-sensitive design, social informatics, and information ethics. However, there are still many areas to explore. Fleischmann (2009) explores two ongoing trends in human-computer interaction writ large: the scale of both social structures and technological systems is greatly increasing, while humans and computers are converging in important ways. Both of these trends have important implications for human agency, since collective agency is a fundamentally different phenomenon from individual agency. Further, the cyborgification of humanity has the potential to develop new agents that combine elements of human and machine. A cyborg may be someone wearing glasses, using a calculator, equipped with a pacemaker, or with sensors embedded within their brain to detect brain waves or nerve impulses and turn them into mechanical actions to control, for example, an artificial limb. Human-computer interaction is no longer about individual humans and computers, and the human and the computer are no longer as distinct as they once were. Finding new ways to study the role of agency and values in these large, hybrid networks is an important challenge that will require much additional research.

Additional research is needed to improve our understanding of the objects of study within the broad domain of values and design, encompassing value-sensitive design, values in design, and other related areas of research. Shilton, Koepfler, and Fleischmann (2013) focus in particular on the holders of values and on the values themselves. The resulting framework included three dimensions for the holders of values: *agency* (objects to subjects), *unit* (individual to collective), and *assemblage* (homogenous to hybrid). These are three of the key components within the sociotechnical and cyborg-cyborg interaction grid (Fleischmann, 2009). The latter illustrates an oversimplification embedded in Figure 6.1; people, information, and technology are not typically independent actors; indeed, information technology delivers information through technology, and even people are blending with information technology, becoming inforgs (Floridi, 2007) or cyborgs (Haraway, 1991). The framework also included three dimensions for values themselves: *salience* (peripheral to central), *intention* (accidental to purposive), and *enactment* (potential to performed). These three dimensions describe the status of values in a particular situation, such as a design process or the development of an ad campaign. These value dimensions can be applied to improve our understanding of how various research methods in the broad area of values and design can be applied (Shilton et al., 2014). These value dimensions make clear that values are not unique properties of non-interacting entities, but rather contested through various sociotechnical processes. Further research in a wide range of contexts, including studying the design, adoption, use, management, and regulation of information technologies, systems, and services is critical.

Research on information and human values can be leveraged in a wide range of application areas. For example, Fleischmann (2010b) explores the need for additional research on the ethical dimensions of computer security practice and education. Computer security is one of the areas where the design of new information technologies can have life or death consequences—imagine, for example, a cyberattack that allowed terrorists to control our electrical grid or transportation system, with almost certain disastrous consequences. Yet, we must walk the same fine line as the U.S. Constitution in terms of ensuring both public safety and privacy for all law-abiding citizens. Clearly, the recent revelations about spying by the National Security Administration (NSA) and other elements of the U.S. government, along with past NSA efforts to embed loopholes in the backbone of the Internet that would allow the NSA to collect data on individuals (Knobel and Bowker, 2011) raise concerns about how these values are being balanced. Here, transparency is key, as citizens have no control over things that they do not know about, so they do have a right to be informed. Even, or perhaps especially, in a post-9/11 world, it is important to consider how we can best balance security and privacy. Not only does research on information and human values have important intellectual implications, but it also has critical practical and societal implications.

One important goal is to popularize value-sensitive design to the point where designers typically consider the values of users, rather than just a relatively small group of designers who currently pay significant consideration to values. However, understanding the values of users involves many challenges that may be daunting for designers. First, users may not be available or willing to be studied or questioned. Second, designers are busy, and often feel that they can't afford the time required to carry out a thorough user-centered design effort. The Content Analysis for Values Elicitation framework (Fleischmann et al., 2012) has significant potential to address these shortcomings, as content analysis is not intrusive, and crowdsourcing and automatic content analysis have the potential to reduce the amount of effort required to understand users' values. This approach has the potential to aid us in making sense and effective use of the vast amount of information now available online.

References

American Library Association (1939/1996). Library Bill of Rights. http://www. ala.org/advocacy/intfreedom/librarybill. 15

American Library Association (1939/2008). Code of Ethics of the American Library Association. http://www.ala.org/advocacy/proethics/codeofethics/ codeethics. 15

American Library Association (1953/2004). The freedom to read statement. http://www.ala.org/advocacy/intfreedom/statementspols/freedomread-statement. 15

American Library Association (1999). Libraries: An American value. http://www. ala.org/advocacy/intfreedom/statementspols/librariesamerican. 15

American Library Association (2004). Core values of librarianship. http://www. ala.org/advocacy/intfreedom/statementspols/corevalues. 16, 17, 18, 23, 28, 29

Beyer, H. and Holtzblatt, K. (1998). *Contextual design: Defining customer-centered systems*. San Francisco: Morgan Kaufmann. 20

Callon, M. (1986). Some elements of a sociology of translation: Domestication of the scallops and the fishermen of St Brieuc Bay. In J. Law (Ed.), *Power, action and belief: A new sociology of knowledge*. London: Routledge & Kegan Paul. 36

Cheng, A.-S. (2012). Values in the Net neutrality debate: Applying content analysis to testimonies from public hearings. Ph.D. diss., University of Maryland. 53

Cheng, A.-S. and Fleischmann, K.R. (2010). Developing a meta-inventory of human values. *Proceedings of the 73rd Annual Meeting of the American Soci-*

ety for Information Science and Technology, Pittsburgh, PA. DOI: 10.1002/ meet.14504701232. 9, 53, 54, 58

Cheng, A.-S., Fleischmann, K.R., Wang, P., Ishita, E., and Oard, D.W. (2012). The role of innovation and wealth in the Net neutrality debate: A content analysis of human values in Congressional and FCC hearings. *Journal of the American Society for Information Science and Technology*, Vol. 63, No. 7, pp. 1360-1373. DOI: 10.1002/asi.22646. 53

Cheng, A.-S., Fleischmann, K.R., Wang, P., and Oard, D.W. (2008). Advancing social science research by applying computational linguistics. *Proceedings of the 71st Annual Meeting of the American Society for Information Science and Technology*, Columbus, OH. 58

Cockton, G. (2006). Designing worth is worth designing. *Proceedings of the 4th Nordic Conference on Human-Computer Interaction*, Oslo, Norway. DOI: 10.1145/1182475.1182493. 20

Department of Health, Education, and Welfare (1979). The Belmont Report. http://www.hhs.gov/ohrp/humansubjects/guidance/belmont.html. 24

Edwards, J.B., Robinson, M.S., and Unger, K.R. (2013). *Transforming libraries, building communities: The community-centered library*. Lanham, MD: Scarecrow Press. 17

Fleischmann, K.R. (2003). Frog and cyberfrog are friends: Dissection simulation and animal advocacy. *Society & Animals*, Vol. 11, No. 2, pp. 123-143. DOI: 10.1163/156853003769233342. 27, 34, 35

Fleischmann, K.R. (2004). Exploring the design-use interface: The agency of boundary objects in educational technology. Ph.D. diss., Rensselaer Polytechnic Institute. 27, 31, 32, 33, 34, 35, 36, 37, 38

Fleischmann, K.R. (2007a). The evolution of agency: Spectra of bioagency and cyberagency. *The Information Society*, Vol. 23, No. 5, pp. 361-371. DOI: 10.1080/01972240701572897. 24

Fleischmann, K.R. (2007b). Standardization from below: Science and technology standards and educational software. *Educational Technology & Society*, Vol. 10, No. 4, pp. 110-117. 36

Fleischmann, K.R. (2009). Sociotechnical interaction and cyborg-cyborg interaction: Transforming the scale and convergence of HCI. *The Information Society*, Vol. 25, No. 4, pp. 227-235. DOI: 10.1080/01972240903028359. 67

Fleischmann, K.R. (2010a). The public library in the life of the Internet: How the core values of librarianship can shape human-centered computing. In J.C. Bertot, P.T. Jaeger, and C. McClure (Eds.), *Public libraries and the Internet*. Santa Barbara, CA: Libraries Unlimited. 15, 18

Fleischmann, K.R. (2010b). Preaching what we practice: Teaching ethical decision-making to computer security professionals. *Lecture Notes in Computer Science*, Vol. 6054, pp. 197-202. DOI: 10.1007/978-3-642-14992-4_18. 68

Fleischmann, K.R., Cheng, A.-S., Templeton, T.C., Koepfler, J.A., Oard, D.W., Boyd-Graber, J., Ishita, E., & Wallace, W.A. (2012). Content analysis for values elicitation. *Proceedings of the ACM SIGCHI Conference on Human Factors in Computing Systems, Workshop on Methods for Accounting for Values in Human-Centered Computing*, Austin, TX. 59, 69

Fleischmann, K.R., Koepfler, J.A., Robbins, R.W., & Wallace, W.A. (2011c). CaseBuilder: A GUI Web app for building interactive teaching cases. *Proceedings of the 74th Annual Meeting of the American Society for Information Science and Technology*, New Orleans, LA. DOI: 10.1002/meet.2011.14504801299. 41

Fleischmann, K.R., Oard, D.W., Cheng, A.-S., Wang, P., & Ishita, E. (2009a). Automatic classification of human values: Applying computational thinking to information ethics. *Proceedings of the 72nd Annual Meeting of the American Society for Information Science and Technology*, Vancouver, BC, Canada. DOI: 10.1002/meet.2009.1450460345. 14, 52, 58

Fleischmann, K.R., Robbins, R.W., and Wallace, W.A. (2009b). Designing educational cases for intercultural information ethics: The importance of diversity, perspectives, values, and pluralism. *Journal of Education for Library and Information Science*, Vol. 50, No. 1, pp. 4-14. 40

Fleischmann, K.R., Robbins, R.W., and Wallace, W.A. (2011a). Information ethics education in a multicultural world. *Journal of Information Systems Education*, Vol. 22, No. 3, pp. 191-202. 40, 41

Fleischmann, K.R., Robbins, R.W., and Wallace, W.A. (2011b). Collaborative learning of ethical decision-making via simulated cases. *Proceedings of the 6th Annual iConference*, Seattle, WA. DOI: 10.1145/1940761.1940805. 40

Fleischmann, K.R., Templeton, T.C., and Boyd-Graber, J. (2011e). Modeling diverse standpoints in text classification: Learning to be human by modeling human values. *Proceedings of the 6th Annual iConference*, Seattle, WA. DOI: 10.1145/1940761.1940863. 55, 59

Fleischmann, K.R. and Wallace, W.A. (2005). A covenant with transparency: Opening the black box of models. *Communications of the ACM*, Vol. 48, No. 5, pp. 93-97. DOI: 10.1145/1060710.1060715. 43, 44, 63

Fleischmann, K.R. and Wallace, W.A. (2009). Ensuring transparency in computational modeling. *Communications of the ACM*, Vol. 52, No. 3, pp. 131-134. DOI: 10.1145/1467247.1467278. 44, 45

Fleischmann, K.R. and Wallace, W.A. (2010). Value conflicts in computational modeling. *Computer*, Vol. 43, No. 7, pp. 57-63. DOI: 10.1109/MC.2010.120. 45, 46, 47

Fleischmann, K.R., Wallace, W.A., and Grimes, J.M. (2010). The values of computational modelers and professional codes of ethics: Results from a field study. *Proceedings of the 43rd Hawai'i International Conference on System Sciences*, Kauai, HI. DOI: 10.1109/HICSS.2010.400. 49

Fleischmann, K.R., Wallace, W.A., and Grimes, J.M. (2011c). Computational modeling and human values: A comparative study of corporate, academic, and government research labs. *Proceedings of the 44th Hawai'i International Conference on System Sciences*, Kauai, HI. DOI: 10.1109/HICSS.2011.123. 47, 48, 49

Fleischmann, K.R., Wallace, W.A., and Grimes, J.M. (2011d). How values can reduce conflicts in the design process: Results from a multi-site mixed-method field study. *Proceedings of the 74th Annual Meeting of the American Society for Information Science and Technology*, New Orleans, LA. DOI: 10.1002/meet.2011.14504801147. 47, 48

Floridi, L. (2007). A look into the future impact of ICT on our lives. *The Information Society*, Vol. 23, No. 1, pp. 59-64. DOI: 10.1080/01972240601059094. 68

Foucault, M. (1973). *The birth of the clinic: An archaeology of medical perception.* New York: Pantheon Books. 37

Friedman, B. (1996). Value-sensitive design. *ACM Interactions*, Vol. 3, No. 6, pp. 17-23. DOI: 10.1145/242485.242493. 20

Friedman, B., and Kahn, P. H., Jr. (2008). Human values, ethics, and design. In J. A. Jacko and A. Sears (Eds.), *The Human-Computer Interaction Handbook*, 2nd Edition, pp. 1241-1266. Mahwah, NJ: Lawrence Erlbaum Associates. 21

Friedman, B., Kahn, P.H., Jr., and Borning, A. (2006). Value sensitive design and information systems. In P. Zhang and D. Galletta (Eds.), *Human-computer interaction and management information systems: Foundations*, pp. 348-372. Armonk, NY: M.E. Sharpe. DOI: 10.1002/9780470281819.ch4. 21, 22, 23, 24, 25, 26, 27, 28, 29, 53, 64

Giddens, A. (1979). *Central problems in social theory: Action, structure, and contradiction in social analysis.* Berkeley: University of California Press. 24

Hakken, D. (1991). Culture-centered computing: Social policy and development of new information technology in England and the United States. *Human Organization*, Vol. 50, No. 4, pp. 406-423. 20

Haraway, D.J. (1988). Situated knowledges: The science question in feminism and the privilege of partial perspective. *Feminist Studies*, Vol. 14, No. 3, pp. 575-599. DOI: 10.2307/3178066. 8

Haraway, D.J. (1991). *Simians, cyborgs, and women: The reinvention of nature*. New York: Routledge. 17, 68

Hitlin, S. and Piliavin, J.A. (2004). Values: Reviving a dormant concept. *Annual Review of Sociology*, Vol. 30, pp. 359-393. DOI: 10.1146/annurev.soc.30.012703.110640. 1, 2, 8, 9

Hofstede, G.H. (2001). *Cultures consequences: Comparing values, behaviors, institutions and organizations across nations*. Thousand Oaks, CA: Sage. 9

Ishita, E., Oard, D.W., Fleischmann, K.R., Cheng, A.-S., & Templeton, T.C. (2010). Investigating multi-label classification for human values. *Proceedings of the 73rd Annual Meeting of the American Society for Information Science and Technology*, Pittsburgh, PA. DOI: 10.1002/meet.14504701116. 58

Jaeger, P. T., and Fleischmann, K.R. (2007). Public libraries, values, trust, and e-government. *Information Technology and Libraries*, Vol. 26, No. 4, pp. 35-43. DOI: 10.6017/ital.v26i4.3268. 18

Johnson, D.G. (1997). Is the global information infrastructure a democratic technology? *Computers and Society*, Vol. 27, No. 3, pp. 20-26. DOI: 10.1145/270858.270865. 2

Kahn, P. H., Jr., Friedman, B., Gill, B. T., Hagman, J., Severson, R. L., Freier, N. G., Feldman, E. N., Carrere, S., and Stolyar, A. (2008). A plasma display window? - The shifting baseline problem in a technologically-mediated natural word. *Journal of Environmental Psychology*, Vol. 28, No. 2, pp. 192-199. DOI: 10.1016/j.jenvp.2007.10.008. 26

Kelton, K., Fleischmann, K.R., and Wallace, W.A. (2008). Trust in digital information. *Journal of the American Society for Information Science and Technology*, Vol. 59, No. 3, pp. 363-374. DOI: 10.1002/asi.20722. 23, 43

Kluckhohn, C. (1951). Values and value-orientations in the theory of action. In T. Parsons (Ed.), *Toward a general theory of action*. New York: Harper. 9

Knobel, C. and Bowker, G.C. (2011). Values in design. *Communications of the ACM*, Vol. 54, No. 7, pp. 26-28. DOI: 10.1145/1965724.1965735. 20, 68

Koepfler, J.A. & Fleischmann, K.R. (2011). Classifying values in informal communication: Adapting the meta-inventory of human values for tweets. *Proceedings of the 74th Annual Meeting of the American Society for Information Science and Technology*, New Orleans, LA. DOI: 10.1002/meet.2011.14504801116. 54

Koepfler, J.A. and Fleischmann, K.R. (2012). Studying the values of hard-to-reach populations: Content analysis of tweets by the 21st Century homeless." *Proceedings of the 7th Annual iConference*, Toronto, Canada. DOI: 10.1145/2132176.2132183. 54

Koepfler, J.A., Templeton, T.C., and Fleischmann, K.R. (2012). Exploration of values and frames in social media texts related to the homeless hotspots debate. *Proceedings of the 75th Annual Meeting of the American Society for Information Science and Technology*, Baltimore, MD. DOI: 10.1002/meet.14504901238. 57

Le Dantec, C.A. and Edwards, W.K. (2008). Designs on dignity: Perceptions of technology among the homeless. *Proceedings of the ACM SIGCHI Conference on Human Factors in Computing Systems*, Florence, Italy. DOI: 10.1145/1357054.1357155. 53

Marini, M.M. (2000). Social values and norms. In E.F. Borgatta and M.L. Borgatta (Eds.), *Encyclopedia of sociology*. New York: Macmillan. 9

Marshall, C.C. and Golovchinsky, G. (2004). Saving private hypertext: Requirements and pragmatic dimensions for preservation. *Proceedings of the 15th ACM Conference on Hypertext and Hypermedia*, Santa Cruz, CA. 19

Mason, R.O. (1994). Morality and models. In W.A. Wallace (Ed.), *Ethics in modeling*. Tarrytown, NY: Elsevier. 43

Nissenbaum, H. (1999). Can trust be secured online? A theoretical perspective. *Etica e Politica*, No. 2, 22, 23

Nissenbaum, H. (2005). Values in technical design. In C. Mitcham (Ed.), *Encyclopedia of science, technology and ethics*. New York: Macmillan, 2005, lxvi-lxx. 20

Obeyesekere, G. (1985). Depression, Buddhism, and the work of culture in Sri Lanka. In A. Kleinman and B. Good (Eds.), *Culture and depression: Studies in the anthropology and cross-cultural psychiatry of affect and disorder*. Berkeley: University of California Press. 11

Pang, B. and Lee, L. (2008). Opinion mining and sentiment analysis. *Foundations and trends in information retrieval*, Vol. 2, Nos. 1-2, pp. 1-135. DOI: 10.1561/1500000011. 57

Parsons, T. (1935). The place of ultimate values in sociological theory. *International Journal of Ethics*, Vol. 45, No. 3, pp. 282-316. DOI: 10.1086/208233. 8

Phenix, K.J. and McCook, K. de la P. (2005). Human rights and librarians. *Reference & User Services Quarterly*, Vol. 45, No. 1, pp. 23-26. 15

Pohl, K. (2010). *Requirements engineering: Fundamentals, principles, and techniques*. New York: Springer. DOI: 10.1007/978-3-642-12578-2. 21

Quinn, M.J. (2013). *Ethics for the information age*. Upper Saddle River, NJ: Pearson. 1, 39

Rogers, Y., Preece, J., and Sharp, H. (2011). *Interaction design: Beyond human-computer interaction*, 3rd Edition. Hoboken, NJ: Wiley. 20

Rokeach, M. (1973). *The nature of human values*. New York: Free Press. 9, 12

Rosson, M.B. and Carroll, J.M., (2002). *Usability engineering: Scenario-based development of human-computer interaction*. San Francisco: Morgan-Kaufmann. 20

Schuler, D. and Namioka, A. (1993). *Participatory design: Principles and practices*. Hillsdale, NJ: Lawrence Erlbaum Associates. 20

Schwartz, S.H. (1994). Are there universal aspects in the structure and contents of human values? *Journal of Social Issues*, Vol. 50, No. 4, pp. 19-45. DOI: 10.1111/j.1540-4560.1994.tb01196.x. 8, 9, 10, 11, 12, 13, 14, 16, 17, 18, 21, 22, 23, 24, 25, 26, 27, 28, 29, 47, 48, 53, 55, 57

Schwartz, S.H. (2007). Value orientations: Measurement, antecedents and consequences across nations. In R. Jowell, C. Roberts, R. Fitzgerald, and G. Eva (Eds.), *Measuring Attitudes Cross-Nationally: Lessons from the European Social Survey*, pp. 169-203. London: Sage. DOI: 10.4135/9781849209458. n9. 2, 9, 55

Senger, P., Boehner, K., David, S., and Kaye, J. (2005). Reflective design. *Proceedings of the 4th Decennial Conference on Critical Computing*, Aarhus, Netherlands. DOI: 10.1145/1094562.1094569. 20

Shilton, K. (2013). Value levers: Building ethics into design. *Science, Technology, and Human Values*, Vol. 38, No. 3, pp. 374-397. DOI: 10.1177/0162243912436985. 44

Shilton, K, Koepfler, J.A., and Fleischmann, K.R. (2013). Charting sociotechnical dimensions of values for design research. *The Information Society*, Vol. 29, No. 5. DOI: 10.1080/01972243.2013.825357. 67

Shilton, K., Koepfler, J.A., and Fleischmann, K.R. (2014). How to see values in social computing: Methods for studying values dimensions. *Proceedings of the 17th ACM Conference on Computer Supported Cooperative Work and Social Computing*, Baltimore, MD. 68

Shneiderman, B. (2000). Universal usability. *Communications of the ACM*, Vol. 43, No. 5, pp. 84-91. DOI: 10.1145/332833.332843. 23

Spates, J.L. (1983). A sociology of values. *Annual Review of Sociology*, Vol. 9, pp. 27-49. DOI: 10.1146/annurev.so.09.080183.000331. 8

Takayama, Y., Tomiura, Y., Ishita, E., Wang, Z., Oard, D.W., Fleischmann, K.R., & Cheng, A.-S. (2013). Automatic annotation of human values behind sentences by using augmented feature vectors. *Proceedings of the Conference of the Pacific Association for Computational Linguistics*, Tokyo, Japan. 58

Templeton, T.C. and Fleischmann, K.R. (2011). The relationship between human values and attitudes toward the Park51 and nuclear power controversies. *Proceedings of the 74th Annual Meeting of the American Society for Information Science and Technology*, New Orleans, LA. DOI: 10.1002/meet.2011.14504801172. 56, 57

Templeton, T.C., Fleischmann, K.R., and Boyd-Graber, J. (2011a). Comparing values and sentiment using Mechanical Turk. *Proceedings of the 6th Annual iConference*, Seattle, WA. DOI: 10.1145/1940761.1940903. 56

Templeton, T.C., Fleischmann, K.R., and Boyd-Graber, J. (2011b). Simulating audiences: Automating analysis of values, attitudes, and sentiment. *Proceedings of the Third IEEE International Conference on Social Computing*. Boston, MA. DOI: 10.1109/PASSAT/SocialCom.2011.238. 59

Wiebe, J. (1994). Tracking point of view in narrative. *Computational Linguistics*, Vol. 20, No. 2, pp. 233-287. 57

Wiegand, W. (1999). Tunnel vision and blind spots: What the past tells us about the present; Reflections on the Twentieth-Century history of American librarianship. *The Library Quarterly*, Vol. 69, No. 1, pp. 1-32. DOI: 10.1086/603022. 15

Winner, L. (1977). *Autonomous technology: Technics-out-of-control as a theme in political thought*. Cambridge, MA: MIT Press. 24

Winner, L. (1987). Technologies as forms of life. In K.S. Shrader-Frechette and L. Westra (Eds.), *Technology and values*. Lanham, MD: Rowman & Littlefield. 4, 39

Woelfer, J. P., Iverson, A., Hendry, D.G., Friedman, B., and Gill, B. (2011). Improving the safety of homeless young people with mobile phones: Values, form and function. *Proceedings of the ACM SIGCHI Confer-*

ence on Human Factors in Computing Systems, Vancouver, Canada. DOI: 10.1145/1978942.1979191. 53

Wright, P. and McCarthy, J. (2010). Experience-centered design: Designers, users, and communities in dialogue. In J.M. Carroll (Ed.), *Synthesis Lectures on Human-Centered Informatics*, San Rafael: Morgan and Claypool. DOI: 10.2200/S00229ED1V01Y201003HCI009. 20

Zhou, Y., Goldberg, M., Magdon Ismail, M., and Wallace, W.A. (2007). Strategies for cleaning organizational e-mails with an application to Enron e-mail dataset. *Proceedings of the 5th Annual Conference of the North American Association for Computational Social and Organization Sciences*, Emory, Atlanta, GA. 57

Zhou, Y., Fleischmann, K.R., and Wallace, W.A. (2010). Automatic text analysis of values in the Enron email dataset: Clustering a social network using the value patterns of actors. *Proceedings of the 43rd Hawai'i International Conference on System Sciences*, Kauai, HI. DOI: 10.1109/HICSS.2010.77. 58

Author Biography

Kenneth R. Fleischmann is an Associate Professor in the School of Information at The University of Texas at Austin. He received his Ph.D. in science and technology studies from Rensselaer Polytechnic Institute. His research has been funded by nine grants and fellowships from the National Science Foundation (NSF) as well as funding from the Intelligence Advanced Research Projects Activity (IARPA), and has been published in journals such as *Journal of the American Society for Information Science and Technology* (JASIST), *Communications of the ACM*, *Computer*, and The *Information Society*. In 2012, his collaborative papers received the iConference Best Paper Award and the ASIS&T SIG-USE Best Paper Award.

Printed in the United States
by Baker & Taylor Publisher Services

To Weronica, for believing in me

—Jack Nutting

To my wonderful wife and soul mate, Madeline, for her amazing love and support

—Dave Wooldridge

To my best friend and partner in life, Deneen

LFU4FREIH

—David Mark

Contents at a Glance

Contents

About the Authors

Jack Nutting has been using Cocoa since the olden days, long before it was even called Cocoa. He has used Cocoa and its predecessors to develop software for a wide range of industries and applications, including gaming, graphic design, online digital distribution, telecommunications, finance, publishing, and travel. When he isn't working on Mac, iPhone, or iPad projects, he is developing web applications with Ruby on Rails. Jack is a passionate proponent of Objective-C and the Cocoa frameworks. At the drop of a hat, he will speak at length on the virtues of dynamic dispatch and runtime class manipulations to anyone who will listen (and even to some who won't). Jack is the principal author of *Learn Cocoa on the Mac* (Apress, 2010). He blogs from time to time at www.nuthole.com, and you can follow his more frequent random musings at twitter.com/jacknutting.

As the founder of Electric Butterfly, **Dave Wooldridge** has been developing award-winning web sites and software for 15 years. When he is not creating Mac and iOS apps, he can be found writing. Dave is the author of *The Business of iPhone App Development: Making and Marketing Apps that Succeed* (Apress, 2010). He also has written numerous articles for leading tech publications, including a monthly software marketing column for *MacTech*. Follow Dave at twitter.com/ebutterfly.

Dave Mark is a longtime Mac developer and author. His books include *Beginning iPhone 3 Development* (Apress, 2009), *Learn C on the Mac* (Apress, 2009), *The Macintosh Programming Primer* series (Addison-Wesley, 1992), and *Ultimate Mac Programming* (Wiley, 1995). Dave loves the water and spends as much time as possible on it, in it, or near it. He lives with his wife and three children in Virginia.

About the Technical Reviewer

 **Mark Dalrymple** is a longtime Mac and Unix programmer, working on cross-platform toolkits, Internet publishing tools, high-performance web servers, and end-user desktop applications. He is the principal author of *Advanced Mac OS X Programming* (Big Nerd Ranch, 2005) and *Learn Objective-C on the Mac* (Apress, 2009). In his spare time, he plays trombone and bassoon and makes balloon animals.

Acknowledgments

The authors wish to thank the editorial staff at Apress who helped make this book possible: Clay Andres, who assembled the team and got the ball rolling; Kelly Moritz, whose vigilance in pulling all of our strings at the appropriate times has been crucial in moving the book forward along its ambitious schedule; Douglas Pundick, who helped to bring coherence and flow to each chapter; and Marilyn Smith, whose expert wordsmithing has helped make us seem like better writers on nearly every page of the book. We are also eternally indebted to Mark Dalrymple, whose keen eye and rapier wit have helped us avoid many technical missteps.

Preface

The world has changed. Since work on this book began, the iPad was released (selling three million units in the first 80 days), and the iPhone OS was renamed to iOS, which debuted as iOS 4 in the new iPhone 4 (which was preordered by 600,000 people the first day). Meanwhile, more than 11,000 apps were released for the iPad—a mix of iPad-only apps and universal apps, which can run on both the iPhone and the iPad. By any measure, the iPad is a runaway hit. It is already inspiring many creative uses far beyond the sort of ultimate media-consumption device that Apple began touting it as back in January.

By the time this book goes to print and reaches your hands, Xcode 4 may be available (throwing a monkey-wrench into our careful descriptions of using Xcode and Interface Builder), Apple will have sold one or two million more iPads, and iOS 4 may even be available for iPad. Apple is keeping iPhone and iPad developers on their toes, and authors are no exception! We've kept all of this in mind while writing this book, and have worked to make a book that will stand the test of time, regardless of OS versions and release dates.

At the end of the day, iPhone and iPad are inherently two different beasts, with different form factors and capabilities that encourage different usage patterns, despite the similarities in their underlying OSes; Beginning iPad Development for iPhone Developers is meant to highlight those differences, helping you build upon your iPhone development knowledge with new tools and techniques to let you create great iPad apps!

Chapter 1

Welcome to the Paradigm Shift

Unless you've been living under a rock, you're well aware that the new darling in Apple's product line is the iPad, a thin, touchscreen tablet that aims to revolutionize mobile computing and portable media consumption. The iPad was undoubtedly one of the most heavily rumored, hyped, and anticipated product launches in recent memory... at least since Apple's introduction of the original iPhone in 2007.

One major difference here is that the first iPhone model did not include an App Store. It wasn't until a little more than a year later that Apple launched the iTunes App Store, with only 500 native apps from third-party developers. Fast-forward to 2010, and you'll find more than 200,000 apps in the App Store. With the iPad's ability to run most of those existing apps without any modifications, users will have access to a vast catalog of software immediately upon powering up their brand-new iPads. But iPhone apps pale in comparison to the sheer beauty and flexibility of native iPad apps!

With the new iPad-only features and user interface elements offered in iPhone SDK 3.2 and the powerful graphics and processing engine under the hood, the iPad represents a much greater business opportunity for developers than even the early days of the iPhone. Unlike the iPhone, with its limited memory constraints and small screen, the iPad offers developers a unique mobile platform for creating truly sophisticated, desktop-quality apps!

But to take advantage of this exciting new opportunity and develop apps that consumers want, it's important to understand who the iPad was designed for.

Reinventing the Tablet

So why a tablet? To carve out a new category that sits between the laptop and the smartphone, the device must satisfy a need that is currently not being delivered by those other products. For the past few years, netbooks have tried to bridge that gap. But as Steve Jobs has famously remarked, netbooks are nothing but cheap laptops in a small form factor. Running Microsoft Windows or a Linux-based operating system, netbooks don't make computing any easier than laptops. Their only advantage is that they're more affordable.

A thin tablet device is much more intimate than a laptop or netbook, and it can be easily held from almost any angle—on a couch or in bed, for example. And I'm willing to bet that some of you even take your iPad into the bathroom for a little quality time, surfing the Web and reading e-books.

The iPad is certainly not the first computer tablet to hit the market, and it won't be the last. Since the early 1990s, countless companies have attempted to lure consumers with feature-packed tablet models, but none of them were ever successful. Why? Because the software was either limited in functionality or too difficult to use.

In 1993, Apple launched the Newton MessagePad, its first stab at a tablet. With its monochrome screen and limited selection of software, it was largely perceived as a big PDA, rather than a true mobile computer. Since the product never seemed to grow beyond a small, yet loyal, cult following, Apple discontinued Newton development in 1998.

Most of the other hardware companies that followed with their own tablets tried a different approach. Running on various flavors of Windows or Linux, those tablets were powerful computers, but were ultimately not the right mobile solution for most consumers. Like Apple's Newton, many of them required the use of a stylus pen in order to accurately tap the tiny on-screen buttons and menu options. The underlying problem was that those desktop operating systems were never designed for a finger-driven touchscreen. From a usability standpoint, a cursor-based desktop operating system is a very cumbersome interface for a mobile tablet device that's typically operated with one hand.

It's All About the Software

When rumors first started circulating back in 2009 about the development of a mysterious Apple tablet, the big question was which operating system it would run. With a larger screen, it could certainly handle Mac OS X, and I must admit, a small part of me had secretly hoped that Apple would announce a Mac-based tablet, so that I could run my favorite Mac apps on it. But as a developer, I'm not the average consumer. If Apple had released the iPad as a Mac OS X-powered device, it would surely have met the same lukewarm reception as the countless tablets that came before it.

But Apple is smarter than that. To succeed, Apple knew this new class of mobile device had to be easier to use than a laptop, yet more powerful than a smartphone. To achieve this, the tablet needed an operating system that was engineered from the ground up for multitouch finger gestures and efficient touchscreen navigation. One of Apple's greatest strengths as a technology company is that it controls the design of both the hardware and the software, always striving for a seamless marriage between the two. The iPad is a perfect example of that ideology.

Powered by a tablet-enhanced version of iOS, the iPad avoids the usual trappings of adapting mouse-driven desktop software to a touchscreen environment. With millions of iPhone and iPod touch users already familiar with the iOS interface, there's an immediate comfort level with the iPad. It looks easy to use because it is. When Apple first announced the iPad, the tablet's emphasis on simplicity seemed to underwhelm some critics, but that is the very element that will make it a game-changer in the world of mobile computing.

The iPad Is *Not* a Big iPod touch

The naysayers who are skeptical of the iPad's future—merely passing it off as a big iPod touch—are the ones who don't get it. They don't see the big picture here. The instant-on iOS proved ideal for a small smartphone device, and it will prove even more effective for the iPad's larger screen. But don't be fooled by its deceptive exterior. Sure, it may *look* like a super-sized iPod touch, but under the hood, the iPad boasts a powerful graphics engine and Apple's speedy, battery-optimized A4 processor.

The iPad is not just about games. Even though games have made the iPod touch a dominant force in portable gaming, and many of those titles will be optimized for Apple's tablet, I believe the iPad will become a popular platform for productivity apps—even more so than the iPhone.

Beyond the convenience of the larger display and full-size touchscreen keyboard, iPhone SDK 3.2 includes iPad support for Core Text and several other exciting new frameworks and user interface niceties that make it much easier to develop feature-rich productivity apps. Apple has set the stage for the iPad to become the portable computer of choice for not only the general public, but also doctors, teachers, students, salespeople, scientists, pilots, engineers, and countless other markets.

Apple hinted as much with its new iWork suite for the iPad (see Figure 1–1). By delivering sophisticated iPad versions of its Mac counterparts (Keynote, Pages, and Numbers), iWork is Apple's shot across the bow at critics, proving its new tablet is so much more than just a glorified iPod.

When a laptop is too unwieldy or too heavy to carry around all day, the iPad is a much more practical form factor, capable of running state-of-the-art, desktop-caliber applications. And with the simplicity of the iOS interface, this new class of mobile apps will increase productivity and provide a much more intimate and immersive experience that is easily accessible to even the most nontechnical neophytes.

 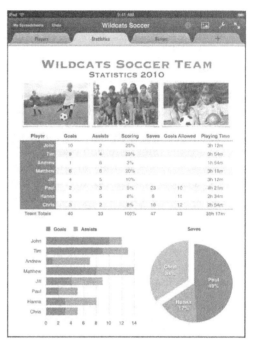

Figure 1–1. *Pages (left) and Numbers (right) are part of Apple's iWork suite for the iPad, a perfect showcase of how sophisticated, desktop-quality apps can be designed for ease of use on a mobile touchscreen.*

Inspired by the iPad's potential, the prominent iPhone development firm, Agile Web Solutions, began working on iPad apps as soon as Apple released the first SDK betas. David Chartier, Chief Media Producer of Agile Web Solutions, says this about the iPad's potential:

> *Some write off the iPad as a "big iPod touch," but that's shortsighted. I think the iOS on a larger screen will allow for a much more engaging multi-touch experience. Just look at all the features Apple included in its iWork [for iPad]. The iPad offers much more powerful hardware and more features for developers. This really could become a secondary computer, or even a primary one for a lot of users, and that's really compelling.*

Personal Computing for the Masses

When exploring the new iPad-centric SDK features in later chapters, you'll immediately see that Apple has provided extensive tools for creating very robust apps. With this newfound power at your fingertips, many of you may be inclined to build apps that mimic traditional desktop interface models, derived from years of programming for Mac OS X, Microsoft Windows, or Linux. Even though the iPad platform removes many of the user interface design restraints and memory limitations that developers grappled with on the iPhone, this would be entirely the wrong approach.

There's a reason Apple used iOS instead of Mac OS X as the iPad's operating system. Beyond the fact that it was designed for a finger-based touchscreen, iOS also serves another valuable role. Unlike traditional desktop operating systems, iOS hides the filesystem from users, placing the focus instead on content.

Although many see the iPad as a mere laptop replacement, I believe Apple's new tablet was designed with a more ambitious goal: to reinvent mainstream personal computing, much like the original Mac did back in 1984. Apple feels that computers have become far too complicated for the average consumer and aims to simplify the experience. Although desktop operating systems like Mac OS X will continue to thrive for years to come, the iPad presents a major paradigm shift in computing.

The iPad was designed for people who don't like using computers. And yet it's packed with enough engineering muscle to easily accommodate the needs of power users. In a nutshell, the iPad is the portable, personal computer for *everyone*.

The genius of the iPad is in its sheer simplicity. I know I've mentioned this a few times already, but it is the single most important factor to remember when developing apps for this new device. A major component in Apple's strategy to deliver a more organic and intuitive user experience is incorporating real-world metaphors into the interface design process. A good example of this is Apple's preinstalled Notes app (see Figure 1–2).

A computer newbie could launch the Notes app for the first time and immediately figure out how to use it, without the need for any instructions or prior computer knowledge. Your grandparents could use this app! To make the experience fun, Apple even added realistic graphical flourishes, such as the stitched-leather binder that holds both the yellow, lined notepad and the white, card-based notes list. And marking the currently selected note with a "hand-drawn" red circle is a nice touch!

Apple encourages developers to embrace this sea change in their own app interface designs as well. Obviously, integrating real-world objects, imagery, and textures to communicate functionality won't be practical in every scenario, but the primary objective is clear: keep it simple. Remember this fundamental rule as you mull over potential app ideas to develop. We'll be exploring additional user interface design considerations in Chapter 3.

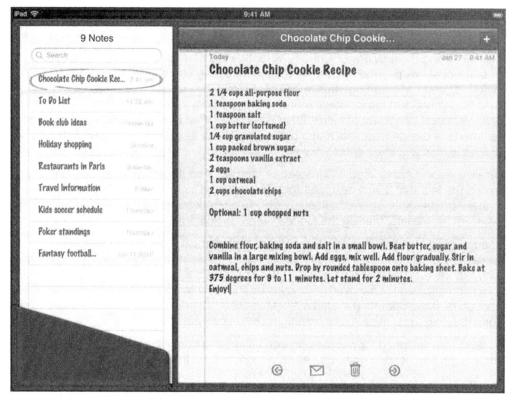

Figure 1–2. *Apple designed the user interface of its Notes app to emulate a physical notepad, eliminating the learning curve for first-time users.*

The continued success of the iPad rests solely on the software that powers it. Apple's revolutionary tablet provides developers with a new opportunity to create apps for people who want a simplified computer experience without having to sacrifice on features. The iPad apps that succeed will be the ones that are packed with functionality while remaining highly intuitive and easy to use.

Like most developers, I constantly find myself serving the role of tech support for family and friends. Most of the time, the problems they encounter involve locating misplaced files and e-mail attachments, deciphering endless configuration options, grappling with arcane software installers, and so on. If they all had iPads—downloading and using apps easily with only a few finger taps—I can guarantee I would be spending a lot more quality time with my family and fewer precious hours troubleshooting their archaic desktop machines. At some point in the near future, everyone will begin to recognize the iPad for what it really is: the next evolutionary step in personal computing for the masses.

Developing Apps for the iPad

Even though most of the 200,000 apps in the App Store will run "as is" on the iPad, the small 320-by-480 pixel dimensions of an iPhone app are less than half the size of the iPad's large 768-by-1024 pixel screen. Although the iPad includes backward-compatibility support for iPhone apps, the end result leaves much to be desired. Apple provides only two options for running iPhone apps on the iPad: displayed at normal size in the center of the screen (the rest of the unused area is left black) or magnified two times to fill the screen. The iPad's scaling algorithm seems to work fairly well, but full-screen iPhone apps still appear rather pixelized. After becoming spoiled by beautiful, high-resolution iPad apps, users will find magnified iPhone apps on the same large screen very crude and unattractive.

When Your iPhone App Is No Longer Good Enough

Although your existing iPhone app may run fine on the iPad, don't settle for an inferior user experience. iPhone apps were designed for the iPhone. The iPad should be treated as an entirely new platform, with its own set of design requirements. Consumers will certainly grow weary of running pixelized iPhone apps on the iPad, especially if iPad-enhanced alternatives are available in the App Store. With this in mind, it's never too soon to begin developing iPad versions of your apps.

Apple is encouraging this new breed of iPad-optimized apps by showcasing them in a special iPad section of the App Store. Obviously, it's in Apple's best interests to champion iPad app development, since an extensive selection of iPad apps will help sell more iPads. And this, in turn, will ultimately help you sell more apps, as the number of new iPad owners increase, all flocking to the App Store to download new software.

As proof of this development push, none of Apple's preinstalled apps were left untouched. Apple took the time to redesign all of them—such as Mail, Calendar, Contacts, Photos, Safari, and even Notes (see Figure 1–2)—to utilize the expanded screen space and new interface capabilities of the iPad platform. And most app developers seem to agree that this is the right direction to take to properly meet user expectations. Here's what David Chartier of Agile Web Solutions had to say on the subject:

> Sure, there's that 2x button for running existing iPhone apps in a full-screen mode on the iPad. But I think that once iPad customers see what's capable with the iPad's increased screen space and hardware and software advantages over the iPhone and iPod touch, you will find that the "2x" mode quickly becomes the Mac OS Classic on the iPad. To succeed on the iPad, there's no question in my mind that developers will need to incorporate the new features and interface tools to provide the best user experience. If you don't, users won't hesitate to check out your competition.

Knowing that iPad users won't be content with running blown-up, pixelized iPhone apps, developers are racing to port their existing iPhone apps into new, enhanced iPad versions. Their efforts go far beyond simply scaling the interface to accommodate the larger screen real estate. Major changes to app navigation and user interface architecture are being implemented to take advantage of the iPad's unique software and hardware features.

There are several important design methodologies and recommended interface guidelines to consider when developing apps for the iPad, all of which will be discussed in great detail in Chapter 3. For now, it's time for a little inspiration to get the creative juices flowing. Let's take a look at how several iPhone developers are retooling their apps for the iPad.

Exploring the Possibilities

A handful of well-known developers were kind enough to share their insights about developing apps for the iPad platform. In taking a closer look at these apps, several iPad-specific user interface elements and concepts are mentioned. If you're unfamiliar with any of them, don't worry. All of the new iPad frameworks and user interface controls available in iPhone SDK 3.2 will be thoroughly explained throughout the rest of the book, starting with Chapter 3.

Brushes

Steve Sprang's acclaimed iPhone app, Brushes (http://brushesapp.com/), is a painting program designed exclusively for the mobile screen. With a deceptively simple interface, Brushes is packed with features, such as an advanced color picker, several realistic brushes, multiple layers, extreme zooming, and even undo/redo options. It is a powerful tool for painting on the iPhone, which has spawned a vast community of mobile digital artists.

Choosing a new color or a different brush requires moving to a new screen view. Due to the iPhone's small size, this is a necessary design strategy to keep the user interface uncluttered and easy to use. Once a selection is made, the artist can then return to the main canvas screen (see Figure 1–3).

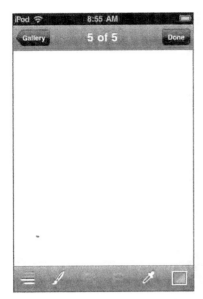 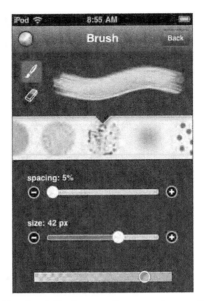

Figure 1–3. *Brushes assigns color picker and brush palettes to separate screen views on the iPhone. This requires users to navigate between various screens, but on such a small device, it's a necessary design to keep the interface uncluttered and easy to use.*

Many people first heard of Brushes when the June 1, 2009, issue of *The New Yorker* featured a beautiful cover by artist Jorge Colombo, created entirely in Brushes on the iPhone. Then in January 2010, Brushes returned to the media spotlight as Steve Sprang was invited to unveil his forthcoming iPad version of Brushes during Apple's iPad keynote announcement. Beyond showcasing the extended drawing space on the iPad's large screen, he also demonstrated how those separate color picker and brush palettes could be made easily accessible from within the main canvas screen by using the new popover controller (see Figure 1–4).

Popovers empower the iPad version of Brushes to behave more like a traditional desktop application, alleviating the need to move back and forth between various screen views, such as on a small iPhone or iPod touch. This is just one of many new user interface features that allowed Sprang to provide a more powerful and simplified Brushes experience on the iPad.

Knowing that Steve Sprang was one of the first developers outside Apple to work with the iPad SDK frameworks and user interface additions, I was curious to learn more about his experience programming for the iPad. I was fortunate enough to steal him away from his busy schedule for a brief interview.

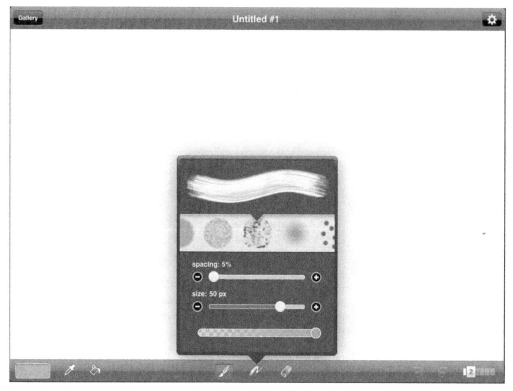

Figure 1–4. *Popovers enabled developer Steve Sprang to integrate the color picker and brush views within the main canvas screen in the iPad version of Brushes.*

Beyond the larger screen size for the Brushes "canvas," what have the new iPad features in the SDK allowed you to do to simplify and enhance the user experience that wasn't possible in the iPhone version?

The larger screen makes it easier to deal with multiple orientations. For example, on the iPhone, the color panel in Brushes would require an alternate layout to work well in landscape mode, but on the iPad, the popover works equally well in any orientation. Popovers are also a big win in terms of workflow, allowing quick access to many controls while still keeping them tucked away when not in use.

In porting Brushes to the iPad, can you share your experience working with the new SDK?

Most of my effort was spent redesigning the interface to work well on the iPad. The gallery view is completely new, as well as the in-app playback feature. Some interface elements from the iPhone were easily reused. For example, the original gallery view from the iPhone now appears as a thumbnail popover in the iPad gallery (for quicker navigation). The painting engine is basically the same, but some optimizations were necessary to deal with the increased number of bits being pushed around on the screen.

Any useful tips or words of wisdom for developers looking to port their own iPhone apps to the iPad platform?

I think it's easy to underestimate the amount of work involved in redesigning an iPhone app to work well on the iPad. In many ways, it's an entirely new design problem. On the iPhone, you could get away with pushing a view controller onto a navigation controller, but on the iPad, you'll likely need a custom transition if you want things to feel right. It's going to take more effort than just scaling up your old interface.

1Password Pro

The best-selling iPhone app, 1Password Pro (http://agile.ws/), securely stores your important information, software licenses, and passwords, and can automatically log you in to web sites with a single tap. Limited by the small screen of the iPhone, Agile Web Solutions employed a navigation controller and tab bar controller in the user interface design, so that users could easily organize and access their stored entries. The goal was to avoid cluttering the small screen with too many elements, but like most iPhone apps, this required navigating back and forth between different screen views (see Figure 1–5).

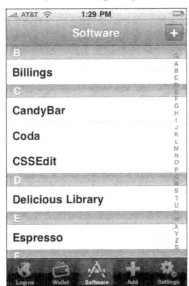

Figure 1–5. *On the small iPhone, Agile Web Solutions used tab bar and navigation controllers to maintain a streamlined 1Password Pro interface across multiple screens.*

Although the iPhone app interface for 1Password Pro was very intuitive and easy to use, Agile Web Solutions developers were eager to take advantage of the iPad's expanded screen size, enabling them to consolidate those primary views into one, multipane interface for the iPad version of 1Password Pro (see Figure 1–6). David Chartier explains the design:

In the big picture, the larger screen space allowed us to design a more cohesive 1Password experience for our users. But really, it's about the little details. We can display a few more of the essential 1Password sections (passwords, secure notes, software licenses, etc.) in a wider toolbar, and present controls in a popover instead of making users tap between multiple screens to create new items. Instead of tapping into a new screen to view an item's details, we can display them in-line in the item list, which can feature web site and application icons to help users pick out the one they need more quickly.

Figure 1–6. *Empowered by the iPad's large screen, Agile Web Solutions consolidated several screen views from the 1Password Pro iPhone app into one, multipane interface for the iPad version.*

Synotes

When Syncode set out to create Synotes (http://www.syncode.com.au/), a note-taking iPhone app that effortlessly "cloud" synchronizes saved notes across multiple devices and the Web, the goal was to provide a stylish and user-friendly interface that was easy to use. As with Brushes and 1Password Pro, this required navigating between several screen views to maintain an uncluttered interface on the small iPhone and iPod touch. A navigation controller manages movement from the main notes list to a selected note, and within a detailed note view, a custom vertical toolbar provides access to additional options, such as assigning an icon to the currently selected note (see Figure 1–7).

 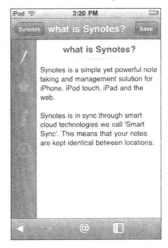 

Figure 1–7. *In the iPhone version of Synotes, several navigation screens are required to preserve an effective and user-friendly experience.*

In redesigning Synotes for the iPad, the larger screen gave the developers the freedom to consolidate those multiple screens into a more unified interface (see Figure 1–8).

Matthew Lesh, cofounder of Syncode, describes their approach:

> *Syncode has found the challenge of porting Synotes to the iPad both exciting and rewarding. The apparent difference between platforms is space, so the question becomes how to most logically utilize the extra screen real estate. Synotes for iPad utilizes three key iPad-specific SDK features. Firstly, UISplitViewController, a key element to Synotes that enables us to follow Apple's "any orientation" style guides and in the process, perfectly fitting the list and content nature of Synotes. Secondly, the UIPopoverController has been vital to display information that doesn't require the entire screen, such as the icon selection screen. Thirdly, UIModalViewControllers have enabled the display of further views that would have traditionally been the third step in a navigation controller, such as settings or history items.*

As evident in the iPad version (Figure 1–8), assigning an icon to the currently selected note is now accomplished with a popover, whereas that feature once required navigating to a separate screen view on the iPhone. Although the landscape orientation is shown here with the notes list displayed in a split-view column, rotating the iPad to portrait mode automatically puts that notes list in a popover view. That way, the narrower portrait view allows more room for the selected note, while the main notes list always remains accessible from the top navigation bar. The beauty here is that the split view controller handles all of this for you, the developer!

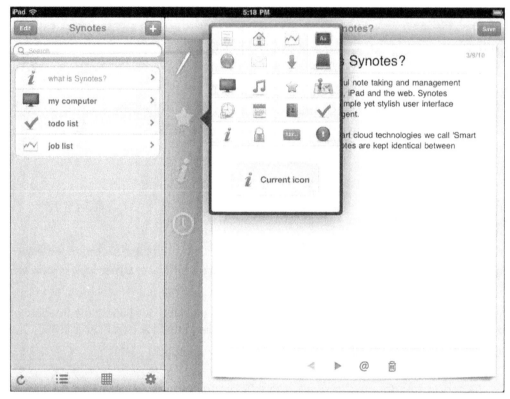

Figure 1–8. *The iPad's new user interface elements and larger screen enabled Syncode to redesign Synotes, so that one optimized screen could accomplish what once required multiple screens on the iPhone.*

ScribattlePad

The tablet's expanded screen size doesn't just benefit productivity apps. It's also a boon for game developers. Coauthor Jack Nutting couldn't wait to start building iPad-optimized versions of his Rebisoft games (http://www.rebisoft.com/).

Remember the stick-figure war games you used to play as a kid with a pencil and some graph paper? Jack has meticulously emulated the authentic look and feel of those paper-based drawings in his fast-paced iPhone game, Scribattle. In preparing a new iPad-optimized version, affectionately named ScribattlePad, he discovered the freedom to include features that had previously proven difficult on the iPhone's smaller screen (see Figure 1–9). He describes the overhaul as follows:

> *The larger screen provides for some interesting new interactions. The main innovation here will be the existence of a new two-player option,*

with each player operating one end of the device, in either a co-op or competitive mode. It will also allow for more strategic play. Each player will have opportunities to move and regroup their guys. If you put them in groups, they'll fire their weapons and activate shields simultaneously, with the challenge of presenting an easier target for enemies to fire upon. This basically brings the game quite a bit closer to my original vision, based on my recollections of childhood play, where we did similar things on paper, but with a whole lot more thrown in as well.

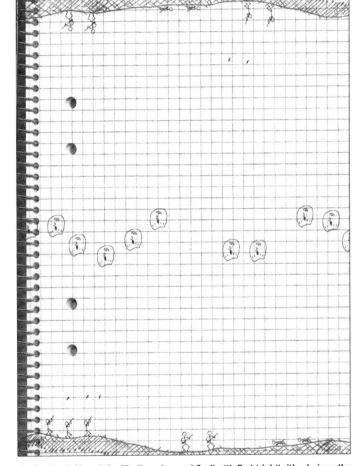

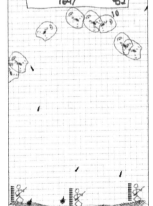

Figure 1–9. *Comparing the iPhone's Scribattle (left) and the iPad's enhanced ScribattlePad (right), it's obvious the iPad's extra screen real estate can make a huge difference in the amount of game play and interaction featured on the screen.*

Zen Bound 2

Secret Exit's Zen Bound (http://zenbound.com/) is a meditative puzzle game that involves wrapping wooden sculptures with rope. Unlike most games, a high score is not the primary goal here. Instead, the intention is to enjoy the process at your own relaxed pace. Many people consider this game to be one of the most beautifully rendered apps currently available on the iPhone.

In planning the sequel, Secret Exit chose to develop Zen Bound 2 exclusively for the iPad, taking advantage of the tablet's powerful graphics engine. The larger screen and superior graphics capabilities enabled the developers to surpass the stunning imagery of the original iPhone game. The result is nothing short of breathtaking (see Figure 1–10). This is definitely an important factor to keep in mind when choosing a platform for your next game!

Figure 1–10. *Taking advantage of the iPad's powerful graphics engine, the stunning Zen Bound 2 (right) far surpasses the imagery in the iPhone's Zen Bound (left).*

Opportunity Awaits

As noted by Syncode's Matthew Lesh, "Apple has provided developers with some powerful and unique tools to create stylish applications for the iPad. The challenge now is to create them."

After exploring the iPad's target market and previewing some of the beautiful apps that developers are building specifically for Apple's new tablet, you're probably pretty fired up to start writing code. Feeling inspired? Good, because you won't want to miss out on another "gold rush" opportunity as new iPad owners flock to the App Store looking to download iPad apps for their devices. It's time to dive into the exciting world of iPad programming!

For those of you interested in a quick refresher course on developing apps with Xcode, Interface Builder, and Apple's iPhone SDK, you'll find Chapter 2 to be a welcome primer before jumping into the rest of the book. If you're an experienced iPhone app developer and have already installed iPhone SDK 3.2, feel free to flip ahead to Chapter 3 to begin your iPad development journey.

Chapter 2

Getting Started with iPad Development

Before you begin working with the new iPad features and frameworks, it's important to have the required tools and preliminary training in place, so that you start your iPad development journey on the right footing. If you've already installed iPhone SDK 3.2 and consider yourself an advanced iPhone developer—perhaps you even have a few apps in the App Store—you may want to skip ahead to Chapter 3. But if you feel your skill set is a little rusty, then take a few minutes to read through this quick refresher course on developing apps with Xcode, Interface Builder, and Cocoa Touch.

Acquiring the Tools of the Trade

As an iPhone developer, you're undoubtedly a frequent visitor to Apple's iPhone Dev Center at http://developer.apple.com/iphone/ and have already downloaded previous versions of the iPhone SDK to build your iPhone apps. Although access to the iPhone SDK, code samples, tutorials, and documentation are free to registered developers, if you eventually plan to submit your apps to the App Store, you'll need to enroll in Apple's iPhone Developer Program.

Enrolling in the iPhone Developer Program

Don't let the name fool you. The iPhone Developer Program encompasses everything related to iOS, so even if you're building only iPad apps, this is the program you want. Enrollment costs an annual $99 fee for individual developers or a small development team. Many newcomers balk at that admission price, but if you're serious about developing iPad and iPhone apps for the lucrative App Store, this will prove to be the easiest $99 you've ever spent in your programming career.

Beyond submitting apps to the App Store, membership also grants you the ability to create provisioning profiles for testing apps on an actual iPhone, iPod touch, and iPad device. The program also provides additional support resources from Apple and enables

you to set up ad hoc distribution for beta testing apps. For details, visit
http://developer.apple.com/programs/iphone.

Do not wait until your iPad app is ready to be submitted to the App Store, since it can
take weeks to receive acceptance into the iPhone Developer Program, which would
delay your progress unnecessarily. After being accepted, pay the $99 fee to complete
your registration. After your payment has been processed, when you log in to the iPhone
Dev Center, you'll see an iPhone Developer Program column on the right side of the
browser screen. Click the iTunes Connect button there.

On the main page of iTunes Connect, be sure to visit the Contracts, Tax, & Banking
Information section to view the contracts you currently have in effect. By default, you
should have the Free Applications contract already activated, which allows you to
submit free apps to the App Store. But if you want to submit paid apps to the App Store,
you'll need to request a Paid Applications contract. Apple needs your bank and tax
information so that it can pay you when you've accrued revenue from app sales. Since
Apple transfers money via secure electronic deposits, make sure your bank supports
electronic transactions with third-party vendors. You'll need to provide your bank's ABA
routing number, name, address, and your account number (along with your bank's
SWIFT code for receiving payments from international App Stores). Until you complete
the required steps (see Figure 2–1), Apple will hold any money it owes you in trust. And
since this can also be a fairly lengthy process, I highly recommend completing the Paid
Applications contract long before submitting your iPad app to the App Store.

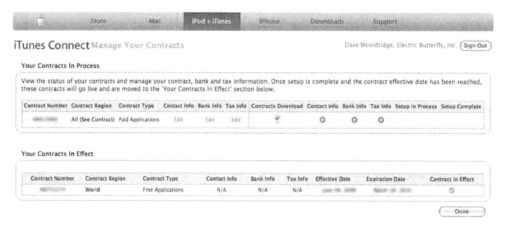

Figure 2–1. *In order to get paid for your App Store sales, make sure you complete Apple's required Paid
Applications contract in the iTunes Connect online portal.*

Installing iPhone SDK 3.2

If you haven't already installed the iPhone SDK 3.2, download it now from Apple's
iPhone Dev Center (http://developer.apple.com/iphone/).

The iPhone SDK 3.2 requires an Intel-based Mac running Mac OS X Snow Leopard
10.6.2 or later. The SDK includes Apple's complete developer tool set, such as Xcode,

Interface Builder, and the iPhone Simulator. The installer provides both the iPhone and iPad frameworks, so you can continue to develop iPhone apps while you work on your new iPad app within the same version of Xcode. You can even test your iPad apps in the iPhone Simulator, which also emulates the iPad environment.

NOTE: During the installation process, be sure to choose the Custom Install option, which will allow you to choose the specific iPhone SDK versions you want to install. Remember that the iPhone SDK 3.2 supports only iPad development. If you also need to work on iPhone apps, also select iPhone SDK 3.1.3 in the Custom Install list. If your iPhone apps need to support older versions of iOS, such as 3.1 and 3.0, select those as well.

Working with Beta Versions of the SDK

With Apple frequently releasing beta versions of forthcoming SDKs, you'll be eager to test and integrate those shiny new features into your apps in anticipation of future iOS releases. Obviously, when compiling your apps for the App Store, you'll need to keep the current, official SDK as well. And beyond that, the beta developer tools may not be stable enough yet for commercial use. In that case, you don't want the beta SDK installer to replace your existing developer tools.

Luckily, there's an easy way around this dilemma—as long as you have plenty of hard drive space to spare. The optimal solution is to maintain two separate sets of Apple's developer tools on your Mac. The primary set is the latest, official SDK and Xcode tools. The second set consists of the beta SDK and Xcode tools that you want to begin experimenting with.

After installing the iPhone SDK 3.2, your primary drive's root directory now includes a new Developer folder. If you attempt to install the latest beta SDK with the default installation settings, the existing SDK 3.2 applications and files in the Developer folder will be overwritten with the new beta tools. To prevent that from happening, you need to direct the installer to place the new beta SDK tools in a different location by following these simple steps:

1. Download the beta SDK from Apple's iPhone Dev Center (an iPhone Developer Program membership is required to download betas).

2. Open/mount the downloaded disk image (.dmg), and then double-click its installer package to launch the installer program.

3. To install the beta developer tools in a directory other than the default Developer folder, choose the Custom Install option. At the top of the Custom Install list, click the Developer folder icon in the Essentials Location column. From the pop-up menu that appears, select Other… and choose a different location.

Your new beta tools folder must be located at the root directory of your primary drive, just like the existing Developer folder. For example, I created a new folder named DevBeta that resides at the same directory level as the Developer folder (see Figure 2–2).

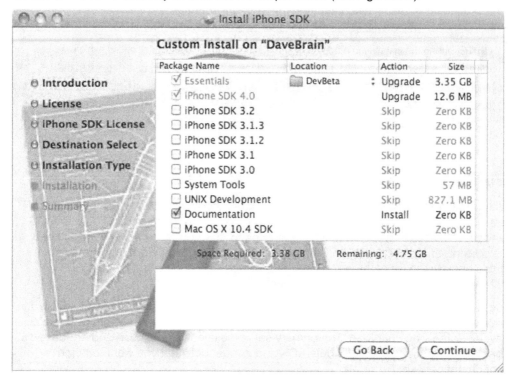

Figure 2–2. *To preserve the previously installed developer tools, use the Custom Install option to install the beta SDK in a different location.*

If the apps you plan to build with the new beta SDK require backward-compatibility with older SDK versions, you can elect to install those as well within that Custom Install list. If you don't need any of those older SDKs, then deselecting them will help conserve valuable hard drive space.

> **Note:** Only one version of the System Tools and UNIX Development packages can be installed on your Mac. Even if you choose a new location for the beta installation, leaving System Tools and UNIX Development selected will replace your existing System Tools and UNIX Development packages with the latest beta versions, which is probably not what you want. To preserve your current System Tools and UNIX Development sets, make sure those items are left unchecked during the custom installation (see Figure 2–2).

If you later need to install multiple beta versions on your hard drive, simply follow the same custom installation process, giving a unique name to each new developer tools folder you create at the root directory. When installing multiple beta releases, it's helpful to include the version number in the directory name for easy reference. For example, instead of the generic DevBeta, you could adopt a naming convention of Developer_4_b1, Developer_4_b2, and so on. Just remember that each installation of developer tools clocks in at around 2GB to 5GB (depending on which components are installed), so multiple sets can quickly consume a lot of hard drive space.

New to Objective-C and Cocoa Touch?

Since this book was designed specifically for iPhone developers, it is assumed that you are already familiar with the Objective-C programming language and the iS frameworks that make up Cocoa Touch. If you're new to iPhone app development, your first step is to acquire that basic foundation before attempting iPad development, which builds on top of the iPhone development core skill set.

Obviously, there's more to learning Objective-C and Cocoa Touch than can be squeezed into a single chapter. Thankfully, quite a few excellent online resources and books will arm you with the necessary knowledge. Apple's iPhone Dev Center offers various guides, including the following:

- *The iPhone OS Reference Library*, which provides comprehensive documentation on Objective-C and Cocoa Touch is available at: http://developer.apple.com/iphone/library/navigation/

- *The Objective-C Programming Language* reference guide can be downloaded as a PDF from: http://developer.apple.com/iphone/library/documentation/Cocoa/C onceptual/ObjectiveC/ObjC.pdf.

If you're finding it difficult to wade through Apple's dense sea of documentation, you may find it easier to learn Objective-C and the iPhone SDK from the proven, step-by-step approaches found in these best-selling Apress books:

- *Learn Objective-C on the Mac* by Mark Dalrymple and Scott Knaster (http://www.apress.com/book/view/9781430218159)

- *Beginning iPhone 3 Development: Exploring the iPhone SDK* by Jeff LaMarche and Dave Mark (http://www.apress.com/book/view/9781430224594)

- *More iPhone 3 Development: Tackling the iPhone SDK 3* by Jeff LaMarche and Dave Mark (http://www.apress.com/book/view/9781430225058)

These references will serve you well as you apply your iPhone knowledge to developing apps for the iPad. That's the nice thing about the iPhone SDK. Sure, the iPad has additional, exclusive APIs (covered extensively in this book), but there are also hundreds of frameworks that work the same on both the iPhone and iPad platforms.

Embracing the Model-View-Controller Concept

After programming in Xcode and arranging user interface (UI) elements in Interface Builder, it becomes apparent that Cocoa Touch was carefully structured to utilize the Model-View-Controller (MVC) design pattern. This approach neatly separates your Xcode project into three distinct pieces of functionality:

- *Model*: This is your application's data, such as the data model object classes in your project. The model also includes any database architecture employed, such as Core Data or working directly with SQLite files.

- *View*: As the name implies, this is your app's visual interface that users see. This encompasses the various UI components constructed in Interface Builder.

- *Controller*: This is the logic that ties the model and view elements together, processing user inputs and UI interactions. Subclasses of UIKit components such as the UINavigationController and UITabBarController first come to mind, but this concept also extends to the application delegate and custom subclasses of NSObject.

Although there will be plenty of interaction between the three MVC elements in your Xcode project (see Figure 2–3), the code and objects you create should be easily defined as belonging to only one of them. Sure, it's easy enough to generate your UI purely within code, or store all your data model methods within the controller classes, but if your source code isn't structured properly, that could drastically blur the line between the model, view, and controller.

You may be thinking, "If the app's performance is fast and works as intended, then why would it matter how the project's infrastructure is crafted?" Besides the fact that it's poor programming form, here's the short answer: *reusability*!

Before the advent of the iPad, your app's structure may not have mattered much at all, especially if you were not planning to reuse any of that code in other projects. At the time, you were developing your app for only one form factor: the iPhone's small 320-by-480 screen. But now you want to port that app to the iPad, taking advantage of the tablet's new features and expanded screen size. If your iPhone app doesn't adhere to the MVC design pattern, porting your Xcode project to the iPad suddenly becomes a daunting task, requiring you to rewrite a lot of code in order to produce an iPad-enhanced version.

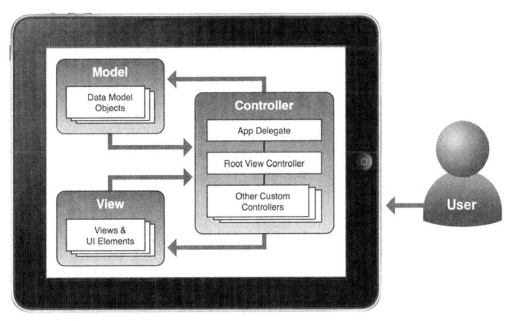

Figure 2–3. *Adhering to Xcode's Model-View-Controller design pattern will greatly simplify the process of converting an iPhone app into an enhanced iPad version.*

For example, let's say your root view controller classes contain all the code for not only retrieving database records through Core Data, but also dynamically generating a UINavigationController and a nested UITableView for displaying those records. That may work fine on the iPhone, but in moving to the iPad, you would want to use a UISplitViewController to display those database records. Yikes! Now you're saddled with the laborious task of manually ripping out all of that UINavigationController code, so that you can add in the new UISplitViewController functionality.

If you had kept your data classes (model) separate from your interface elements (view) and controller objects (controller), then porting the project to the iPad would have been a much simpler, streamlined process.

Reusability in Xcode

The majority of the work you'll be doing when porting an existing iPhone app to the iPad platform entails redesigning your app's UI to utilize new iPad UI components. Following the MVC design pattern from the very beginning enables you to focus most of your development time on converting the UI to the iPad, rather than losing countless hours reengineering your entire codebase. But the importance of MVC doesn't end there. Ah, yes, the plot thickens…

The iPhone SDK 3.2 introduces a new universal app format. This provides developers with a convenient path for distributing a single application package that contains both iPhone and iPad versions—hence the appropriate *universal* name. As you might expect, if the app is downloaded on the iPad, the iPad version will run; if downloaded on the iPhone, the iPhone version will run. Obviously, you can opt to compile your app as only a stand-alone iPad app or iPhone app as well. Which format should you choose? There are unique business and marketing advantages to both scenarios, which will be touched upon in Chapter 3.

For now, let's say you decide to build your application as a universal app. As a basic example, go ahead and create a new project in Xcode by choosing Window-based Application from the iPhone OS Application templates and selecting **Universal** from the related product menu (see Figure 2–4).

Figure 2–4. *To create a new universal app project, choose the Window-based Application template and select Universal from the product menu.*

Once you've given your project a name, the main Xcode project window that appears is where you'll spend most of your development time. As you may already know, the Xcode integrated development environment (IDE) is the central application in Apple's developer tools arsenal. Here, you manage your project's files and resources, as well as debug and test your app via the iPhone Simulator or a connected device.

In the Universal version of the Window-based Application template, you'll notice that the default project that's generated organizes the source files into distinct folders. In the Groups & Files list, iPad-specific files are located in an iPad folder, and iPhone-specific files are located in an iPhone folder (see Figure 2–5). So far, this doesn't look any different from maintaining two different codebases within the same project, but wait! See that Shared folder? Beyond sharing a common .plist file, a Universal project can also share common classes, databases, resources, and select controllers and UI views!

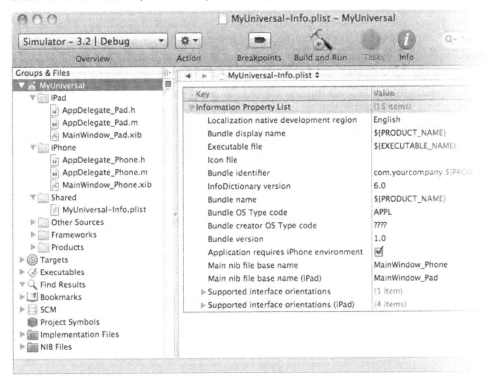

Figure 2–5. *Sharing common source files and resources for both iPhone and iPad platforms within a single Universal project is yet another reason why utilizing the MVC design pattern is so important.*

By sharing common classes between both iPhone and iPad versions, you'll not only remove redundant code from your project, but moving forward, your codebase will also be much easier to maintain. This becomes extremely useful when adding a new feature that needs to be made available to both platforms. And what if Apple decides to someday extend iOS to yet another hardware device configuration, which might require adding a third platform to your Universal project? By adhering to the MVC approach, your codebase will be much easier to adapt to whatever the future may hold.

You will learn more about creating universal apps in Chapters 3 and Chapter 11.

> **NOTE:** If you're interested in improving your knowledge of Apple's Xcode tools beyond what's offered in the embedded help, check out the Apress book *Learn Xcode Tools for Mac OS X and iPhone Development* by Ian Piper (http://www.apress.com/book/view/9781430272212).

Designing in Interface Builder

Interface Builder provides an easy way to quickly create your app's UI by customizing the various view controllers, views, and UI components. As part of this brief refresher on using Apple's developer tools, let's create a new project, so that we can explore the power of Interface Builder.

In Xcode, choose **File ➤ New Project**. From the New Project window, choose the View-based Application template from the iPhone OS list. Select **iPad** from the related product menu, and name the project MyWeb.

In the main Xcode project window that appears, the Groups & Files pane lists all of your project's source files and resources. The template generates some basic class files in the Classes folder and the corresponding user interface .xib files in the Resources folder.

For this example, we'll build a very simple iPad app with a button that loads the Apress.com web site into a UIWebView. The complete project can be downloaded along with the rest of the examples in this book from http://www.apress.com/book/view/9781430230212.

Double-click the *MyWebViewController.xib* file, and that UI view will open in Interface Builder. Drag a UIToolbar from the Library window to the top of the View window. Select the default UIBarButtonItem that is included in the toolbar. In the attribute inspector window, rename the button's title to **Display Web Site** (see Figure 2–6).

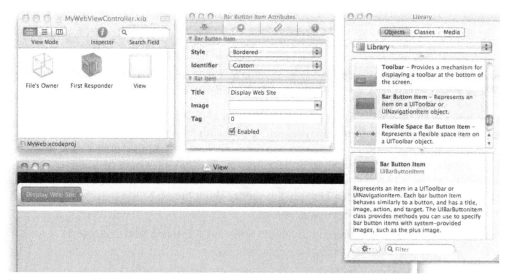

Figure 2–6. *Create a UI in Interface Builder by dragging components from the Library onto the View window. Selecting the button enables you to customize its properties in the attribute inspector.*

Why use a toolbar? Since the rest of the screen will hold the UIWebView, encapsulating the button in a toolbar will look much nicer than a lonely UIButton in the corner of the screen. So you've probably guessed what's next—it's time to drag a UIWebView from the

Library onto the View window. Grab the selection points on the ends of the UIWebView and make sure it covers the remaining screen space below the toolbar.

Now that the UI has been designed, save the *MyWebViewController.xib* file, exit from Interface Builder, and return to Xcode.

Right now, the new UI has no connections to the project's source code. If you run the app in the iPhone Simulator, you'll be able to tap the button in the toolbar, but nothing will happen. So now it's time to add some interaction between the model, view, and controller pieces of our project.

Within Xcode, open the *MyWebViewController.h* header file and add the following new lines of code (highlighted in bold):

```
// MyWebViewController.h
#import <UIKit/UIKit.h>

@interface MyWebViewController : UIViewController {
    UIWebView *mywebView;
    UIBarButtonItem *urlButton;
}

@property (nonatomic, retain) IBOutlet UIWebView *mywebView;

-(IBAction)urlbuttonTapped;

@end
```

Notice that we added a mywebView reference to the UIWebView, as well as an IBOutlet for this object. There are also references to an urlButton as the UIBarButtonItem and urlbuttonTapped as an IBAction. If the purposes of IBOutlet and IBAction are a little fuzzy to you, don't worry—I'll explain how outlets and actions work in a moment.

After saving the *MyWebViewController.h* file, open the corresponding *MyWebViewController.m* implementation file and add the following bold code (with the exception of the viewDidLoad event, which was simply uncommented):

```
// MyWebViewController.m
#import "MyWebViewController.h"

@implementation MyWebViewController

@synthesize mywebView;

// Implement viewDidLoad for additional setup after loading the view.
- (void)viewDidLoad {
    [super viewDidLoad];
}

- (IBAction)urlbuttonTapped {
    // The button was tapped, so display the specified web site.
    NSURL *url = [NSURL URLWithString:@"http://www.apress.com/"];
    NSURLRequest *request = [NSURLRequest requestWithURL:url];
    [self.mywebView loadRequest:request];
}
```

```
// Override to allow orientations other than the default portrait orientation.
- (BOOL)shouldAutorotateToInterfaceOrientation:(UIInterfaceOrientation)
interfaceOrientation {
    return YES;
}

- (void)didReceiveMemoryWarning {
    // Releases the view if it doesn't have a superview.
    [super didReceiveMemoryWarning];
    // Release any cached data, images, etc that aren't in use.
}

- (void)dealloc {
    [mywebView release];
    [super dealloc];
}

@end
```

We added the urlbuttonTapped method with code for loading the Apress.com URL in the UIWebView. Also, since we've instantiated the mywebView reference in memory, once our code is finished with it, we should properly release the reference in the dealloc event, freeing up that precious memory for other uses.

Even after saving the *MyWebViewController.m* file, we're not quite finished yet. True, we've added the necessary code to power our app, but our UI is still not aware of that functionality. In order to bind the UI with the relevant items in our source code, we must connect the IBAction and IBOutlet to the appropriate UI components in Interface Builder.

Wiring Actions

Double-click the *MyWebViewController.xib* file to open it again in Interface Builder. In the View window, control-click (or right-click) the UIBarButtonItem, and a dark-gray contextual menu will appear with a list of items. Click the selector's empty dot (listed under **Sent Actions**), and while holding down the mouse button, drag the cursor over to the File's Owner icon in the main window. You'll see a blue line connecting the button to your cursor's location (see Figure 2–7). After you release the mouse button, a dark-gray menu will appear above File's Owner. Select urlbuttonTapped from that hovering menu to bind the UIBarButtonItem to the urlbuttonTapped method. This "wires" the button's action, so that if a user taps that button, the urlbuttonTapped method will be called.

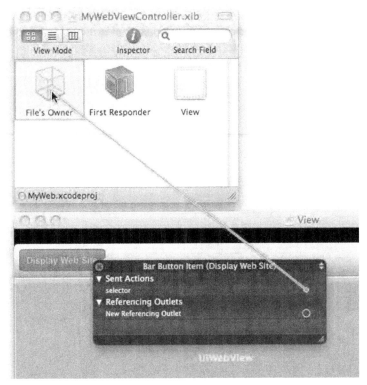

Figure 2–7. *To wire the button's action, drag a connector from the button's selector (sent action) to the File Owner's urlbuttonTapped (received action).*

Although it may seem like it took several steps within Xcode and Interface Builder to assign only a single action to a button, this approach provides a very flexible connection between your data and your UI that can be easily modified. If you decide to redesign your app in the future, replacing the existing interface with a completely new set of UI elements, you can easily control-click the UIBarButtonItem, remove that wired binding to the urlbuttonTapped method in the contextual menu, and then assign that action to a different button.

Wiring Outlets

Now that tapping the button successfully calls urlbuttonTapped, that method aims to load the Apress.com web site into the UIWebView. In order to send this URL request to the UIWebView, the MyWebViewController class needs to connect an outlet to it. Similar to how you wired the button's action, the outlet runs in the opposite direction.

In the main window, control-click (or right-click) the File's Owner icon, and a dark-gray contextual menu will appear. Click the mywebView's empty dot (listed under **Outlets**) and, while holding down the mouse button, drag the cursor over to the UIWebView in the View window. Just as when you are wiring an action, you'll see a blue line flowing from the File's Owner icon to your cursor's location (see Figure 2–8). Release the mouse button above the UIWebView to complete the outlet connection. And last, but not least, save the *MyWebViewController.xib* file before returning to Xcode.

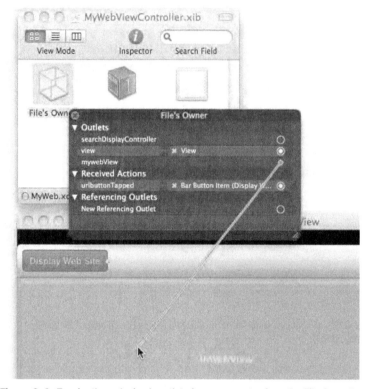

Figure 2–8. *To wire the web view's outlet, drag a connector from the File Owner's mywebView (outlet) to the UIWebView on the View window.*

With all of the functionality connected through the appropriate actions and outlets, your app is now ready to rock! To test it, ensure the **Overview** pull-down menu (in the top-right corner of the Xcode project window) is set to **Simulator - 3.2 I Debug**, and then click Build and Run to launch the iPad app in the iPhone Simulator. In the simulator's iPad window, tap the Display Web Site button, and the Apress.com home page should load into the web view (see Figure 2-9).

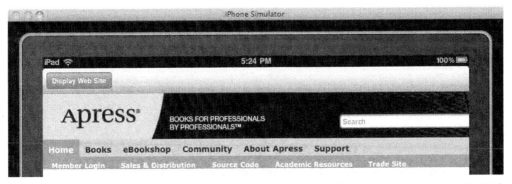

Figure 2-9. *With your project's actions and outlets wired to the UI, the MyWeb iPad app now works as intended in the iPhone Simulator.*

The Importance of Delegates

Cocoa Touch relies heavily on delegates, so it's vital that you're comfortable using them. Delegates allow one object to receive messages or modify the behavior or another object, without needing to inherit or subclass it. This is an extremely handy design pattern that helps alleviate a lot of extra coding.

A very simple example of delegation is the UIWebView component that we implemented in the MyWeb project. Besides the fact that Apple recommends not to subclass UIWebView, the easiest way to communicate with UIWebView directly is via delegation.

Let's say we want the MyWeb app to notify the user when the Apress.com home page finishes loading into the web view. We will designate the MyWebViewController class as the UIWebViewDelegate for its mywebView instance so that it can receive events from the web view and act accordingly.

Open the *MyWebViewController.h* header file and add <UIWebViewDelegate> to the end of the @interface line (see the bold code):

```
// MyWebViewController.h
#import <UIKit/UIKit.h>

@interface MyWebViewController : UIViewController <UIWebViewDelegate> {
    UIBarButtonItem *urlButton;
    UIWebView *mywebView;
}

@property (nonatomic, retain) IBOutlet UIWebView *mywebView;

-(IBAction)urlbuttonTapped;

@end
```

Save this file, and then open the *MyWebViewController.m* implementation file. Add the following (again, new code is shown in bold):

```
// MyWebViewController.m
```

```
#import "MyWebViewController.h"

@implementation MyWebViewController

@synthesize mywebView;

// Implement viewDidLoad for additional setup after loading the view.
- (void)viewDidLoad {
    self.mywebView.delegate = self;
    [super viewDidLoad];
}

- (IBAction)urlbuttonTapped {
    // The button was tapped, so display the specified web site.
    NSURL *url = [NSURL URLWithString:@"http://www.apress.com/"];
    NSURLRequest *request = [NSURLRequest requestWithURL:url];
    [self.mywebView loadRequest:request];
}

#pragma mark -
#pragma mark UIWebViewDelegate

- (void)webViewDidFinishLoad:(UIWebView *)webView {
    // Web view finished loading, so notify the user.
    UIAlertView *buttonAlert = [[UIAlertView alloc] initWithTitle:@"Welcome to
Apress.com" message:@"The home page has finished loading. Thanks for visiting!"
delegate:nil cancelButtonTitle:@"Continue" otherButtonTitles:nil];
    [buttonAlert show];
    [buttonAlert release];
}

// Override to allow orientations other than the default portrait orientation.
- (BOOL)shouldAutorotateToInterfaceOrientation:(UIInterfaceOrientation)
interfaceOrientation {
    return YES;
}

- (void)didReceiveMemoryWarning {
    // Releases the view if it doesn't have a superview.
    [super didReceiveMemoryWarning];
    // Release any cached data, images, etc that aren't in use.
}

- (void)dealloc {
    mywebView.delegate = nil;
    [mywebView release];
    [super dealloc];
}

@end
```

In the viewDidLoad event, the mywebView.delegate is assigned to the
MyWebViewController class (self). And when finished, mywebView.delegate is set to nil
in the dealloc event. The UIWebView includes several events, but the one we're
interested in is webViewDidFinishLoad. Since this class is the designated delegate, it can
add its own custom behavior when receiving that event. Simply add that

webViewDidFinishLoad receiver to the *MyWebViewController.m* file. Any custom code added to that receiver will be called when that event fires. In this case, we're notifying the user that the web page finished loading via a UIAlertView (see Figure 2-10).

Figure 2–10. *Designating MyWebViewController as a UIWebViewDelegate enables the class to receive UIWebView events and add custom behavior, such as notifying the user with a UIAlertView when a web page has finished loading.*

NOTE: Delegation isn't confined to the existing Cocoa Touch framework. You can modify your own custom classes to offer a delegate protocol, so that other objects can become delegates. For details, read the section "Delegates and Data Sources" in Apple's *Cocoa Fundamentals Guide*, which can be downloaded as a PDF from http://developer.apple.com/iphone/library/documentation/Cocoa/Conceptual /CocoaFundamentals/CocoaFundamentals.pdf.

Improving App Usability with UIKit

Apple has supplied a vast library of ready-made UI components and controllers in Cocoa Touch's UIKit. Since users are already familiar with how these common UI elements work, employing them in your own iPhone apps not only enhances usability, but also helps save you valuable time during the development process. For example, on the iPhone's small screen, utilizing Apple's UINavigationController or UITabBarController is an efficient method for moving between different compact views within an app.

On the iPad's much larger 768-by-1024 screen, you may be tempted to be a little more creative in your interface design choices. It's true that the iPad offers a much more robust platform for creating sophisticated, desktop-caliber apps, but it would be a huge mistake to attempt to mimic traditional desktop interface models. Just because you have a larger screen to work with doesn't mean that you can forget why the iPad is such a powerful mobile device: simplicity. Regardless of the expanded real estate, you're still dealing with a touchscreen and multifinger gestures. Let the interface breathe with plenty of space for trouble-free finger tapping. Less is more!

As with its efforts for the iPhone, Apple has provided some wonderful new iPad-centric interface elements in UIKit. Along with new UI components that have been added to

Interface Builder's Library, Xcode also provides new iPad project templates, such as the Split View-based Application template (see Figure 2–11).

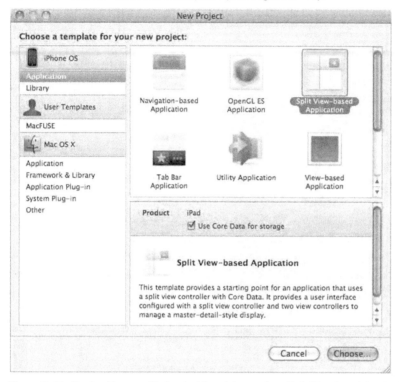

Figure 2–11. *Xcode offers new iPad project templates, such as Split View-based Application, to aid in generating an initial codebase for your new iPad app, which you can then further customize.*

The new iPad-exclusive `UISplitViewController` is employed in dozens of popular iPad apps, such as The Iconfactory's Twitterriffic and Apple's Mail. Like most of the Xcode templates, the Split View-based Application template generates a working project that you can further customize. The template offers a prebuilt split view-based app interface, configured with a `UITableView` in the master pane and a `UIView` in the detail pane. And if you select the Use Core Data for storage check box, the new project will even include sample code for populating the `UITableView` with Core Data entries. You can learn a lot about programming for the iPad by examining the code generated by these handy project templates! If this new UI controller interests you, then don't miss Chapter 8, which provides extensive coverage of using `UISplitViewController` in your own iPad apps.

With so many great interface items available in `UIKit`, why reinvent the wheel with your own UI experiments that may feel foreign to new users? Yes, you want to give your iPad app a unique interface, but if you stray too far from familiar user interactions, you run the risk of diminishing your app's immediate usability. Unless you're developing an app that requires a completely custom UI, such as a game, it's in your best interest to utilize the `UIKit` when appropriate.

The beauty of the ready-made project templates and UI components is that they are fully customizable. Modify their existing attributes or subclass them, and tweak to your heart's content to give your app its own personalized polish. Your users will find your iPad app much easier to operate with an interface that is already familiar to them.

Primed for Programming

This chapter presented a quick refresher on iPhone app development. If any of this was new to you, I highly recommend reading the books and online resources listed in the "New to Objective-C and Cocoa Touch?" section before continuing. Since this book was designed for iPhone app developers, subsequent chapters assume a working knowledge of common iPhone development tasks, such as how to build and populate the rows of a UITableView. Having that basic foundation under your belt will help you quickly grasp and enjoy your iPad development journey!

Next up in Chapter 3, I'll introduce you to all of the new iPad frameworks and UI elements, how they relate to existing iOS features, and the proper context for using them within your own iPad apps.

Chapter 3

Exploring the iPhone SDK's New iPad Features

iOS 3.2 includes many new features that are currently supported on only the iPad. Because of these special iPad-exclusive features, apps compiled for 3.2 will not run on the iPhone or iPod touch. This enables developers to produce apps specifically designed for the iPad, taking advantage of the tablet's unique form factor and capabilities. This chapter provides an introduction to the new iPad offerings in iPhone SDK 3.2, as well as how to best utilize them within your apps.

Optimizing Apps for the iPad

Before diving into the new software features available to developers, let's take a look at the hardware environment that powers the operating system and installed apps. You already know about the iPad's amazing 10-hour battery life and other much-publicized selling points, so I won't bore you by listing all of the iPad's hardware specifications. Here, we'll review some of the key factors that may impact your development efforts.

Examining the Tablet

The first thing you'll notice is the iPad's brilliant display. With a 9.7-inch (diagonal) backlit in-plane switching (IPS) display, the beautiful screen boasts a 1024-by-768 pixel resolution at 132 pixels per inch. By comparison, the iPhone has a 320-by-480 pixel screen at 163 pixels per inch.

Like the display of the iPhone and iPod touch, the iPad's display is multitouch, but the big difference here is that the iPad's screen is fully capacitive, with a much greater number of touch sensors, supporting several fingers at once. With the larger screen and the almost full-size virtual keyboard (in landscape orientation), this is a significant milestone.

Whereas you may typically operate an iPhone with one hand or only two thumbs, the iPad is much more immersive and often invites you to use two hands while the device rests in your lap. In a few informal tests, some independent developers have reported that the iPad's multitouch display has successfully recorded more than ten simultaneous finger taps. This is important, not only for building complex two-player games with users playing head-to-head on both ends of the tablet, but also for the ability to more efficiently track fast keyboard typing and multifinger gestures for a vast array of touch commands.

As you would expect, the iPad also includes the accelerometer, an embedded microphone, a headphone jack, and a built-in speaker. Unlike the iPhone's tiny speaker, the iPad's enhanced speaker is actually quite decent, so games, videos, and music are enjoyable even without headphones.

The iPad features the same 30-pin dock connector and wireless Bluetooth support as the iPhone, which should be welcome news for developers who utilize the iPhone SDK's existing Accessory APIs to communicate with add-on accessories.

> **NOTE:** If you're interested in building apps that work with external hardware, check out the Apress book *Building iPhone OS Accessories: Use the iPhone Accessories API to Control and Monitor Devices* by Ken Maskrey (http://www.apress.com/book/view/9781430229315).

Although the 3G models support assisted GPS, keep in mind that the most popular iPad is the 16GB Wi-Fi only model. If you're developing an app that requires GPS capabilities, that particular functionality may not work quite as well on those Wi-Fi only models.

Last, but not least, the iPad is fast! Apple's custom-designed A4 processor chip provides a lightning-quick, high-performance experience that's surprisingly battery-efficient.

The iPad is so much faster than the iPhone 3GS that you might assume it also packs more RAM, but that may not be the case. Even though Apple has not published the amount of RAM in the iPad, early benchmarks from industry experts report that the iPad sports the same GPU and 256MB of RAM as the iPhone 3GS. This is important to remember when designing memory-intensive apps, such as graphics-heavy games with full-screen animation.

Managing Memory

It's true that Apple's new A4 chip is blazingly quick, and games do run much faster on the iPad, but it's not yet the Holy Grail of hardware that game developers might have been hoping for. Without any significant boost in RAM or GPU speed, creating apps for the iPad requires the same attention to memory management as previous efforts on the iPhone 3GS and iPod touch. In some regards, memory optimization is even more important on the iPad than on smaller iOS devices.

With its larger screen, the iPad's GPU is forced to push around a lot more pixels, especially when running full-screen animations in games. In converting iPhone games into enhanced iPad versions, some developers have encountered noticeable animation frame rate issues, requiring them to make additional optimizations to avoid dropped frames during game play.

Obviously, the amazing graphics in Firemint's Real Racing HD and other best-selling games are proof that the iPad is a stellar game platform. The fast A4 chip definitely helps in this regard, but proactive memory management is key when programming your iPad project. Even if you plan to build productivity apps that don't include graphics-intensive animations, optimizing your app to maintain a small memory footprint is still very important.

Unlike Objective-C 2.0 for Mac OS X development, Cocoa Touch's Objective-C does not include built-in garbage collection. You need to keep track of your app's memory usage in iOS, paying close attention to your code to ensure instantiated objects are released after being used. While memory management is certainly important when optimizing apps for the iPad's limited RAM, it will become especially critical in the future when iOS 4's multitasking functionality eventually comes to the iPad, enabling multiple apps to run in the background.

Testing Your Apps on an iPad

While it's always helpful to know the iPad's hardware specifications, never assume your app will perform well on the device, just because it runs flawlessly in Xcode's iPhone Simulator. The Simulator does not support several features, such as the accelerometer, multitouch gestures, and In App Purchase. But even if you don't use any of those elements in your app, you should always, always, always test it on an actual iPad as well.

> **NOTE:** Don't yet have an iPad? Since you're reading this book, it's a safe assumption that you're serious about iPad app development, so you really should own an iPad or have direct access to an iPad for testing. If iPads are not sold where you live, you can easily purchase one from an online retailer that can ship it to your location.

Running your app in the iPhone Simulator is great for general debugging, but as a Mac-based software emulator, it's not a true test of how your app will perform on an actual device. Beyond testing the many features that are not supported in the iPhone Simulator, running your app on an iPad will also reveal any issues that arise from the constraints of the device's fixed memory and processing power.

Yes, I know the process of creating and installing provisioning profiles and development certificates is frustrating and tedious, but it's well worth the effort in the long run, especially if your goal is to eventually release your iPad app in the iTunes App Store. You'll want to discover and squash as many bugs and performance problems as possible to help ensure that your app is well received by customers.

As an iPhone developer, you should already have experience configuring a test device with your development certificate and a new provisioning profile. The process is the same for an iPad. If this is all new to you, then log in to Apple's iPhone Dev Center and read the documentation in the iPhone Provisioning Portal, at http://developer.apple. com/iphone/manage/overview/index.action. The iPhone Provisioning Portal even includes a handy online Provisioning Assistant that can guide you through the process.

> **NOTE:** The Apress book *The Business of iPhone App Development: Making and Marketing Apps that Succeed* by Dave Wooldridge with Michael Schneider
> (http://www.apress.com/book/view/9781430227335) features an extensive chapter on testing, with easy step-by-step instructions on how to set up a development device with provisioning profiles. It also explains how to configure and compile your app for beta testing via ad hoc distribution.

What's New in iPhone SDK 3.2 for the iPad

Now for the fun part! This section will walk you through the new iPad features in iPhone SDK 3.2, as well as touch on how to best use them within your own apps. Subsequent chapters will drill deeper into each subject, showing you step by step how to implement each of these new features in your Xcode projects with extensive code examples.

Shape Drawing

The new UIBezierPath class may not be one of the most talked about or publicized new features in iPhone SDK 3.2, but if you do any kind of 2D drawing in your app, its inclusion is actually a pretty big deal. Similar to the vector-based drawing tools found in Adobe Illustrator and Photoshop, the UIBezierPath class enables you to draw straight lines, circles, rectangles, and curved shapes with complete control over the line's stroke color and thickness, as well as the fill color of enclosed objects.

The process of constructing a shape is relatively simple. After creating a new UIBezierPath object, you set the starting point via the moveToPoint method, and then use the addLineToPoint method for each additional connected line you wish to add to your shape. Calling the closePath method closes the shape, drawing a final line between the first point and last point. True to its name, the UIBezierPath class is also capable of creating Bézier curves. You can pass control points to the addCurveToPoint method to set the angle of the line's curve.

The aforementioned methods define the shape of your UIBezierPath. In order to render the object to your current graphics context, you call the fill and stroke methods. Before doing so, you'll want to assign a unique UIColor to setFill and setStroke, and adjust the thickness of the line stroke by designating an integer to your path's lineWidth property. To avoid having your fill path overlap the stroke path, you'll want to draw the fill color before drawing the stroke outline. This is as easy as calling the `fill` method before calling the `stroke` method.

I've outlined the basics of `UIBezierPath`, but you're probably itching to see how all of this works in code. In Chapter 4, you'll learn how to draw several types of objects using the `UIBezierPath` class in the process of creating a fun drawing app project called Dudel. Figure 3–1 is a preview of drawing with Dudel.

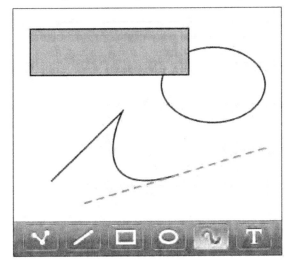

Figure 3–1. *Beyond standard objects like lines, ovals, rectangles, and custom shapes, the UIBezierPath class also enables you to draw curved lines by setting arc control points.*

Why is this graphics functionality so important? Even if you have no aspirations to develop a drawing app like Dudel, there are other practical uses for this graphics class. If you need a simple shape drawn on the screen, utilizing `UIBezierPath` requires much less memory than a PNG resource image of the same shape. With a vector-based object, only the instructions on how to draw that shape are needed. In contrast, a bitmap image file may consume several kilobytes (or more) when loaded into memory.

For example, let's say you're building a task management app. To visually indicate the priority status, your interface design places a colored dot next to each task name. A red dot represents a high priority, an orange dot indicates medium priority, and a yellow dot shows low priority. Using bitmap images, the three different dots would need to be stored in your project's Resources folder as either three separate PNG files or consolidated within one large PNG file. Changing the priority color of a task would require your app to load a new image resource into memory. But if you used `UIBezierPath` instead, you could create a very simple method that draws the colored dot. Need a different color? Just pass the new color to your custom method, which redraws the dot with the requested color.

Since conserving memory is the name of the game, this is a very economical approach to displaying simple 2D shapes on the screen. Limiting the number of bitmap image resources needed is one of many ways to help reduce the memory overhead of your app.

PDF Files

If you're developing an app that creates content, then you'll find the new PDF-creation feature to be a very welcome addition to the iPad arsenal. iOS 3.2 enables developers to generate and save PDFs within their apps—all natively supported within the UIKit framework. Apple has done a great job of making this process very straightforward and elegant.

First, you create a PDF graphics context by calling one of two available functions. UIGraphicsBeginPDFContextToData stores the PDF content in an NSMutableData object. The more commonly used function is UIGraphicsBeginPDFContextToFile, which saves the PDF content as a PDF file (using your requested filename parameter) to your app's sandboxed files directory.

Unlike on-screen views, which can scroll for miles if needed, PDFs are structured as pages with a set width and height. After establishing the PDF graphics context, you must then create a new PDF page, so that you can draw content into that defined area. If you wish to create a new page using the previous default page size, then call UIGraphicsBeginPDFPage. But if you prefer to customize the page's size and various attributes, you should call the UIGraphicsBeginPDFPageWithInfo function instead.

The beauty of this new API is that all of the content you pass to the PDF graphics context is automatically translated into PDF data. After creating a new page, anything you can draw into a custom view can be drawn into your PDF, including text, bitmap images, and even vector-based shapes. For content that might not fit within the bounding box of a single PDF page, such as a large amount of text, you can call UIGraphicsBeginPDFPage or UIGraphicsBeginPDFPageWithInfo every time you need to close the current page and start a new page.

When you're finished drawing your content into the PDF graphics context, you call UIGraphicsEndPDFContext, which closes the current page and saves the PDF content to either an NSMutableData object or a PDF file, depending on whether you originally created the PDF graphics context via UIGraphicsBeginPDFContextToData or UIGraphicsBeginPDFContextToFile. Once those tasks have been completed, the UIGraphicsEndPDFContext function also performs a little housecleaning by automatically clearing your PDF data in memory from the graphics context stack.

You'll learn more about generating PDFs in Chapter 4. Building on the Dudel app example that showcases the new UIBezierPath class, you'll follow step-by-step instructions to add the ability to produce and save drawings as PDF files.

If your app needs to distribute only a single image, then exporting it as a PNG or JPEG may be the obvious path. The same holds true for plain text that's much easier to edit when saved as an ASCII text document. But what if your app needs to export a rendered web page or a sales report full of visual graphs and charts? For more complex layouts that include multiple images, tables, and styled text, saving the data as a multipage PDF file is a great solution.

That's right, I mentioned styled text! You're not dreaming, and it's not a typo. Keep reading!

Core Text

As an iPhone developer, the lack of any easy-to-use text styling functionality has probably annoyed you on countless occasions. Sure, you can display styled text as HTML in a UIWebView, but what about editing that styled text? For years, you've been jealous of the wonderful Core Text APIs that were available only to Mac OS X developers, wishing you could tap into that same functionality within Cocoa Touch. As of iOS 3.2, your wish has finally been granted!

Even though Apple has never officially confirmed that it utilizes Core Text in its stunning word processor app, Pages for iPad (see Figure 3–2), the arrival of Core Text in iPhone SDK 3.2 enables you to add similar sophisticated styled text features to your own iPad apps.

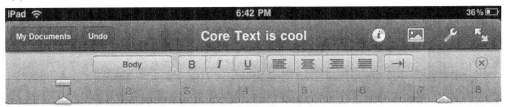

Figure 3–2. *With Core Text, you can build styled text features into your app, similar to Apple's Pages for iPad.*

Although all of us would love to use a word processor interface like Pages in our own apps, UIKit does not include a ready-made word processing control for easily editing text. To emulate such a beast, you'll need to build your own from scratch. Rendering portions of a text string with different styles, fonts, sizes, or colors will require quite a bit of work on your part, but the result is well worth the effort.

Using Core Text, you draw styled text into a graphics context. To assign custom font styles to specific segments of your text, you collect the text with this associated style metadata in a special attributed string, appropriately named NSAttributedString. To add that text information via Core Text, you then create a CTFramesetter by passing that attributed string to the function, CTFramesetterCreateWithAttributedString. Next, you construct a CTFrame object by passing your CTFramesetter (the styled text) and a CGPath (a bounding rectangle area) to the CTFramesetterCreateFrame function. Lastly, call the CTFrameDraw function to draw the styled text into the designated graphics context.

Of course, I've oversimplified the steps here in order to give you a general idea of how Core Text is structured. Working with Core Text can be rather complicated, so I wouldn't recommend utilizing it for trivial text-input fields. But if you're determined to build the next great mobile word processing powerhouse for the iPad, then Core Text is your answer.

Of all the new features in iPhone SDK 3.2, the Core Text classes are probably the most difficult to grasp. That's where Jack Nutting swings to the rescue! My esteemed coauthor breaks it all down in Chapter 5 by showing you how to add a Core Text-driven text tool to the Dudel drawing app. Complete with code examples and expert guidance, that chapter provides the basic building blocks needed to begin using Core Text in your own iPad apps.

Popovers

With iPhone apps, the small screen real estate could display only a very limited amount of controls and content. To keep the interface clean and easy to use, access to additional settings and elements were presented in separate views. This required shuffling back and forth between various screens.

Even though the iPad's larger screen size gives developers room to include more functionality into a single, consolidated screen, the design objective still remains the same: keep it simple. Rather than clutter the screen with an overly complex interface, your goal should be to minimize the interface where ever possible, allowing users to focus on your app's primary purpose and content. To solve this problem, popovers were introduced in iPhone SDK 3.2. Exclusive to the iPad, popovers display a secondary view on top of the main view. Typically, this subview contains user-selectable settings or additional contents that do not require the full screen.

Remember the iPad apps showcased in Chapter 1? On the iPad, both Brushes (Figure 1–4) and Synotes (Figure 1–8) utilize popovers to display views that previously required navigating between separate iPhone screens. A popover controller can contain almost any kind of view you want. Although popovers are most commonly displayed when users tap toolbar buttons, you can program a popover to appear when tapping other types of objects, such as an image, a map item, or a custom interface element. In The Iconfactory's Twitterrific for iPad, tapping on a Twitter user's avatar icon conveniently presents a popover view of that user's Twitter profile information.

The iPad places an increased importance on toolbars. Unlike the iPhone, where toolbars are limited to the bottom of the screen, iPad apps support toolbar placement on both the top and bottom of your interface. In fact, since the split view controller (introduced later in this chapter) relies on a top toolbar layout, Apple recommends placing your toolbars at the top. In many aspects, this actually brings iPad interface design much closer to a traditional desktop application layout than that of an iPhone app.

In Apple's Pages for iPad, the toolbar's buttons present popovers for choosing various document styles and settings. In Figure 3–3, the Tools popover shows a UITableView with several options. Some of the items even include user-selectable controls.

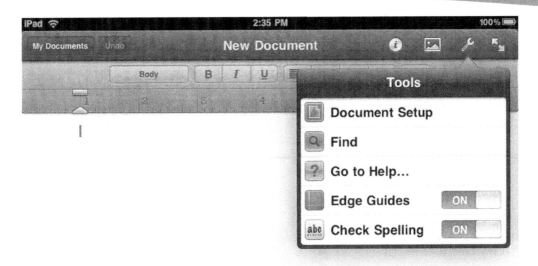

Figure 3–3. *Popovers are a great way to display user-selectable options that don't require a modal view. An effective use of popovers can be seen in Apple's Pages for iPad.*

If your app's main toolbar (or navigation bar) is configured with a default color, then a toolbar within a popover will inherit the popover's native dark-blue outline. If you assign a custom color to the toolbar, that custom color is shown instead, with the popover's dark-blue outline surrounding the view. With that in mind, if you insist on using a custom toolbar color, make sure it's a color that complements the popover outline coloring.

For best results, I recommend sticking with a default color for your app's main toolbar, unless you modify your popover code to enforce a default color for its own popover toolbar. For example, even though Pages uses a custom brown color for its main toolbar, Apple decided not to implement that custom color in its popover toolbars. This also allows a popover to visually contrast with the interface behind it, making its hovering box easily distinguishable from its parent view. If your popovers don't contain their own toolbars, then this won't be an issue for you.

Think strategically when designing your app's interface with popovers. Is your app overflowing with features? Instead of piling several buttons into a toolbar, with each one displaying a separate popover, try to consolidate all your subviews into only a few popovers. This can be done within a popover view by adding a segmented control to a toolbar. Each segmented tab loads a different view into the same popover. The feature-rich Pages for iPad effectively utilizes this concept, as shown in the example in Figure 3–4.

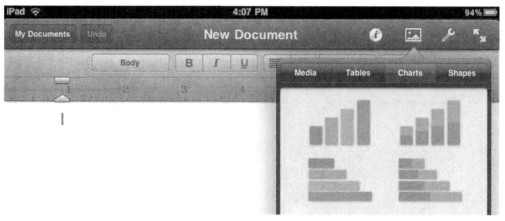

Figure 3–4. *Simplify your interface design! Within a popover, use a segmented control in a toolbar to consolidate multiple, related subviews.*

Beyond displaying custom views, popovers are also handy for presenting only a few options. Instead of showing an alert sheet, a popover is the more appropriate method on the iPad for presenting those options. A good example of this is tapping the Add Bookmark button in Mobile Safari. On the iPhone, an alert sheet is called. But on the iPad, alert sheets are displayed as popovers, as shown in Figure 3–5.

Figure 3–5. *Although an alert sheet is a good choice for displaying a few options on the iPhone (left), presenting those options as a popover is a better solution on the iPad (right).*

Unlike an alert sheet, a popover should never include a Cancel (or Close) button. If a user taps outside a popover, the popover will disappear. But any selections made within the popover will not automatically dismiss the popover, requiring you to programmatically close the popover yourself. Since Apple recommends using popovers for user-selectable options, you may wonder why this is the case. There is actually a good reason for this design. Since popovers generally include not only user-selectable items, but also other tappable elements like segmented controls (as shown in Figure 3–4), you don't want the popover disappearing after just any finger tap. With control over the closing of the popover, you can designate exactly how and when the popover is dismissed based on a user's selection.

If you need users to make a specific choice before allowing them to return to the main view, you can force the popover to be modal (dimming the screen area behind it), but depending on your needs, a popover may not be the ideal solution for that use case. For many situations where that behavior is needed, your best bet may be to present a modal view instead, as discussed in the "Modal Presentation Styles" section later in this chapter.

Displaying a popover in your code is actually quite easy. In a nutshell, you create a new instance of UIPopoverController and pass a custom view controller to it (which will be loaded into the popover view). The parent view should be assigned to the popover's delegate, so that communication can take place between the two. To show the popover when a user taps a toolbar button, you call the presentPopoverFromBarButtonItem method. If the popover is being displayed when a user taps another interface element such as an image, you should call presentPopoverFromRect instead.

The default size of a popover is 320 pixels wide and 1100 pixels tall, but you can easily customize the width and height with the popoverContentSize property. But you may find it interesting that the default 320-pixel width is the same size as the iPhone's portrait mode width. That's no coincidence! With that default width, it's much easier to convert most existing iPhone app views into popovers when creating an iPad version—you won't need to redesign much (if any) of the view's original layout.

There are a few additional configuration options and considerations when using popovers, which are covered at length in Chapter 6. You'll walk through the creation of several popovers as you continue to develop the Dudel drawing app, so that chapter is a must-read.

Popovers might just be one of the most important new features of iPhone SDK 3.2. Certainly, this new interface component will prove to be a very useful new weapon in your iPad development arsenal.

Video Playback and Display Options

As of iOS 3.2, Apple has changed the way the MPMoviePlayerController class works. In previous versions, videos were always played in a full-screen player interface. The iPad now offers an enhanced movie player that can be displayed in either full-screen mode or embedded within your app's views.

The YouTube app that's included on the iPad is a perfect example of this new video functionality. In landscape orientation, videos play full-screen as usual, but in portrait orientation, videos play within the app's interface, as shown in Figure 3–6.

Figure 3–6. *The iPad's YouTube app showcases the MPMoviePlayerController's new embedded video playback functionality.*

One of the many advantages of this embedded player feature is that it gives you the option to allow users to interact with other elements in the app while the selected video plays. The enhanced movie controller also enables developers to change videos without initiating new controllers, overlay additional views on top of the current movie, generate thumbnail images from video frames, control the playback options via code, and much more.

It's important to note that in order to provide these new capabilities and the improved playback interface, some of MPMoviePlayerController's previous API has been deprecated, replaced with new methods and properties. This was necessary in order to provide developers with more granular control over the presentation of the movie. For example, instead of the movie player controller handling the video's presentation on the screen, it now provides a view object that acts as a container for your video content, giving you much more control over the movie's overall display and playback within your app. If you're porting existing iPhone movie player code to an iPad app, you'll need to modify that code to ensure that it works properly in iOS 3.2.

Beyond the iPad's display, there's also new support for presenting content on an external monitor or projector when connected to an iPad. Using the screens method of the UIScreen class, you can program your iPad app to detect if an external display device is connected via a compatible cable. UIScreen also includes methods and properties for not only accessing the external screen's resolution, but also for configuring your app's content for proper viewing on the connected device. But this feature isn't limited to mirroring your iPad's screen. You can also project any additional view onto the external display by assigning it to that screen object. This will prove to be a very valuable feature for iPad developers building business and media apps that need to present content on a desktop computer monitor, a projector screen, or even a TV.

In Chapter 7, you'll learn how to program your iPad apps to utilize the enhanced MPMoviePlayerController class, as well as how to communicate with external display devices connected to the iPad using UIScreen.

Split View Controller

After popovers, the new split view controller is the second most distinctive feature that distinguishes iPad apps from their iPhone siblings. Navigating back and forth between various views is a good solution for the small iPhone screen, but on the much larger iPad display, that interface mechanism is no longer necessary. To make efficient use of the iPad's extra screen real estate, while also helping developers migrate existing iPhone navigation systems to the tablet, Apple introduced a new view controller called the UISplitViewController.

True to its name, a split view controller contains two panes: master and detail. The master pane typically holds the navigation or primary table view for the app. Within the master pane, users can make selections. If a chosen item requires a display, then its data is loaded into the detail pane. For example, in a note-taking app, the master pane would list all of the user's saved notes. Selecting a note would open it in the detail pane, where it could be read and edited by the user.

The master pane is fixed at 320 pixels wide, while the detail pane consumes the remaining width of the window. Notice the recurring 320-pixel width? Just like the default width of popovers, this was a strategic design decision by Apple to make the conversion of iPhone apps into iPad apps as painless as possible. A navigation bar from an iPhone app could be repurposed for use within the master pane of a split view-based iPad app.

As discussed in Chapter 2, the Xcode Split View-based Application project template provides a convenient starting point. Although that template populates the master pane with a table view list, you can just as easily add a navigation bar controller, if you need to provide the ability to drill down through a few levels of content within the master pane before displaying a selection in the detail pane.

In landscape orientation, the master pane is located on the left side, and the detail pane is on the right side of the screen, as shown in Figure 3–7. See how the detail pane includes a toolbar at the top of the view to match the toolbar or navigation bar in the master pane? Not only does the consistency provide a visually pleasing and balanced interface design, but this layout also reinforces Apple's push for consolidating an iPad app's primary buttons into a top-aligned toolbar.

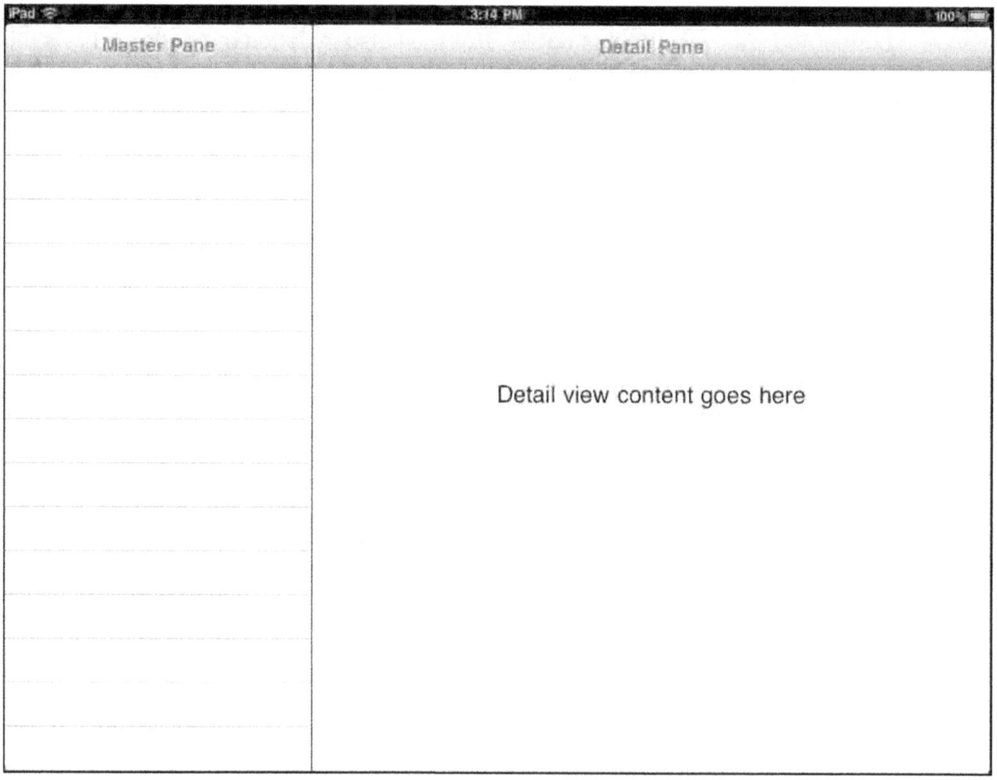

Figure 3–7. *The two-pane layout of a split view controller in landscape orientation*

Beyond aesthetics, the detail pane's toolbar serves another important purpose for the split view controller. To help preserve your interface design within the detail pane, rotating the tablet to the portrait orientation allows the detail pane to use the entire screen. In order to keep the master pane accessible to users, the split view controller automatically adds a UIBarButtonItem to the left side of the detail pane's toolbar. Tap that button, and a popover displays the master pane's view, as shown in Figure 3–8.

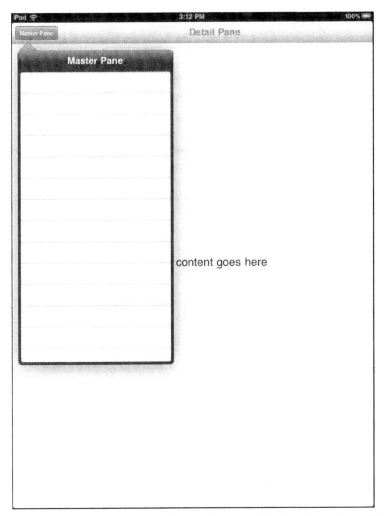

Figure 3–8. *When a split view-based app is in portrait orientation, the contents of the master pane are accessible by tapping its toolbar button to reveal a popover.*

Since the detail pane usually represents the detailed data of the item selected, the master pane should reflect the current selection. So if it's a table view row, then your code should ensure the selection remains persistent. In a simple notes app, for example, if the user is viewing a specific note in the detail pane, the master pane could visually indicate the current selection by maintaining a highlighted or checked table view row of that listed note.

Although the split view controller handles much of its functionality for you, there are some essential implementation details worth learning in order to customize it for use with your own interface needs. Going beyond the basic Split View-based Application template, Chapter 8 walks you through the steps of manually adding a UISplitViewController to your Xcode project.

Modal Presentation Styles

As an iPhone developer, you're already familiar with how to make a UIViewController modal, which prevents the user from returning to the parent window until the modal view is closed. A modal view is a great solution when you need to present a much more sophisticated layout than what's possible in a limited UIAlertView.

On the iPhone, a modal view fills the entire screen, which is perfectly fine with only 320 by 480 pixels. But on an iPad, there's considerably more display space, so you may not always want a modal view that stretches the full 1024 by 768 pixels. To accommodate the larger surface area, Apple has introduced four new modal style options, which can be assigned to a new UIViewController class property called modalPresentationStyle. As on the iPhone, you still call a modal view via presentModalViewController, but before doing so, you simply assign one of the new style options to the view controller's modalPresentationStyle property.

For example, let's say your code already has an instance of UIViewController named myController. You could assign a modal style to it before presenting it on the screen, like this:

```
myController.modalPresentationStyle = UIModalPresentationFormSheet;
[self presentModalViewController:myController animated:YES];
```

As you can see from that code snippet, one of the new style options is UIModalPresentationFormSheet, which has a fixed size of 540 pixels wide by 620 pixels tall. Being smaller than the iPad's window, it is displayed in the center of the screen, with the parent view dimmed gray behind it, as shown in Figure 3–9.

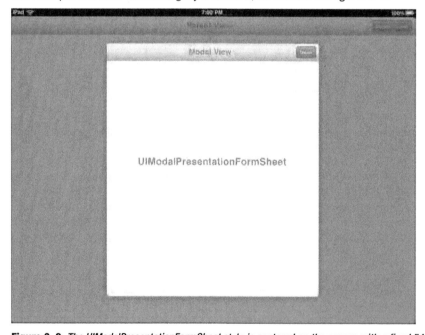

Figure 3–9. *The UIModalPresentationFormSheet style is centered on the screen with a fixed 540-by- 620 size.*

The next option is UIModalPresentationPageSheet, which assumes the current height of the screen and a fixed width of 768 pixels. This means that in portrait orientation, it appears to fill the entire screen, but in landscape orientation, the dimmed gray parent view can be seen in the background on both sides, as shown in Figure 3–10.

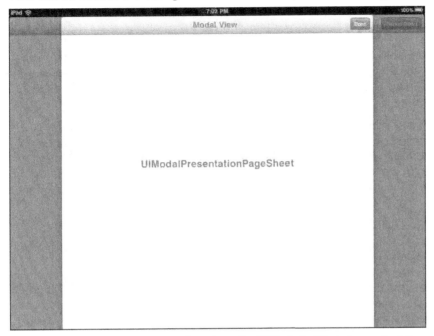

Figure 3–10. *UIModalPresentationPageSheet has a fixed 768-pixel width, but spans the full screen height.*

If you do need the modal view to utilize the entire screen, you can set the modalPresentationStyle property to UIModalPresentationFullScreen. But what do you do when the rare need arises to display a modal view within a popover or one of the split view panes? That's where UIModalPresentationCurrentContext comes to the rescue, presenting the modal view in the same size as the parent view that called it. For example, a UIModalPresentationCurrentContext-assigned modal view shown within a popover would use the same width and height dimensions as the popover.

Even though tapping outside a popover will automatically dismiss it, that won't work with modal views. Just like its counterpart on the iPhone, a modal view needs to be programmatically closed on the iPad. This can be achieved by including a Done button (as shown in Figures 3-9 and 3-10) or by designating this task to some other user interaction within the modal view.

In Chapter 8, you will learn how to put these new modal view styles to good use in your own iPad apps.

Advanced Input Methods

iOS 3.2 also includes a new set of custom input methods that developers can use in their apps: edit menu actions, keyboard layouts, and gesture recognizers.

Edit Menu Actions

Depending on the object you tap and hold your finger on, the small, black edit menu that appears on the screen will display one or more of the default menu actions, such as **Copy**, **Cut**, **Paste**, **Select**, **Select All**, and **Delete**. Now, with access to the UIMenuController, you can insert your own custom actions into the edit menu for a specific object.

A custom menu action consists of a UIMenuItem with a title property and an action selector. You then assign your UIMenuItem to the UIMenuController of the appropriate object type. In order to facilitate the target action behavior, you also need to identify a target for your new menu item by setting the applicable view as the first responder for that action. The last step is to write the actual action method for handling that task if the user selects it.

For example, if you wanted to add a custom menu item for a thesaurus when a text word is selected, you could create a new UIMenuItem instance with the title Thesaurus that points to an action selector thesaurusLookup. Add that UIMenuItem to the UIMenuController assigned to that text object, and your custom **Thesaurus** menu item will appear along with the default **Copy**, **Cut**, and **Paste** options in the edit menu. The assigned target would be the parent view of that text object. The parent view controller's source code would need to include your action method, thesaurusLookup, so that when a user selects that menu item, your app knows how to respond.

When you add custom items, keep their menu titles short, with no more than one or two words per item. To prevent users from being overwhelmed, try not to add too many additional items to an edit menu. If you need to provide several options to the user, you should consider presenting them in a popover action sheet instead.

Eager to add custom menu items (such as the one shown in Figure 3–11) to your own iPad apps? In Chapter 9, you'll learn how to accomplish this with only a handful of code lines.

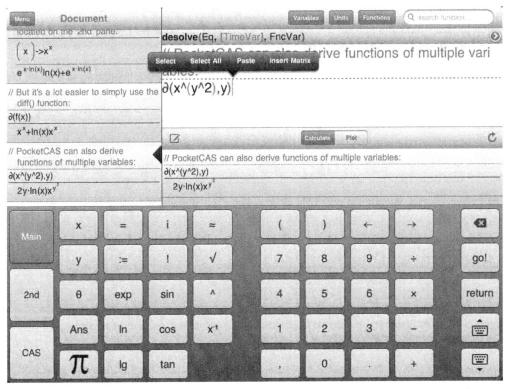

Figure 3–11. *Daniel Alm and Thomas Osthege used custom edit menu items and keyboard layouts in their PocketCAS graphics calculator iPad app. Alongside the standard edit menu commands is a custom Insert Matrix menu item.*

Keyboard Layouts

Did you notice the unique keyboard in Figure 3–11? No, it's not an interface trick. No longer limited to only the standard keyboard, you now have a way to present your own keyboard layout, which is nothing more than a custom view. To replace the system keyboard, you assign the view to the `inputView` property of a `UITextField`, a `UITextView`, or any compatible responder object.

Since users are already familiar with the system keyboard, don't stray too far from the default design when creating your own custom keyboard. Make sure the buttons appear tappable and automatically size to display well in both portrait and landscape orientations. The background of your view should extend to the full width of the screen. The height is flexible, but Apple recommends sticking with the same height as the system keyboard for consistency when possible. As an example, the PocketCAS app shown in Figure 3–11 does a nice job of emulating the look and feel of Apple's virtual keyboard design, which reduces the learning curve for first-time users.

If you need to insert only a few additional buttons to the existing system keyboard, another option is to add a keyboard extension, called an input accessory view. If you've ever filled out a web form in Mobile Safari, you may have noticed the extra translucent black toolbar that runs across the top of the keyboard, as shown in Figure 3–12. As with a custom keyboard, this is accomplished by creating a view that contains the additional interface elements you want displayed above the keyboard. Whereas a keyboard replacement uses inputView, your input accessory view should be assigned to the inputAccessoryView property instead.

Figure 3–12. *When filling out a web form in Mobile Safari, the keyboard includes an input accessory view, which is a toolbar-like interface added to the top of the keyboard.*

Programming your app to utilize a custom keyboard layout or input accessory view can be somewhat complicated, but Chapter 9 takes you step by step through the process with helpful sample projects.

Gesture Recognizers

The user interface components in the UIKit framework include handling for basic touch events, such as tapping a UIButton, but what if you need to add event handling for specific touch behavior to a custom view or object? To help simplify what was previously a laborious task, Apple has provided iPad developers with a new UIGestureRecognizer class for easily detecting touch gestures. UIKit includes six common gesture recognizers, which are subclasses of UIGestureRecognizer:

- ▩ UITapGestureRecognizer: Finger taps.
- ▩ UILongPressGestureRecognizer: Holding a finger down on one spot.
- ▩ UIPinchGestureRegnizer: Pinching fingers in and out.
- ▩ UIPanGestureRecognizer: Dragging a finger.
- ▩ UISwipeGestureRecognizer: A quick finger swipe.
- ▩ UIRotationGestureRecognizer: Rotating two fingers in opposite directions.

To add a gesture recognizer to a view, you first create a new instance of one of the six UIGestureRecognizer subclasses. Like a custom edit menu, an action selector is assigned to the gesture recognizer instance. This informs the view which method to call when the user performs that gesture. Some gesture recognizers have configurable attributes, such as numberOfTapsRequired, which sets the number of taps for a UITapGestureRecognizer. In order to give the gesture recognizer a target, it needs to be attached to the view by calling the addGestureRecognizer method.

If you do use one of the standard six gesture recognizers in your app, it's important to use it for an action that users associate with that gesture. For example, people know that finger pinching is typically used for zooming in and out of an image. If your app uses that UIPinchGestureRecognizer for deleting files, the unorthodox use of that gesture will only lead to confusion (and possibly even rejection from the App Store).

If you need a unique gesture recognizer, you can create your own subclass of UIGestureRecognizer and override all of its methods (such as touchesBegan, touchesMoved, touchesEnded, touchesCancelled, and reset) with your desired functionality. The drawback to implementing support for custom gestures is that they are unknown touch commands. It becomes your app's responsibility to properly educate users on how to use the new gestures. Unless you have a compelling reason to go this route, sticking with the well-known, common gestures is usually the best approach.

In Chapter 9, you'll add undo support to the Dudel drawing app by implementing a gesture recognizer.

Document Support

The iOS does a good job of hiding the underlying filesystem, so that users can focus on creating and consuming content. But the iPad's larger screen encourages greater productivity, so situations arise where users will want to control how some files are opened and shared between apps.

In the past, this was always tricky due to how each app was limited to its own "sandbox" directory, but with iOS 3.2, Apple introduced a new file-handling mechanism called Document Support. Apple's built-in Mail app is a good example of this new feature. If an e-mail contains a file attachment, it's displayed as a file icon at the bottom of the message. If you currently have an installed app that has registered itself with iOS as the "owner" of that file format, the e-mail attachment's file icon will reflect that app's icon. For example, if the e-mail attachment is a Microsoft Word document and you have Apple's Pages installed on your iPad, the file icon may look like the Pages app icon. As expected, if you tap the file, it will open in Pages. Since both Mail and Pages are Apple apps running on an Apple tablet, this comes as no surprise.

But the real beauty of Document Support is the power it provides to developers. It also allows a user to open that e-mail attachment in any other registered app that supports that file type! If you hold your finger on the e-mail attachment icon, a popover will appear with a few options. One option, of course, is to open the file in its owner app. In the case of the Word document, that option might be Open in Pages. But one of the other options is **Open In**.... Selecting **Open In**... replaces that popover with a new popover, listing all of the registered apps that can open Word documents. I happen to have the excellent app, GoodReader, installed on my iPad, which also supports Word files, so it's listed alongside Pages in that Open In... popover, as shown in Figure 3–13.

Figure 3–13. *Document Support enables the Mail app to suggest opening an e-mail attachment in other registered apps that are capable of opening that file type.*

If I select GoodReader from the list, the Word document not only opens in GoodReader, but a copy of the file is also stored in GoodReader's file directory, accessible to me any time I run GoodReader. This is a safe and sanctioned way to transfer a file from one app to another, without sacrificing the security of an app's sandbox.

So how does this all work? There are actually two factors that make this functionality possible: the sender app and the receiver app, both of which require different development steps. In Figure 3–13, the Mail app is the sender app, and Pages and GoodReader are receiver apps.

In order for your app to send a file to another app (as Mail does), you need to use the `UIDocumentInteractionController` class. A document interaction controller communicates with the iOS to see if the selected file can be previewed by the system and if any other installed apps are registered to open that file format (the Open In... popover list).

If you want your app to act as a receiver, it needs to notify the iOS registry of the specific file types that it can open. This is done by including each supported file type in the `CFBundleDocumentTypes` key of your app's *Info.plist* file. Each file type declaration consists of four attributes: name, the related uniform type identifier (UTI), handler rank, and file image icon. The handler rank informs the system whether your app is the owner of the file type (such as your own proprietary file format) or is simply capable of opening that kind of file. The image icon is optional for file type owners (which will be discussed later in the section "Required Project Resources for iPad Apps").

If your app is registered with iOS as supporting a particular file type, then it will need to be able to field requests to open related files upon app launch. If another app, such as Mail, uses a document interaction controller for that file type and a user selects your app from the Open In... list, your app needs to be ready to handle that request, which is delivered to the `application:didFinishLaunchingWithOptions` method in your application delegate. The request arrives with an options dictionary that includes important information about the file your app needs to open, such as the file's location, the sender app's bundle identifier, and an annotations property list object that contains additional data about the file.

If your iPad app opens and saves files, you really should take advantage of the new Document Support feature. It provides greater flexibility for your app's offerings and better interoperability with other installed apps. To learn more about utilizing Document Support, be sure to read Chapter 10. Your users will thank you for it!

Universal Applications

Even though most iPhone apps will run on the iPad, their smaller dimensions appear rather pixelized and inferior to native iPad apps. But some developers may not want to maintain two separate Xcode projects for essentially the same product in order to properly support both platforms. To solve this problem, iPhone SDK 3.2 introduced a new universal application format that runs on both iPhone and iPad devices. Depending on the device running the universal application, the appropriate version of the app is launched. This way, you can maintain one Xcode project with shared source code, but design separate user interfaces specifically tailored for each platform. For example, your iPhone app may use a navigation controller for organizing content, yet on an iPad, you would most likely want to display a split view controller instead. Both versions use the same data, but present it in different ways that best suit the chosen device.

For developers targeting both platforms, Apple highly recommends building universal applications. Managing and updating only one application in the App Store makes it much easier for customers who use your app on both their iPhone and iPad. But if your iPad version is radically different from your iPhone app, with dozens of new features that require a fairly hefty code rewrite, a universal application may not be the ideal choice. If the two versions don't share much in the way of code, it may make more sense to build them as two stand-alone products: one for the iPhone and one for the iPad. There are also business and marketing factors that come into play as well, which we'll explore in the upcoming "To Be or Not to Be Universal" section. If you do make the decision to distribute your product as a universal application, it requires some extra planning and effort on your part.

Universal App Requirements

The first minor hurdle for universal app development is orientation. With the iPhone's small screen, providing an efficient user interface design often requires a dedicated orientation, such as a portrait-only app. That's perfectly acceptable on the iPhone, but the iPad's larger display allows more of your interface elements to be consolidated into a single window, providing enough screen space in both portrait and landscape views. In fact, Apple insists that iPad apps should support all orientations. If your iPhone app is locked into a single orientation, you'll need to configure your universal app project to accommodate multiple orientations when displaying your iPad version's user interface.

So how does the app differentiate between your iPhone code and your iPad code? This is where we encounter the next hurdle in developing universal applications. Not only does your app need to detect the current platform and run the appropriate code, but when compiling your project in Xcode, you'll need to properly "wrap" your iPad code to prevent compiler errors. Remember that in producing a universal application, the iPad features exclusive to iPhone SDK 3.2 will cause compiler errors when Xcode is building the iPhone portion of the app, so you'll need to use conditional coding to prevent that from happening.

Although you may be tempted to simply check the user's device type or operating system version, with Apple constantly releasing new devices and iOS versions, that's not the way to go. A better approach is to test for the availability of exclusive iPad classes using NSClassFromString. If you pass an iPad-only class name, such as UISplitViewController to NSClassString and a valid object is returned, you'll know the user's device is an iPad. If nil is returned, then that iPad class doesn't exist, so the user's device is an iPhone or iPod touch.

For new iPad functions that have been added to existing frameworks, checking the class name's existence will not be effective. In those cases, you can compare a specific function name with NULL. If an iPad-only function is equal to NULL, then the user's device is not an iPad.

You'll also need to perform similar code checks if your app utilizes hardware features that are available on only one of the platforms, such as the iPhone's camera. And don't forget your .xib interface files and images that are uniquely designed for a specific screen size. Since your iPad app may require a different interface and graphics than your iPhone app, your view controller classes will need to be programmed to load the correct resources.

All of this talk about conditional coding may sound like a lot of work, and truthfully, it is fairly time-consuming to implement at first. But your efforts will prove worthwhile when working on future updates of your app. Adding new features to a single Xcode project that shares common code between the two platforms is much more time-efficient than needing to add the same code to separate projects.

Chapter 11 covers the process of creating a universal application, complete with expert tips and conditional coding examples. You'll also learn how to convert an existing iPhone project into a universal app using Xcode's new Upgrade Current Target for iPad feature.

To Be or Not to Be Universal

From a development standpoint, there are many advantages to creating a universal application, but is it the right choice for you? If your app is free, then your goal is to provide the most convenient, user-friendly access to it. A universal application makes it easy for users to download your app across all of their Apple mobile devices. But paid apps are a different story. Putting aside the technical benefits for a moment, let's look at the business factors involved.

If your iPad app represents an enhanced edition, offering dozens of exclusive new features that are not available in your iPhone version, it may make more sense to release it as a separate, stand-alone iPad app. As a universal application, existing owners of your iPhone app will be able to access the iPad version for free, since there's no official upgrade mechanism supported in universal applications. By selling the iPad app as a separate product, you have the opportunity to recoup your development costs. And if it provides additional value above and beyond your iPhone edition, then most customers won't have a problem with paying for it, even after they've already purchased the iPhone version. I say "most" because there will always be a select few users protesting that they should receive all app versions for all applicable Apple devices for free. Ironically, the loudest complaints usually come from people who paid only 99 cents for your original iPhone app. But don't cut off a potential revenue stream that could help support your continued development just because you're worried about keeping everyone happy. Here's a little secret: It's not possible to please everyone. Just build the best features and user experience possible. If you provide your customers with additional value, most of them will be more than happy to pay for the enhanced iPad version.

On the other hand, if your iPad app does not offer anything new beyond an iPad-optimized interface slapped on top of the same iPhone feature set, you may want to consider a universal application. If you can't justify the iPad app price with additional iPad-exclusive functionality, selling it as a separate product will definitely attract an angry mob of customers, wielding pitchforks and writing negative App Store reviews! And Apple may just agree with them. Apple has been known to reject stand-alone iPad apps that don't add any significant value beyond what's available from their iPhone counterparts. In these situations, Apple usually advises the developer to convert it into a universal application before resubmitting it to the App Store.

Another major issue to consider is the file size of your app. A universal application combines the incremental code and separate *.xib* files and image resources for both the iPhone and iPad versions into one package, which means it can often be nearly double the file size of a single platform app. Although Apple recently raised the cellular 3G download limit from 10MB to 20MB to help accommodate universal applications, some content-heavy apps such as games may still exceed that file size. If your universal application is larger than 20MB, that drastically reduces your app's potential audience to only people within Wi-Fi range. Whether your app is free or a paid product, this factor alone may force you to release separate iPhone and iPad versions to ensure that your app can be downloaded by both Wi-Fi and cellular 3G connections.

Required Project Images for iPad Apps

For an iPhone app compiled for iOS 3.1.3 or an earlier version, you were required to include a 57-by-57-pixel app icon and a default launch image sized for portrait orientation in your Xcode project. With iOS 3.2 and the iPad's support for multiple orientations, the project images that an iPad app or a universal application requires are much different.

App Icon Images

Beyond the usual 512-by-512-pixel app icon that's required by the App Store, you'll need to add the following iPad icon files to your Xcode project's Resources folder:

- *72-by-72-pixel PNG image*: The app icon displayed on the iPad's home screen.

- *50-by-50-pixel PNG image*: The app icon shown if your app name is listed in iPad Spotlight Search results. It's important to note that iOS crops 1 pixel from all sides of this icon, so only the inner 48 by 48 pixels are displayed.

- *29-by-29-pixel PNG image*: This app icon is required only if your application places settings options in iOS Settings app.

Don't worry about the rounded edges and glossy beveled look that iPad app icons typically have. iOS and the App Store automatically add those elements to the icon for you. Although you can't do anything about the dynamically added rounded edges, you do have the option to disable the default beveled gloss effect from your app icon if your app icon looks better without it.

After you've added your 72-by-72-pixel icon PNG file to the Resources folder of your iPad app project in Xcode, you'll need to open your project's *plist* file. Once you've added the icon's filename to the Icon property, click the gray plus symbol (+) button on the bottom-right side of the list to add a new entry to the *plist* file. In the new, blank row, click the tiny arrows in the left Key column to display a contextual menu of additional properties. Select **Icon already includes gloss and bevel effects** from that menu. Setting its value to True will disable the default beveled gloss effect from your app icon, as shown in Figure 3–14. When displaying your 72-by-72-pixel app icon on the iPad or the 512-by-512-pixel icon in the App Store, Apple checks your app's *plist* file first, so your preferred setting is always honored.

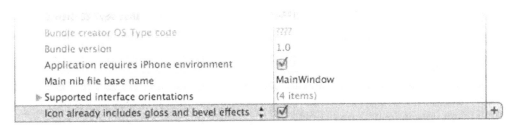

Figure 3–14. *Adding a new plist property, Icon already includes gloss and bevel effects, and setting it to True will disable the default beveled gloss effect from your iPad app icon.*

Document Type Icon Images

If your iPad app utilizes the new Document Support feature and registers a custom file type with the iOS registry, you should assign a custom document icon to it, so that users can visually identify that file type as belonging to your app. Remember the Pages document icon shown in Figure 3–13? If you don't assign a custom icon to your app's file type, iOS will display your app icon inside a white document (with a top-right corner page curl). Most apps simply rely on that system default, but if you would prefer to design your own document icon, you'll need to save your custom icon in two sizes: a 64-by-64-pixel PNG image and a 320-by-320-pixel PNG image.

Do not design your icon to emulate a document with a page curl. iOS automatically adds the document border, drop shadow, and top-right corner page curl. Due to these system-supplied graphics effects, you must take special care to place your icon's main imagery within the "safe zone" area. For the 64-by-64-pixel icon, stay within 1 pixel from the top, 4 pixels from the bottom, and 10 pixels from both sides. For the 320-by-320-pixel icon, stay within 5 pixels from the top, 20 pixels from the bottom, and 50 pixels from both sides.

Default Launch Images

A launch image is briefly displayed on the screen when an app is first loading. This means the image should represent only the basic user interface elements of the app's initial window. For example, if your app's first screen shows a split view controller, then your default launch image should reflect the same controller layout, without any text or any content.

On the iPhone, your app needed to provide only a single portrait orientation image named *Default.png*. But on the iPad, Apple wants your app to support multiple orientations. Since a user could launch your iPad app in any orientation, your Xcode project will need to include multiple default launch images. Even though the iPad screen is 768 pixels by 1024 pixels, the launch images should not include the status bar, which accounts for the top 20 pixels.

The *Default* filename is still employed, but the orientation label is appended to the name with a hyphen, as follows:

- *Default-Portrait.png*: This 768-by-1004-pixel image represents the first view in portrait orientation.

- *Default-PortraitUpsideDown.png*: Unless your initial portrait window is different if viewed upside down, this image is not needed. In its absence, *Default-Portrait.png* will be shown.

- *Default-Landscape.png*: This 1024-by-748-pixel image represents the first view in landscape orientation.

- *Default-LandscapeLeft.png* and *Default-LandscapeRight.png*: Unless your initial landscape window is different depending on whether the device is rotated left or right, these images are not needed. In the absence of either (or both) of these images, *Default-Landscape.png* will be shown.

If you're building a universal application, you'll need to designate unique prefixes to your launch image filenames, so that your Xcode project can properly identify which PNG files to use for the iPhone and the iPad, respectively. This is configured via the UILaunchImageFile key in your app's *plist* file. In order to differentiate between the two platforms, attach a device-specific value to the UILaunchImageFile key title, connected with a tilde character (no spaces). The UILaunchImageFile~iphone key's string is for the iPhone, so it would remain as *Default*. You would use a different iPad-related name for the UILaunchImageFile~ipad key's string, such as *iPadDefault*. In the universal application's *plist* file, the key-string syntax would look like this:

```
<key>UILaunchImageFile~iphone</key>
<string>Default</string>
<key>UILaunchImageFile~ipad</key>
<string>iPadDefault</string>
```

With these *plist* keys in place, you then want your launch image filenames to adhere to that assigned prefix. For example, your iPad launch images would be named *iPadDefault-Portrait.png*, *iPadDefault-Landscape.png*, and so on. Your iPhone launch image would remain *Default.png*.

Drilling Deeper

Don't worry if you're feeling a bit overwhelmed. We certainly covered a lot of ground in this chapter! This was merely an introduction to the vast array of new iPad classes and functions in iPhone SDK 3.2. The rest of the book covers the major iPad features in detail. You can read each chapter at your own pace, easily absorbing the step-by-step explanations on how to develop cool apps with these new features. You'll be an iPad code master in no time!

All of the code examples listed in this book, along with the full source code of the iPad drawing app, Dudel, can be downloaded from http://www.apress.com/book/view/9781430230212.

New Graphics Functionality

Starting with version 3.2, iOS includes some compelling new graphics capabilities. Besides the larger screen in the iPad, the software has also been updated with some new features that will help developers make their apps even better. This chapter covers two of these new features: the UIBezierPath class, which can be used to draw and fill shapes of all kinds, and the ability to render directly to PDF format—anything that you can draw on the screen, you can also send straight to a PDF file!

One bit of graphics functionality that apparently hasn't changed is OpenGL. The iPad uses the same graphics hardware, and the same OpenGL ES 2.0, that the iPhone 3GS uses. Therefore, any OpenGL code you've written for iPhone in the past should work with little or no changes on the iPad (for that matter, any Quartz/CoreGraphics drawing code should also be functionally equivalent).

Bezier Paths

One great new feature of iOS 3.2 is the inclusion of the UIBezierPath class, which gives you the ability to draw paths of arbitrary complexity. Anyone who has used a vector-drawing program such as Adobe Illustrator is probably familiar with the path tool, which lets you define a curve by clicking on points. You define a start and end point for the curve, along with two control points, giving you a smooth curve from one point to the other. The curve you create in this way is actually several Bézier paths linked together. However, a Bézier path can also define straight lines, rectangles, and basically any other 2D shape you have in mind. Figure 4–1 shows some examples of paths drawn using UIBezierPath.

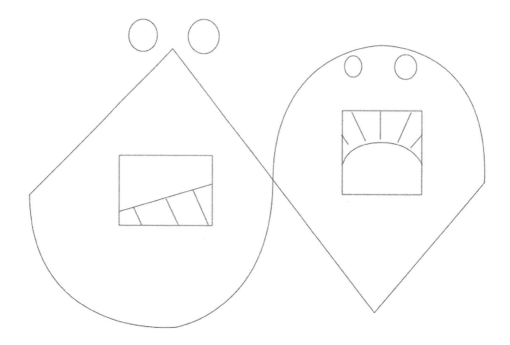

Figure 4–1. *Various paths constructed from Bézier curves*

In this chapter, we're going to build an example that demonstrates various uses of UIBezierPath. You'll learn how to create complex paths, define drawing characteristics for the paths you create, and use different colors to draw a path's outline (with the stroke color) and its interior (with the fill color).

Introducing Dudel

The sample iPad app we'll create will let the user create some on-screen graphics using a handful of tools, similar to what you might see in a vector-drawing application like Adobe Illustrator. We'll call it Dudel. See Figure 4–2 for a glimpse of Dudel in action.

Apart from showing the use of Bézier paths, this application will serve as the foundation for demonstrating other technologies throughout the book. We'll add one piece at a time as we work through the book, evolving and improving the app as we introduce new features. This means that in this chapter, we'll need to do a bit of project setup before we get to the actual Bézier paths. Please bear with me—it's going to be worth the wait!

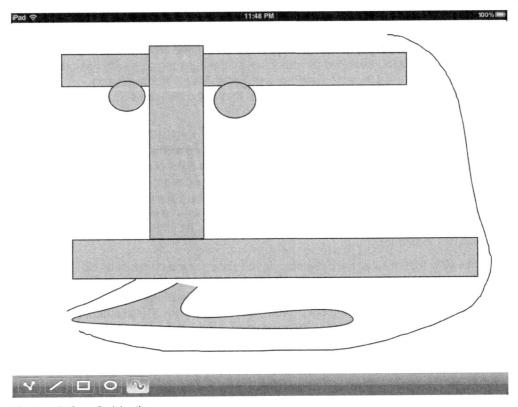

Figure 4–2. *Some Dudel action*

Creating the Dudel Project

Launch Xcode, and use the menu or Xcode's friendly startup panel to create a new project. Select iPhone OS Application in the upper left, which will bring up the familiar set of application templates in the main section. Here, you'll see a few changes compared to older SDKs. First is the addition of the new Split View-based Application template, which we'll cover in Chapter 8.

Click around to explore the various application templates. You'll see that each shows a product type in the center of the window. Some project types are only for the iPhone or only for the iPad; for those, the product type (iPhone or iPad) is displayed in a label. Other project types can apply to either platform; for those, you get a popup menu that lets you choose iPhone, iPad, or Universal (to support both). Of course, our focus is iPad apps, but in Chapter 11, you'll learn how to have your app support both the iPhone and the iPad.

For our project, pick the View-based Application template, select iPad from the product menu, and click the Choose... button. Tell the familiar save panel where you want to save this new project, and name it Dudel.

Xcode will make a new project for you, containing *.h* and *.m* files for the DudelAppDelegate and DudelViewController classes. These contain the exact same sort of boilerplate code that you would typically find in an iPhone project. You'll also see that the project has a Resources-iPad directory, which contains the same kind of Interface Builder files you're used to seeing in iPhone projects: *MainWindow.xib* and *DudelViewController.xib*. The main difference is that these files are set up for iPad, with windows and views that are already iPad-sized.

The default *DudelViewController.xib* file contains a top-level UIView instance, but we're going to make our own view subclass, capable of drawing all the shapes a user creates in the app. In Xcode, add a new class to your project by right-clicking the folder where the new class should be added (the Classes folder is the classic choice) and choosing **Add ➤ New File** from the context menu. In the assistant that appears, choose Cocoa Touch Class from the iPhone section, use the pop-up menu to make it a subclass of UIView, and then click Next. Name the file *DudelView.m*, hit Finish, and a basic view class will be created for you.

Now, this view that does all the drawing is sure to have some complexity. Obviously, it will need to have some sort of interaction with the controller class. So let's do this the standard Cocoa way, and define a delegate outlet for connecting to the controller class. We'll also take the step of defining a protocol for this delegate. The protocol won't have any methods yet. We will add those after we figure out what sort of things we need to delegate! For now, make sure your *DudelView.h* looks like this (the lines in bold are the ones you need to add to the template-generated header file):

```
// DudelView.h
#import <UIKit/UIKit.h>

@protocol DudelViewDelegate
@end

@interface DudelView : UIView {
    IBOutlet id <DudelViewDelegate> delegate;
}
@end
```

That defines just enough for us to be able to hook it up in Interface Builder. Now we will continue to pull together the rest of the pieces for the nib-based portion of the app. Later on, we'll go back and implement the view itself.

The source code archive accompanying this book includes a set of buttons meant for use in Dudel. If you don't have the archive at hand, use your favorite graphics editor (I'm partial to GIMP) to create buttons similar to what you see in Table 4-1. They don't need to be pixel-perfect, but should be roughly similar so that your version of the app looks and feels about the same as mine. The button images shown here are 46 by 32, and you should try to stick to a similar size.

Table 4-1. *Buttons for the Main Dudel View*

Filename	Image
button_bezier.png	
button_bezier_selected.png	
button_cdots.png	
button_cdots_selected.png	
button_ellipse.png	
button_ellipse_selected.png	
button_line.png	
button_line_selected.png	
button_rectangle.png	
button_rectangle_selected.png	

NOTE: If you're making your own button images, keep in mind the way that UIToolbar renders its button images. Rather than drawing their content directly, it uses the brightness as a sort of transparency mask. White areas are completely transparent (letting the UIToolbar itself show through), black areas show up as a solid color that contrasts well against the UIToolbar's background color (e.g., black on a light-gray background or white on a dark-gray background), and all gray values are treated somewhere in between. In the graphics supplied for this example, the "normal" images for each button are mostly completely transparent, with just a border and the contained symbol, and the "selected" images have a gradient background to make them stand out clearly.

Drag all of the button image files into the Resources-iPad folder in your Xcode project. Be sure to check the Copy items into destination group's folder check box before clicking the Add button. Once those images are in place, they'll be ready to use within your application code and nib files.

Next, we need to define the interface for our controller. For now, we just want to set up enough to allow us to hook up the few components we need in the nib file.

As you saw in Figure 4–2, Dudel will contain a row of buttons that let the user select a drawing tool. These buttons are actually instances of UIBarButtonItem, which will be placed on a UIToolbar. We'll need to have an outlet for each button so that we can control its appearance, and we'll need an action for each button to trigger, all of which will be set up in Interface Builder. We'll also create an outlet to point at a DudelView instance, which will be initialized when the nib file is loaded. Last but not least, we'll declare our class to conform with the DudelViewDelegate protocol, so that Interface Builder will let us hook it up.

Open *DudelViewController.h* and add the code shown in bold.

```objc
// DudelViewController.h
#import <UIKit/UIKit.h>
#import "DudelView.h"

@interface DudelViewController : UIViewController <DudelViewDelegate> {
  IBOutlet DudelView *dudelView;
  IBOutlet UIBarButtonItem *freehandButton;
  IBOutlet UIBarButtonItem *ellipseButton;
  IBOutlet UIBarButtonItem *rectangleButton;
  IBOutlet UIBarButtonItem *lineButton;
  IBOutlet UIBarButtonItem *pencilButton;
}
- (IBAction)touchFreehandItem:(id)sender;
- (IBAction)touchEllipseItem:(id)sender;
- (IBAction)touchRectangleItem:(id)sender;
- (IBAction)touchLineItem:(id)sender;
- (IBAction)touchPencilItem:(id)sender;
@end
```

For the sake of having an app that we're able to build without errors at any time, let's go ahead and add some minimal implementations of those action methods to *DudelViewController.m*. They won't have any functionality yet, but their presence will let the compiler compile this class without complaint.

```
// DudelViewController.m
#import "DudelViewController.h"

@implementation DudelViewController

- (IBAction)touchFreehandItem:(id)sender {}
- (IBAction)touchEllipseItem:(id)sender {}
- (IBAction)touchRectangleItem:(id)sender {}
- (IBAction)touchLineItem:(id)sender {}
- (IBAction)touchPencilItem:(id)sender {}

// skipping the boilerplate code that's part of the template
// [...]

@end
```

We'll add more to this class later on, but this is all we need to create and hook up the GUI in Interface Builder.

Adding a Simple GUI

Now let's move to Interface Builder and construct a simple GUI. Double-click *DudelViewController.xib* to open it in Interface Builder.

First, let's make sure that the nib file uses our DudelView class instead of just a plain-old UIView. Select the UIView object and open the identity inspector (⌘4). At the top of the panel, click the Class combo box and change the selection from UIView to DudelView. While we're still looking at it, let's create the connections between this view and the controller. Start by control-dragging from the Dudel View icon to the File's Owner icon, which represents the DudelViewController that loads this nib. Release the mouse button, and in the context menu that appears, pick **delegate**. Now control-drag from the File's Owner icon back to DudelView, and select **dudelView** from the resulting context menu.

With that out of the way, we can focus on those all-important buttons at the bottom of the screen. Start by making sure you can see the DudelView layout window. If not, double-click the Dudel View icon in the main *.nib* window so that the layout window appears. If your screen isn't large enough to display the entire window, scroll down so that you can see the bottom. Now find UIToolbar in the Library, and drag one out to the DudelView layout window, placing it at the bottom of the window. Open the attribute inspector (⌘1) and change the toolbar's style to Black Translucent.

The toolbar you just created includes a single UIBarButtonItem, which we'll use as a starting point for all our toolbar buttons. Use the attribute inspector to set the button item's Style to Plain (since the images we're using have a border of their own), and then press ⌘D to duplicate the item. And duplicate it again and again and again. We want to have five of these items, and we want them all to be Plain, so this is quicker than dragging a button item out from the Library five times and setting the style each time.

These button items need to be assigned some imagery. Click the left-hand button and use the attribute inspector to set its Image to *button_cdots_selected.png*. This first button is going to be selected by default, so we'll start it off with the selected image. Now go through the remaining buttons and set their images to *button_line.png*, *button_rectangle.png*, *button_ellipse.png*, and *button_bezier.png*. These are the normal (unselected) versions of the images. You should now see something like Figure 4–3.

Figure 4–3. *The buttons are all in place.*

Now all that's left is to connect each of those buttons to an action method in the controller, and connect an outlet from the controller back to each button. Start with the button item on the left. Control-drag from it to the File's Owner icon, and select the touchPencilItem: action. Then control-drag from the File's Owner icon back to that button item, and select the pencilButton outlet. Go to the next button (the one with the straight line icon), control-drag from it to the File's Owner icon and select the touchLineItem: action, and then control-drag from File's Owner back to that button item and select the lineButton outlet. Do the same for the three remaining button items, so that each is set to trigger the appropriate action method in the controller, and each of the controller's outlets is connected to the correct button item.

With all this in place, you should now be able to build and run your app in the iPhone Simulator. If you get a big, blank canvas with a row of buttons at the bottom that don't do anything when you touch them, then you've achieved the goal for this portion of our project. Congratulations!

The Basic Drawing Architecture

Now it's time to talk about how Dudel is going to draw. Instead of dealing with an underlying pixel-buffer canvas on which all operations are performed, we're going to maintain a list of drawing operations, defined by the user's actions. Each object that the user draws will be added to an array, and each of the objects in the array will be drawn when necessary.

For maximum modularity, let's decide that each drawing operation should know how to draw itself. Then all our DudelView class really needs to do is hang onto an array and pass along a draw request whenever it's time to redraw. We'll try to maintain some sort of order here by defining a protocol called Drawable, which contains a single method called draw. Any object that represents a drawing operation should conform to this protocol. Also, there will be times—such as while the user is creating a drawing operation by dragging a finger around the screen—that some temporary drawing will need to be done. The view class won't be responsible for this, however. We'll pass that to our delegate object, the DudelViewController. So, we'll add a method to the DudelViewDelegate method, giving the controller a chance to do some temporary, context-based drawing.

Create a new protocol header file (one of the file types found in the Cocoa Touch Class section of the New File Assistant) in your project, name it *Drawable.h*, and give it the following content:

```
//  Drawable.h

@protocol Drawable
- (void)draw;
@end
```

Now we're ready to flesh out the DudelView class. First, add a few lines to *DudelView.h*:

```
//  DudelView.h
#import <UIKit/UIKit.h>

@protocol DudelViewDelegate
- (void)drawTemporary;
@end

@interface DudelView : UIView {
  NSMutableArray *drawables;
  IBOutlet id <DudelViewDelegate> delegate;
}
@property (retain, nonatomic) NSMutableArray *drawables;
@end
```

Then define the *DudelView.m* file as follows:

```
// DudelView.m
#import "DudelView.h"
#import "Drawable.h"

@implementation DudelView
@synthesize drawables;
- (id)initWithFrame:(CGRect)frame {
  if ((self = [super initWithFrame:frame])) {
    drawables = [[NSMutableArray alloc] initWithCapacity:100];
  }
  return self;
}
- (id)initWithCoder:(NSCoder *)aDecoder {
  if ((self = [super initWithCoder:aDecoder])) {
    drawables = [[NSMutableArray alloc] initWithCapacity:100];
  }
  return self;
}
- (void)drawRect:(CGRect)rect {
  for (<Drawable> d in drawables) {
    [d draw];
  }
  [delegate drawTemporary];
}
```

```
- (void)dealloc {
  [drawables release];
  [super dealloc];
}
@end
```

You'll notice that we define two different initialization methods. The first is normally called within code; the second is called when an object is being instantiated from a nib file. In our current implementation, only the nib file version is being used, but we may as well cover the other possibility as well.

Apart from that, this code is quite straightforward. Other objects can directly add drawable display operations to the view's array. Whenever drawRect: is called (as a result of someone, somewhere, calling setNeedsDisplay on the view), the view just calls draw everywhere else.

We Are All Tool Users

At this point, it's time to deal with an interesting aspect of our application's architecture: the representation and use of tools corresponding to the buttons we put in the GUI. We'll define a number of tool classes, each conforming to a particular protocol so that our controller can talk to them all. Our controller will keep a pointer to the active tool, based on the user's selection, and will pass all touch events along to the active tool, which will deal with the events in whatever way is appropriate for it. It will also pass along the drawTemporary message from the view, so that the tool can draw a representation of the work in progress if it's a multistage creation action. Our controller doesn't need to know any specifics about how a tool interprets events, defines drawing operations, or anything else.

In addition, DudelViewController will maintain state information about other potential user-selected values, such as the current fill color (used to fill the inside of the shape that's being drawn) and the current stroke color (used to draw the edge of the shape). That information will be available for the active tool to access when it's doing its temporary drawing and when it's creating a completed drawing operation to give to the view. For now, we're not going to provide any mechanism for setting the fill and stroke colors. We'll just give them predefined values. Later, in Chapter 6, we'll demonstrate a nice way to let the user specify these colors using the latest version of the SDK.

The final piece of functionality that DudelView will include is responding to presses of the UIBarButtonItems in the toolbar, which will result in a new tool being set as the active tool. To get started, add a few lines to *DudelViewController.h*:

```
// DudelViewController.h
#import <UIKit/UIKit.h>
#import "Tool.h"
#import "DudelView.h"

@interface DudelViewController : UIViewController <ToolDelegate, DudelViewDelegate> {
  id <Tool> currentTool;
  IBOutlet DudelView *dudelView;
```

```
    IBOutlet UIBarButtonItem *freehandButton;
    IBOutlet UIBarButtonItem *ellipseButton;
    IBOutlet UIBarButtonItem *rectangleButton;
    IBOutlet UIBarButtonItem *lineButton;
    IBOutlet UIBarButtonItem *pencilButton;
    UIColor *strokeColor;
    UIColor *fillColor;
    CGFloat strokeWidth;
}

@property (retain, nonatomic) id <Tool> currentTool;
@property (retain, nonatomic) UIColor *strokeColor;
@property (retain, nonatomic) UIColor *fillColor;
@property (assign, nonatomic) CGFloat strokeWidth;
- (IBAction)touchFreehandItem:(id)sender;
- (IBAction)touchEllipseItem:(id)sender;
- (IBAction)touchRectangleItem:(id)sender;
- (IBAction)touchLineItem:(id)sender;
- (IBAction)touchPencilItem:(id)sender;
@end
```

Next, move to *DudelViewController.m*. This is where the real changes take place. Among other things, this file contains implementations for all the action methods we defined in the header file. These are all empty for now, but will be filled in later as we cover each new tool. It also defines a few utility methods for internal use, for taking care of some repetitive tasks that we'll need to do for each of those action methods.

```
//  DudelViewController.m
#import "DudelViewController.h"

#import "DudelView.h"

@implementation DudelViewController

@synthesize currentTool, fillColor, strokeColor, strokeWidth;

- (void)deselectAllToolButtons {
    [textButton setImage:[UIImage imageNamed:@"button_text.png"]];
    [freehandButton setImage:[UIImage imageNamed:@"button_bezier.png"]];
    [ellipseButton setImage:[UIImage imageNamed:@"button_ellipse.png"]];
    [rectangleButton setImage:[UIImage imageNamed:@"button_rectangle.png"]];
    [lineButton setImage:[UIImage imageNamed:@"button_line.png"]];
    [pencilButton setImage:[UIImage imageNamed:@"button_cdots.png"]];
}
- (void)setCurrentTool:(id <Tool>)t {
    [currentTool deactivate];
    if (t != currentTool) {
        [currentTool release];
        currentTool = [t retain];
        currentTool.delegate = self;
        [self deselectAllToolButtons];
    }
    [currentTool activate];
    [dudelView setNeedsDisplay];
}
```

```objc
- (IBAction)touchFreehandItem:(id)sender {
}
- (IBAction)touchEllipseItem:(id)sender {
}
- (IBAction)touchRectangleItem:(id)sender {
}
- (IBAction)touchLineItem:(id)sender {
}
- (IBAction)touchPencilItem:(id)sender {
}

- (void)touchesBegan:(NSSet *)touches withEvent:(UIEvent *)event {
  [currentTool touchesBegan:touches withEvent:event];
  [dudelView setNeedsDisplay];
}
- (void)touchesCancelled:(NSSet *)touches withEvent:(UIEvent *)event {
  [currentTool touchesCancelled:touches withEvent:event];
  [dudelView setNeedsDisplay];
}
- (void)touchesEnded:(NSSet *)touches withEvent:(UIEvent *)event {
  [currentTool touchesEnded:touches withEvent:event];
  [dudelView setNeedsDisplay];
}
- (void)touchesMoved:(NSSet *)touches withEvent:(UIEvent *)event {
  [currentTool touchesMoved:touches withEvent:event];
  [dudelView setNeedsDisplay];
}
- (void)addDrawable:(id <Drawable>)d {
  [dudelView.drawables addObject:d];
  [dudelView setNeedsDisplay];
}
- (UIView *)viewForUseWithTool:(id <Tool>)t {
  return self.view;
}
- (void)drawTemporary {
  [self.currentTool drawTemporary];
}
- (void)viewDidLoad {
  [super viewDidLoad];
  self.fillColor = [UIColor lightGrayColor];
  self.strokeColor = [UIColor blackColor];
  self.strokeWidth = 2.0;
}
// Override to allow orientations other than the default portrait orientation.
- (BOOL)shouldAutorotateToInterfaceOrientation:(UIInterfaceOrientation)orientation {
    return YES;
}
- (void)dealloc {
  self.currentTool = nil;
  self.fillColor = nil;
  self.strokeColor = nil;
  [super dealloc];
}
@end
```

That code also refers to a file called *Tool.h*, and the Tool protocol it defines. That's the protocol with which the controller communicates with the selected tool. Create a new protocol header file in your project, name it *Tool.h*, and fill it with this:

```
// Tool.h
#import <UIKit/UIKit.h>

@protocol ToolDelegate;
@protocol Drawable;

@protocol Tool <NSObject>

@property (assign, nonatomic) id <ToolDelegate> delegate;
- (void)activate;
- (void)deactivate;

- (void)touchesBegan:(NSSet *)touches withEvent:(UIEvent *)event;
- (void)touchesCancelled:(NSSet *)touches withEvent:(UIEvent *)event;
- (void)touchesEnded:(NSSet *)touches withEvent:(UIEvent *)event;
- (void)touchesMoved:(NSSet *)touches withEvent:(UIEvent *)event;

- (void)drawTemporary;
@end

@protocol ToolDelegate

- (void)addDrawable:(id <Drawable>)d;
- (UIView *)viewForUseWithTool:(id <Tool>)t;
- (UIColor *)strokeColor;
- (UIColor *)fillColor;

@end
```

This also defines the ToolDelegate protocol, with which each tool can communicate back to the controller.

At this point, you should be able to build and run your app. You'll still wind up with a blank slate that doesn't do anything, but doing so will at least verify that you're on track.

Next, let's tackle the tools.

The Pencil Tool

The Pencil tool is the simplest one we're going to create. It will place a small dot wherever you tap the screen, or a continuous squiggly line if you continue to drag your finger around.

Make a new NSObject subclass named PencilTool and give it the following content:

```
// PencilTool.h
#import <Foundation/Foundation.h>
#import "Tool.h"
@interface PencilTool : NSObject <Tool> {
  id <ToolDelegate> delegate;
```

```objc
  NSMutableArray *trackingTouches;
  NSMutableArray *startPoints;
  NSMutableArray *paths;
 }
+ (PencilTool *)sharedPencilTool;
@end

//  PencilTool.m
#import "PencilTool.h"
#import "PathDrawingInfo.h"
#import "SynthesizeSingleton.h"
@implementation PencilTool
@synthesize delegate;
SYNTHESIZE_SINGLETON_FOR_CLASS(PencilTool);
- init {
  if ((self = [super init])) {
    trackingTouches = [[NSMutableArray array] retain];
    startPoints = [[NSMutableArray array] retain];
    paths = [[NSMutableArray array] retain];
  }
  return self;
}
- (void)activate {
}
- (void)deactivate {
  [trackingTouches removeAllObjects];
  [startPoints removeAllObjects];
  [paths removeAllObjects];
}
- (void)touchesBegan:(NSSet *)touches withEvent:(UIEvent *)event {
  UIView *touchedView = [delegate viewForUseWithTool:self];
  for (UITouch *touch in [event allTouches]) {
    // remember the touch, and its original start point, for future
    [trackingTouches addObject:touch];
    CGPoint location = [touch locationInView:touchedView];
    [startPoints addObject:[NSValue valueWithCGPoint:location]];
    UIBezierPath *path = [UIBezierPath bezierPath];
    path.lineCapStyle = kCGLineCapRound;
    [path moveToPoint:location];
    [path setLineWidth:delegate.strokeWidth];
    [path addLineToPoint:location];
    [paths addObject:path];
  }
}
- (void)touchesCancelled:(NSSet *)touches withEvent:(UIEvent *)event {
  [self deactivate];
}
- (void)touchesEnded:(NSSet *)touches withEvent:(UIEvent *)event {
  for (UITouch *touch in [event allTouches]) {
    // make a line from the start point to the current point
    NSUInteger touchIndex = [trackingTouches indexOfObject:touch];
    // only if we actually remember the start of this touch...
    if (touchIndex != NSNotFound) {
      UIBezierPath *path = [paths objectAtIndex:touchIndex];
      PathDrawingInfo *info = [PathDrawingInfo pathDrawingInfoWithPath:path
        fillColor:[UIColor clearColor] strokeColor:delegate.strokeColor];
      [delegate addDrawable:info];
```

```
        [trackingTouches removeObjectAtIndex:touchIndex];
        [startPoints removeObjectAtIndex:touchIndex];
        [paths removeObjectAtIndex:touchIndex];
      }
    }
  }
- (void)touchesMoved:(NSSet *)touches withEvent:(UIEvent *)event {
    UIView *touchedView = [delegate viewForUseWithTool:self];
    for (UITouch *touch in [event allTouches]) {
      // make a line from the start point to the current point
      NSUInteger touchIndex = [trackingTouches indexOfObject:touch];
      // only if we actually remember the start of this touch...
      if (touchIndex != NSNotFound) {
        CGPoint location = [touch locationInView:touchedView];
        UIBezierPath *path = [paths objectAtIndex:touchIndex];
        [path addLineToPoint:location];
      }
    }
  }
- (void)drawTemporary {
    for (UIBezierPath *path in paths) {
      [delegate.strokeColor setStroke];
      [path stroke];
    }
  }
- (void)dealloc {
    [trackingTouches release];
    [startPoints release];
    [paths release];
    self.delegate = nil;
    [super dealloc];
  }
@end
```

The interesting parts of this code are all contained in the various "touches" methods, which look at all the current touches (yes, this will work with multitouch just fine). In each case, these methods create or modify a Bézier path, or prepare a completed path, using the fill color from the delegate to create a new instance of a Drawable object called PathDrawingInfo, and pass that to the controller as a complete drawing operation, ready to be added to the DudelView's stack of Drawable objects.

PathDrawingInfo is a simple class that conforms to the Drawable protocol we defined earlier. It encapsulates a UIBezierPath and two UIColor values for the stroke and fill. Add a new class called PathDrawingInfo to your project, and give it the following content:

```
// PathDrawingInfo.h
#import <Foundation/Foundation.h>
#import "Drawable.h"
@interface PathDrawingInfo : NSObject <Drawable> {
  UIBezierPath *path;
  UIColor *fillColor;
  UIColor *strokeColor;
}
@property (retain, nonatomic) UIBezierPath *path;
@property (retain, nonatomic) UIColor *fillColor;
```

```
@property (retain, nonatomic) UIColor *strokeColor;
- (id)initWithPath:(UIBezierPath *)p fillColor:(UIColor *)f strokeColor:(UIColor *)s;
+ (id)pathDrawingInfoWithPath:(UIBezierPath *)p fillColor:(UIColor *)f
strokeColor:(UIColor *)s;
@end

//  PathDrawingInfo.m
#import "PathDrawingInfo.h"
@implementation PathDrawingInfo
@synthesize path, fillColor, strokeColor;
- (id)initWithPath:(UIBezierPath *)p fillColor:(UIColor *)f strokeColor:(UIColor *)s {
  if ((self = [self init])) {
    path = [p retain];
    fillColor = [f retain];
    strokeColor = [s retain];
  }
  return self;
}
+ (id)pathDrawingInfoWithPath:(UIBezierPath *)p fillColor:(UIColor *)f
strokeColor:(UIColor *)s {
  return [[[self alloc] initWithPath:p fillColor:f strokeColor:s] autorelease];
}
- (void)dealloc {
  self.path = nil;
  self.fillColor = nil;
  self.strokeColor = nil;
  [super dealloc];
}
- (void)draw {
  CGContextRef context = UIGraphicsGetCurrentContext();
  CGContextSaveGState(context);
  if (self.fillColor) {
    [self.fillColor setFill];
    [self.path fill];
  }
  if (self.strokeColor) {
    [self.strokeColor setStroke];
    [self.path stroke];
  }
  CGContextRestoreGState(context);
}
@end
```

The PencilTool class, and all the rest of the Tool classes, also makes use of the SYNTHESIZE_SINGLETON_FOR_CLASS macro. This chunk of code, which comes from Matt Gallagher's Cocoa with Love blog, provides a standardized way to make any class into a singleton. This is perfect for Dudel's tools, since we never need more than one of each kind. This macro overrides all of the methods that deal with memory management, making sure that only one instance of this class is ever created. To use it, add a new header file called *SynthesizeSingleton.h* to your project, with the following content:

```
//
//  SynthesizeSingleton.h
//  CocoaWithLove
//
//  Created by Matt Gallagher on 20/10/08.
```

```
#define SYNTHESIZE_SINGLETON_FOR_CLASS(classname) \
 \
static classname *shared##classname = nil; \
 \
+ (classname *)shared##classname \
{ \
        @synchronized(self) \
        { \
                if (shared##classname == nil) \
                { \
                        shared##classname = [[self alloc] init]; \
                } \
        } \
         \
        return shared##classname; \
} \
 \
+ (id)allocWithZone:(NSZone *)zone \
{ \
        @synchronized(self) \
        { \
                if (shared##classname == nil) \
                { \
                        shared##classname = [super allocWithZone:zone]; \
                        return shared##classname; \
                } \
        } \
         \
        return nil; \
} \
 \
- (id)copyWithZone:(NSZone *)zone \
{ \
        return self; \
} \
 \
- (id)retain \
{ \
        return self; \
} \
 \
- (NSUInteger)retainCount \
{ \
        return NSUIntegerMax; \
} \
 \
- (void)release \
{ \
```

```
} \
 \
- (id)autorelease \
{ \
        return self; \
}
```

> **NOTE:** This sort of macro definition is inherently sort of tricky to type in on your own, since the backslash character on each line must come right at the end of the line, without any trailing spaces. Your best bet is to copy this file from the book's source code archive.

You're now very close to being able to try things out! At this point, all that's left to enable the Pencil tool is the addition of a few lines in *DudelViewController.m*. Start by importing the header:

```
#import "PencilTool.h"
```

Then populate the touchPencilItem: method as follows:

```
- (IBAction)touchPencilItem:(id)sender {
  self.currentTool = [PencilTool sharedPencilTool];
  [pencilButton setImage:[UIImage imageNamed:@"button_cdots_selected.png"]];
}
```

Finally, to arrange that this tool is selected by default when the app starts, add a line to the viewDidLoad method:

```
- (void)viewDidLoad {
  [super viewDidLoad];
  self.currentTool = [PencilTool sharedPencilTool];
  self.fillColor = [UIColor lightGrayColor];
  self.strokeColor = [UIColor blackColor];
  self.strokeWidth = 2.0;
}
```

You should now be able to build and run your app. Try tapping and dragging all over the screen with the Pencil tool, making dots and squiggles. Figure 4–4 shows an example of a drawing made with our new tool.

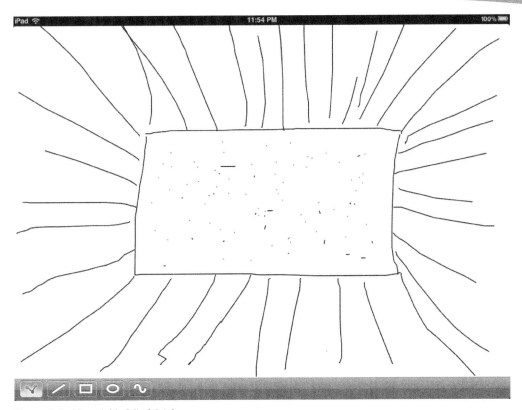

Figure 4–4. *My god, it's full of dots!*

The Line Tool

The Line tool works by letting you touch the screen in one spot and drag to another, creating a line between the two spots when you let go. While you're dragging, a temporary line is drawn between the two points.

Make a new NSObject subclass named LineTool in your Xcode project. Both the header and implementation files are shown here:

```
// LineTool.h
#import <Foundation/Foundation.h>
#import "Tool.h"
@interface LineTool : NSObject <Tool> {
  id <ToolDelegate> delegate;
  NSMutableArray *trackingTouches;
  NSMutableArray *startPoints;
}
+ (LineTool *)sharedLineTool;
@end

// LineTool.m
#import "LineTool.h"
```

```objc
#import "PathDrawingInfo.h"
#import "SynthesizeSingleton.h"

@implementation LineTool
@synthesize delegate;
SYNTHESIZE_SINGLETON_FOR_CLASS(LineTool);
- init {
  if ((self = [super init])) {
    trackingTouches = [[NSMutableArray array] retain];
    startPoints = [[NSMutableArray array] retain];
  }
  return self;
}
- (void)activate {
}
- (void)deactivate {
  [trackingTouches removeAllObjects];
  [startPoints removeAllObjects];
}
- (void)touchesBegan:(NSSet *)touches withEvent:(UIEvent *)event {
  UIView *touchedView = [delegate viewForUseWithTool:self];
  for (UITouch *touch in [event allTouches]) {
    // remember the touch, and its original start point, for future
    [trackingTouches addObject:touch];
    CGPoint location = [touch locationInView:touchedView];
    [startPoints addObject:[NSValue valueWithCGPoint:location]];
  }
}
- (void)touchesCancelled:(NSSet *)touches withEvent:(UIEvent *)event {}
- (void)touchesEnded:(NSSet *)touches withEvent:(UIEvent *)event {
  UIView *touchedView = [delegate viewForUseWithTool:self];
  for (UITouch *touch in [event allTouches]) {
    // make a line from the start point to the current point
    NSUInteger touchIndex = [trackingTouches indexOfObject:touch];
    // only if we actually remember the start of this touch...
    if (touchIndex != NSNotFound) {
      CGPoint startPoint = [[startPoints objectAtIndex:touchIndex] CGPointValue];
      CGPoint endPoint = [touch locationInView:touchedView];
      UIBezierPath *path = [UIBezierPath bezierPath];
      [path moveToPoint:startPoint];
      [path addLineToPoint:endPoint];
      PathDrawingInfo *info = [PathDrawingInfo pathDrawingInfoWithPath:path
fillColor:delegate.fillColor strokeColor:delegate.strokeColor];
      [delegate addDrawable:info];
      [trackingTouches removeObjectAtIndex:touchIndex];
      [startPoints removeObjectAtIndex:touchIndex];
    }
  }
}
- (void)touchesMoved:(NSSet *)touches withEvent:(UIEvent *)event {}
- (void)drawTemporary {
  UIView *touchedView = [delegate viewForUseWithTool:self];
  for (int i = 0; i<[trackingTouches count]; i++) {
    UITouch *touch = [trackingTouches objectAtIndex:i];
    CGPoint startPoint = [[startPoints objectAtIndex:i] CGPointValue];
    CGPoint endPoint = [touch locationInView:touchedView];
    UIBezierPath *path = [UIBezierPath bezierPath];
```

```
        [path moveToPoint:startPoint];
        [path addLineToPoint:endPoint];
        [delegate.strokeColor setStroke];
        [path stroke];
    }
}
- (void)dealloc {
    [trackingTouches release];
    [startPoints release];
    self.delegate = nil;
    [super dealloc];
}
@end
```

This is pretty similar to the Pencil tool. We keep track of all the current touches, as well as the start point for each of them, so that we can make a proper line path for each line segment. We use the touchesBegan:withEvent: method to save a reference to each touch we're tracking, as well as each start point. Then in touchesEnded:withEvent:, we create a new path object and send it to the delegate.

Now we need to add a bit to DudelViewController, so that it knows about this class and can work with it. Start off with another import line, somewhere near the top:

```
#import "LineTool.h"
```

Then fill in the touchLineItem: action method, like this:

```
- (IBAction)touchLineItem:(id)sender {
    self.currentTool = [LineTool sharedLineTool];
    [lineButton setImage:[UIImage imageNamed:@"button_line_selected.png"]];
}
```

Again, build and run your app, and try out our new tool. One nice feature of this implementation is that since you're tracking multiple touch points, you can touch and drag with several fingers at once, dragging out lines behind each of them. If you're running on the simulator instead of an actual iPad, you can test this a little by holding down the Option key while you're clicking, which simulates an additional click on the other side of the screen. This is mainly in place to help simulate twist and pinch gestures, but we can use it here as well. Figure 4–5 shows some lines.

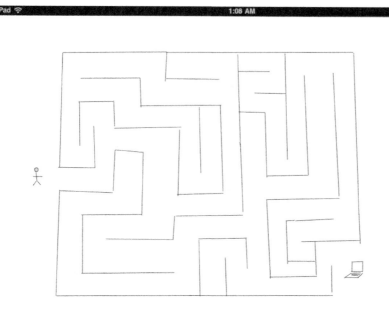

Figure 4–5. *The tyranny of straight lines is keeping this poor fellow away from his beloved MacBook Pro.*

The Ellipse and Rectangle Tools

Next up are the Ellipse and Rectangle tools. They are extremely similar to one another, and also to the Line tool. From a user standpoint, they function similarly: you touch in one corner, drag, and release to define the opposite corner. The Rectangle tool creates a rectangle, and the Ellipse tool creates (you guessed it) an ellipse.

Make a new RectangleTool class, and give it this code:

```
//  RectangleTool.h
#import <Foundation/Foundation.h>
#import "Tool.h"
@interface RectangleTool : NSObject <Tool> {
  id <ToolDelegate> delegate;
  NSMutableArray *trackingTouches;
  NSMutableArray *startPoints;
}
+ (RectangleTool *)sharedRectangleTool;
@end

//  RectangleTool.m
#import "RectangleTool.h"
```

```
#import "PathDrawingInfo.h"
#import "SynthesizeSingleton.h"
@implementation RectangleTool
@synthesize delegate;
SYNTHESIZE_SINGLETON_FOR_CLASS(RectangleTool);
- init {
  if ((self = [super init])) {
    trackingTouches = [[NSMutableArray array] retain];
    startPoints = [[NSMutableArray array] retain];
  }
  return self;
}
- (void)activate {
}
- (void)deactivate {
  [trackingTouches removeAllObjects];
  [startPoints removeAllObjects];
}
```

As you can see, like the LineTool class, this class maintains arrays of startingPoints and trackingTouches.

The "touches" methods are where the interesting work of this class is done. Like the Line tool, the Rectangle tool is capable of tracking multiple simultaneous touches, ultimately creating a new line for each of them.

```
- (void)touchesBegan:(NSSet *)touches withEvent:(UIEvent *)event {
  UIView *touchedView = [delegate viewForUseWithTool:self];
  for (UITouch *touch in [event allTouches]) {
    // remember the touch, and its original start point, for future
    [trackingTouches addObject:touch];
    CGPoint location = [touch locationInView:touchedView];
    [startPoints addObject:[NSValue valueWithCGPoint:location]];
  }
}
- (void)touchesCancelled:(NSSet *)touches withEvent:(UIEvent *)event {
}
- (void)touchesEnded:(NSSet *)touches withEvent:(UIEvent *)event {
  UIView *touchedView = [delegate viewForUseWithTool:self];
  for (UITouch *touch in [event allTouches]) {
    // make a rect from the start point to the current point
    NSUInteger touchIndex = [trackingTouches indexOfObject:touch];
    // only if we actually remember the start of this touch...
    if (touchIndex != NSNotFound) {
      CGPoint startPoint = [[startPoints objectAtIndex:touchIndex] CGPointValue];
      CGPoint endPoint = [touch locationInView:touchedView];
      CGRect rect = CGRectMake(startPoint.x, startPoint.y, endPoint.x - startPoint.x,
endPoint.y - startPoint.y);
      UIBezierPath *path = [UIBezierPath bezierPathWithRect:rect];
      PathDrawingInfo *info = [PathDrawingInfo pathDrawingInfoWithPath:path
fillColor:delegate.fillColor strokeColor:delegate.strokeColor];
      [delegate addDrawable:info];
      [trackingTouches removeObjectAtIndex:touchIndex];
      [startPoints removeObjectAtIndex:touchIndex];
    }
  }
}
```

```
- (void)touchesMoved:(NSSet *)touches withEvent:(UIEvent *)event {
}
```

The following method draws the current state of the rectangle while you are still dragging it around. Only later does the object being drawn here get added to the view's list of drawable items.

```
- (void)drawTemporary {
  UIView *touchedView = [delegate viewForUseWithTool:self];
  for (int i = 0; i<[trackingTouches count]; i++) {
    UITouch *touch = [trackingTouches objectAtIndex:i];
    CGPoint startPoint = [[startPoints objectAtIndex:i] CGPointValue];
    CGPoint endPoint = [touch locationInView:touchedView];
    CGRect rect = CGRectMake(startPoint.x, startPoint.y, endPoint.x - startPoint.x,
endPoint.y - startPoint.y);
    UIBezierPath *path = [UIBezierPath bezierPathWithRect:rect];
    [delegate.fillColor setFill];
    [path fill];
    [delegate.strokeColor setStroke];
    [path stroke];
  }
}
- (void)dealloc {
  [trackingTouches release];
  [startPoints release];
  self.delegate = nil;
  [super dealloc];
}
@end
```

Now for the Ellipse tool. Its only substantial difference from the Rectangle tool is the creation of UIBezierPaths in touchesEnded:withEvent: and drawTemporary.

```
// EllipseTool.h
#import <Foundation/Foundation.h>
#import "Tool.h"
@interface EllipseTool : NSObject <Tool> {
  id <ToolDelegate> delegate;
  NSMutableArray *trackingTouches;
  NSMutableArray *startPoints;
}
+ (EllipseTool *)sharedEllipseTool;
@end


// EllipseTool.m
#import "EllipseTool.h"
#import "PathDrawingInfo.h"
#import "SynthesizeSingleton.h"
@implementation EllipseTool
@synthesize delegate;
SYNTHESIZE_SINGLETON_FOR_CLASS(EllipseTool);
- init {
  if ((self = [super init])) {
    trackingTouches = [[NSMutableArray arrayWithCapacity:100] retain];
    startPoints = [[NSMutableArray arrayWithCapacity:100] retain];
  }
  return self;
```

```
}
- (void)activate {
}
- (void)deactivate {
  [trackingTouches removeAllObjects];
  [startPoints removeAllObjects];
}
- (void)touchesBegan:(NSSet *)touches withEvent:(UIEvent *)event {
  UIView *touchedView = [delegate viewForUseWithTool:self];
  for (UITouch *touch in [event allTouches]) {
    // remember the touch, and its original start point, for future
    [trackingTouches addObject:touch];
    CGPoint location = [touch locationInView:touchedView];
    [startPoints addObject:[NSValue valueWithCGPoint:location]];
  }
}
- (void)touchesCancelled:(NSSet *)touches withEvent:(UIEvent *)event {
}
- (void)touchesEnded:(NSSet *)touches withEvent:(UIEvent *)event {
  UIView *touchedView = [delegate viewForUseWithTool:self];
  for (UITouch *touch in [event allTouches]) {
    // make an ellipse/oval from the start point to the current point
    NSUInteger touchIndex = [trackingTouches indexOfObject:touch];
    // only if we actually remember the start of this touch...
    if (touchIndex != NSNotFound) {
      CGPoint startPoint = [[startPoints objectAtIndex:touchIndex] CGPointValue];
      CGPoint endPoint = [touch locationInView:touchedView];
      CGRect rect = CGRectMake(startPoint.x, startPoint.y, endPoint.x - startPoint.x,
endPoint.y - startPoint.y);
      UIBezierPath *path = [UIBezierPath bezierPathWithOvalInRect:rect];
      PathDrawingInfo *info = [PathDrawingInfo pathDrawingInfoWithPath:path
fillColor:delegate.fillColor strokeColor:delegate.strokeColor];
      [delegate addDrawable:info];
      [trackingTouches removeObjectAtIndex:touchIndex];
      [startPoints removeObjectAtIndex:touchIndex];
    }
  }
}
- (void)touchesMoved:(NSSet *)touches withEvent:(UIEvent *)event {
}
- (void)drawTemporary {
  UIView *touchedView = [delegate viewForUseWithTool:self];
  for (int i = 0; i<[trackingTouches count]; i++) {
    UITouch *touch = [trackingTouches objectAtIndex:i];
    CGPoint startPoint = [[startPoints objectAtIndex:i] CGPointValue];
    CGPoint endPoint = [touch locationInView:touchedView];
    CGRect rect = CGRectMake(startPoint.x, startPoint.y, endPoint.x - startPoint.x,
endPoint.y - startPoint.y);
    UIBezierPath *path = [UIBezierPath bezierPathWithOvalInRect:rect];
    [delegate.fillColor setFill];
    [path fill];
    [delegate.strokeColor setStroke];
    [path stroke];
  }
}
- (void)dealloc {
  [trackingTouches release];
```

```
    [startPoints release];
    self.delegate = nil;
    [super dealloc];
}
@end
```

Here are the necessary changes to *DudelViewController.m*:

```
#import "RectangleTool.h"
#import "EllipseTool.h"

- (IBAction)touchEllipseItem:(id)sender {
    self.currentTool = [EllipseTool sharedEllipseTool];
    [ellipseButton setImage:[UIImage imageNamed:@"button_ellipse_selected.png"]];
}
- (IBAction)touchRectangleItem:(id)sender {
    self.currentTool = [RectangleTool sharedRectangleTool];
    [rectangleButton setImage:[UIImage imageNamed:@"button_rectangle_selected.png"]];
}
```

With those in place, the next two buttons at the bottom of the GUI should now be working. Figure 4–6 shows some of the kinds of shapes that can be created with these tools. As with the previous tools, these also work with multitouch, so you should be able to drag multiple fingers at once to create several rectangles or ellipses simultaneously.

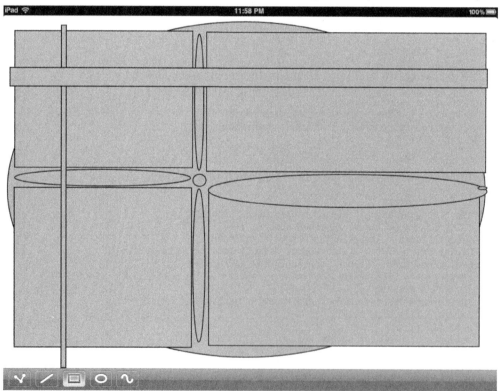

Figure 4–6. *Overlapping blocks and curves*

The Freehand Tool

Our final tool, the Freehand tool, lets you create a Bézier path. With this tool, you can draw a big string of curved sections by tapping and dragging. Each touch defines a new point on the curve, and dragging immediately after the touch lets you define control points that determine the curvature around that point. While you're dragging a control point around, it's shown with a dashed red line connecting it to the last point you touched, just to make it stand out a little more. To finish off a path, touch the Freehand button in the toolbar (or any other tool button, for that matter). This Freehand tool corresponds to what most people think of as Bézier curves (if they're thinking of Bézier curves at all).

Due to the additional complexity of the interaction with the Freehand tool, we're not going to consider the use of multitouch here. The Freehand tool relies on making a series of points by touching and releasing multiple times, and if we were to track multiple touches, it would be impossible to guess which subsequent touch belonged with which previous touch. Instead, we have a different set of instance variables that are used to hold the state of the current in-progress curve segment, if there is one. As each curve segment is created, it's added to a workingPath object, which is finally sent to the delegate when it's done.

Create a new class called FreehandTool, with the following code:

```
// FreehandTool.h
#import <Foundation/Foundation.h>
#import "Tool.h"
@interface FreehandTool : NSObject <Tool> {
  id <ToolDelegate> delegate;
  UIBezierPath *workingPath;
  CGPoint nextSegmentPoint1;
  CGPoint nextSegmentPoint2;
  CGPoint nextSegmentCp1;
  CGPoint nextSegmentCp2;
  BOOL isDragging;
  BOOL settingFirstPoint;
}
@property (retain, nonatomic) UIBezierPath *workingPath;
+ (FreehandTool *)sharedFreehandTool;
@end

// FreehandTool.m
#import "FreehandTool.h"
#import "PathDrawingInfo.h"
#import "SynthesizeSingleton.h"
@implementation FreehandTool
@synthesize delegate, workingPath;
SYNTHESIZE_SINGLETON_FOR_CLASS(FreehandTool);
- init {
  if ((self = [super init])) {
  }
  return self;
}
- (void)activate {
  self.workingPath = [UIBezierPath bezierPath];
```

```
    settingFirstPoint = YES;
}
- (void)deactivate {
  // this is where we finally tell about our path
  PathDrawingInfo *info = [PathDrawingInfo pathDrawingInfoWithPath:self.workingPath
fillColor:delegate.fillColor strokeColor:delegate.strokeColor];
  [delegate addDrawable:info];
}
- (void)touchesBegan:(NSSet *)touches withEvent:(UIEvent *)event {
  isDragging = YES;
  UIView *touchedView = [delegate viewForUseWithTool:self];
  UITouch *touch = [[event allTouches] anyObject];
  CGPoint touchPoint = [touch locationInView:touchedView];
  // set nextSegmentPoint2
  nextSegmentPoint2 = touchPoint;
  // establish nextSegmentCp2
  nextSegmentCp2 = touchPoint;
  if (workingPath.empty) {
    // this is the first touch in a path, so set the "1" variables as well
    nextSegmentCp1 = touchPoint;
    nextSegmentPoint1 = touchPoint;
    [workingPath moveToPoint:touchPoint];
  }
}
- (void)touchesCancelled:(NSSet *)touches withEvent:(UIEvent *)event {
  isDragging = NO;
}

- (void)touchesEnded:(NSSet *)touches withEvent:(UIEvent *)event {
  isDragging = NO;
  UIView *touchedView = [delegate viewForUseWithTool:self];
  UITouch *touch = [[event allTouches] anyObject];
  CGPoint touchPoint = [touch locationInView:touchedView];
  nextSegmentCp2 = touchPoint;
  // complete segment and add to list
  if (settingFirstPoint) {
    // the first touch'n'drag doesn't complete a segment, we just
    // note the change of state and move along
    settingFirstPoint = NO;
  } else {
    // nextSegmentCp2, which we've been dragging around, is translated
    // around nextSegmentPoint2 for creation of this segment.
    CGPoint shiftedNextSegmentCp2 = CGPointMake(
      nextSegmentPoint2.x + (nextSegmentPoint2.x - nextSegmentCp2.x),
      nextSegmentPoint2.y + (nextSegmentPoint2.y - nextSegmentCp2.y));
    [workingPath addCurveToPoint:nextSegmentPoint2 controlPoint1:nextSegmentCp1
controlPoint2:shiftedNextSegmentCp2];
    // the "2" values are now copied to the "1" variables
    nextSegmentPoint1 = nextSegmentPoint2;
    nextSegmentCp1 = nextSegmentCp2;
  }
}
- (void)touchesMoved:(NSSet *)touches withEvent:(UIEvent *)event {
  UIView *touchedView = [delegate viewForUseWithTool:self];
  UITouch *touch = [[event allTouches] anyObject];
  CGPoint touchPoint = [touch locationInView:touchedView];
  if (settingFirstPoint) {
```

```
      nextSegmentCp1 = touchPoint;
    } else {
      // adjust nextSegmentCp2
      nextSegmentCp2 = touchPoint;
    }
  }
}
- (void)drawTemporary {
  // draw all the segments we've finished so far
  [workingPath stroke];
  if (isDragging) {
    // draw the current segment that's being created
    if (settingFirstPoint) {
      // just draw a line
      UIBezierPath *currentWorkingSegment = [UIBezierPath bezierPath];
      [currentWorkingSegment moveToPoint:nextSegmentPoint1];
      [currentWorkingSegment addLineToPoint:nextSegmentCp1];
      [[delegate strokeColor] setStroke];
      [currentWorkingSegment stroke];
    } else {
      // nextSegmentCp2, which we've
      // been dragging around, is translated around nextSegmentPoint2
      // for creation of this segment
      CGPoint shiftedNextSegmentCp2 = CGPointMake(
        nextSegmentPoint2.x + (nextSegmentPoint2.x - nextSegmentCp2.x),
        nextSegmentPoint2.y + (nextSegmentPoint2.y - nextSegmentCp2.y));
      UIBezierPath *currentWorkingSegment = [UIBezierPath bezierPath];
      [currentWorkingSegment moveToPoint:nextSegmentPoint1];
      [currentWorkingSegment addCurveToPoint:nextSegmentPoint2
controlPoint1:nextSegmentCp1 controlPoint2:shiftedNextSegmentCp2];
      [[delegate strokeColor] setStroke];
      [currentWorkingSegment stroke];
    }
  }
  if (!CGPointEqualToPoint(nextSegmentCp2, nextSegmentPoint2) && !settingFirstPoint) {
    // draw the guideline to the next segment
    UIBezierPath *currentWorkingSegment = [UIBezierPath bezierPath];
    [currentWorkingSegment moveToPoint:nextSegmentCp2];
    CGPoint shiftedNextSegmentCp2 = CGPointMake(
      nextSegmentPoint2.x + (nextSegmentPoint2.x - nextSegmentCp2.x),
      nextSegmentPoint2.y + (nextSegmentPoint2.y - nextSegmentCp2.y));
    [currentWorkingSegment addLineToPoint:shiftedNextSegmentCp2];
```

To display the temporary curve that the user is dragging around, we will use a dashed line instead of a solid line, to help make it stand out from the background. This dash pattern specifies that the line will be drawn with 10 pixels in the stroke color we set, then skip 7 pixels, repeating forever.

```
    float dashPattern[] = {10.0, 7.0};
    [currentWorkingSegment setLineDash:dashPattern count:2 phase:0.0];
    [[UIColor redColor] setStroke];
    [currentWorkingSegment stroke];
  }
}
- (void)dealloc {
  self.workingPath = nil;
  self.delegate = nil;
  [super dealloc];
```

```
}
@end
```

Now add a few lines to *DudelViewController.m* to bring it together:

```
#import "FreehandTool.h"
- (IBAction)touchFreehandItem:(id)sender {
  self.currentTool = [FreehandTool sharedFreehandTool];
  [freehandButton setImage:[UIImage imageNamed:@"button_bezier_selected.png"]];
}
```

That's it! The final drawing tool button in our toolbar is complete. Try it out and see how it works. Figure 4–7 shows a bit of "art" created with our Dudel tools.

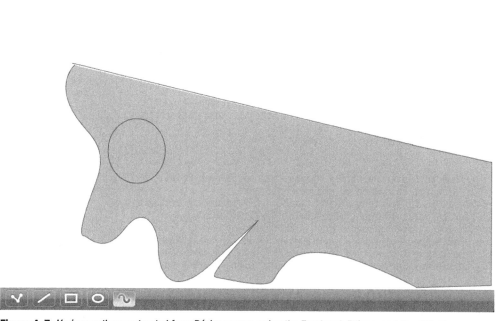

Figure 4–7. *Various paths constructed from Bézier curves, using the Freehand, Ellipse, and Pencil tools*

PDF Generation

The iOS new functionality for rendering to a PDF file means that anything you can draw to the screen using UIView can now be drawn straight into a PDF file. Here, you'll learn how to do so by "wrapping" your drawing code in a special PDF-generation context.

Generating a PDF is great, but you may ask, "What am I going to do with that PDF file?" In Chapter 10, you'll learn about some of the new things you can do with files in iOS 3.2 and beyond. For now, we'll stick to technology that has been a part of iOS ever since *way* back in version 3.0—sending an e-mail message with an attachment using MFMailComposeViewController.

We'll add this new functionality to our Dudel app. First, in the header file for our controller class, we'll need a new action method, to be triggered from the GUI. We're also going to declare that our controller conforms to the MFMailComposeViewControllerDelegate protocol, so that we'll be notified when the user has composed and sent the e-mail message or hit Cancel to discard it. We need to include the relevant header for accessing the mail composition GUI. Here's the updated version of *DudelViewController.h*, containing those changes:

```
// DudelViewController.h
#import <UIKit/UIKit.h>
#import <MessageUI/MessageUI.h>
#import "Tool.h"
#import "DudelView.h"
@interface DudelViewController : UIViewController <ToolDelegate, DudelViewDelegate,
MFMailComposeViewControllerDelegate> {
    id <Tool> currentTool;
    IBOutlet DudelView *dudelView;
    IBOutlet UIBarButtonItem *freehandButton;
    IBOutlet UIBarButtonItem *ellipseButton;
    IBOutlet UIBarButtonItem *rectangleButton;
    IBOutlet UIBarButtonItem *lineButton;
    IBOutlet UIBarButtonItem *pencilButton;
    UIColor *strokeColor;
    UIColor *fillColor;
}
@property (retain, nonatomic) id <Tool> currentTool;
@property (retain, nonatomic) UIColor *strokeColor;
@property (retain, nonatomic) UIColor *fillColor;
- (IBAction)touchFreehandItem:(id)sender;
- (IBAction)touchEllipseItem:(id)sender;
- (IBAction)touchRectangleItem:(id)sender;
- (IBAction)touchLineItem:(id)sender;
- (IBAction)touchPencilItem:(id)sender;
- (IBAction)touchSendPdfEmailItem:(id)sender;
@end
```

Now go back to project navigation pane in Xcode, and look for the Frameworks section. Right-click it and select **Add ➤ Existing Frameworks…** from the context menu, then double-click MessageUI.framework so that Dudel can make use of it.

Next, let's take care of what we need to hook up in Interface Builder. Open *DudelViewController.xib*, and take a look at the toolbar at the bottom of the window. We want to put a new item in the toolbar that will call our new method, but it should be separated from the drawing tools, so we need some space there as well.

Use the Library to search for "bar button item," and you'll see all the sorts of things that you can put into your toolbars. For this example, drag a Flexible Space Bar Button Item out and place it in our toolbar, to the right of everything else. You'll see it expand to fill all of the available space in the toolbar. Then drag a Bar Button Item from the Library to the far-right end of the toolbar. While it's still selected, use the attribute inspector to make sure its Style is set to Bordered, and set its Title to **Email PDF**. Then control-drag from the new item to File's Owner in the main .nib window, and select touchSendPdfEmailItem: from the context menu that appears. We're finished with Interface Builder for now, so save your work and go back to Xcode.

It's time to implement the code that will initiate the PDF rendering. Add the following method:

```
- (IBAction)touchSendPdfEmailItem:(id)sender {
  // set up PDF rendering context
  NSMutableData *pdfData = [NSMutableData data];
  UIGraphicsBeginPDFContextToData(pdfData, dudelView.bounds, nil);
  UIGraphicsBeginPDFPage();

  // tell our view to draw
  [dudelView drawRect:dudelView.bounds];

  // remove PDF rendering context
  UIGraphicsEndPDFContext();

  // send PDF data in mail message
  MFMailComposeViewController *mailComposer = [[[MFMailComposeViewController alloc]
init] autorelease];
  mailComposer.mailComposeDelegate = self;
  [mailComposer addAttachmentData:pdfData mimeType:@"application/pdf" fileName:@"Dudel
creation.pdf"];
  [self presentModalViewController:mailComposer animated:YES];
}
```

All we do here is set up a special context using an NSMutableData object to contain the PDF content, and call our view object's drawRect: method. When we're finished, we pass the PDF data off to the message-composing window.

We also need to implement the following method, so that the e-mail composer can let us know that the user has clicked either Send or Cancel in the window. It's our duty to end the modal session here.

```
- (void)mailComposeController:(MFMailComposeViewController*)controller
didFinishWithResult:(MFMailComposeResult)result error:(NSError*)error {
  [self dismissModalViewControllerAnimated:YES];
}
```

Now you're all set! Build and run, create something with the tools, and then hit the Email PDF button. You'll see that the content of your view is a visible attachment in a new e-mail window, ready for you to send to your admirers!

Things to See and Do

We've covered a lot of ground in this chapter! You've seen several uses of the NSBezierPath class, learned how to "print" the content of a UIView, and laid the foundation for a fun and functional graphics app. We'll continue building on this foundation throughout the book. Next, in Chapter 5, you'll learn about rendering text on the screen using Core Text.

Chapter 5

Using Core Text

This chapter introduces Core Text, a new API available in iOS 3.2. If you're familiar with programming on Mac OS X, you may realize that Core Text isn't really a new API. It has been part of Mac OS X for years, and has now made the transition to iOS.

Here, you'll learn what Core Text is, how it's structured, and how to use it to render text in your applications, by adding a new Text tool to Dudel. After that's in place, you'll see how to use NSAttributedString to style your text, letting you change fonts and colors for portions of your string, which Core Text will render with equal ease. In this chapter, we'll keep the text rendering pretty simple, but in Chapter 6, we'll get a little fancier, adding GUI elements for selecting fonts (among other things).

Why Core Text?

Earlier versions of iOS provided a few ways to render text in your own custom views: make a UILabel of your view, or tell an NSString to draw its contents in a view. But these approaches are somewhat limited. There's no way to specify font, color, or other attributes of a substring to be rendered, for instance. So, if you wanted to render some bold text within a paragraph, you would need to first render everything that came before the bold text, determine the CGPoint where the rendering ended, render the bold portion, calculate its end point, start rendering the next piece, and so on. And, of course, at each step, you would need to check to see if you're wrapping to the next line; if so, you would need to start over from there with the rest of the string.

In short, dealing with long strings, or strings with varied styles throughout, has really been kind of a pain in iOS. The level of complexity in laying out rich text is almost on par with laying out a web page, which is the solution that many iPhone applications are built around when displaying styled text, using a UIWebView to do the layout. But there are problems with that approach as well. UIWebView is a fairly "heavy" class, which can take a while to load and display content—even content that's stored locally on the device.

With Core Text, you now have a chance to skip the web view, and just draw text directly into any graphics context you like. Figure 5–1 shows an example of some text rendered in Dudel using Core Text.

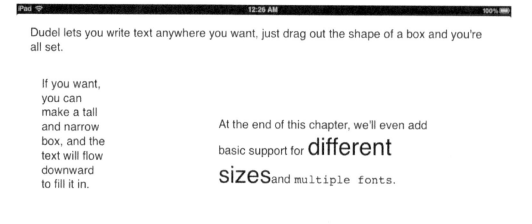

Figure 5–1. *Dudel now includes basic text rendering.*

Note that Core Text is a fairly low-level way to deal with a piece of text. iOS still doesn't offer anything that is as versatile as the NSTextView class in Mac OS X, which will also let you edit rich text, setting fonts and colors as you like. The presence of Core Text is, however, a good step in the right direction. And it's quite possible that Apple or a third party will soon leverage it to provide a general-purpose GUI class for editing rich text.

The Structure of Core Text

Before we start making use of Core Text in our code, an overview of how it works is in order. Unlike most of the new APIs discussed in the book, Core Text is a C-based API, rather than a set of Objective-C classes. For its "home environment" of Mac OS X, it was designed to be a unified API that could be used easily from both Cocoa applications written in Objective-C and Carbon applications written mainly in C and C++. However, like most other modern C-based APIs present in Mac OS X and iOS, Core Text is written in a way that is as close to object-orientation with C as possible, using opaque types for all its structures and accessing those structures only through a comprehensive set of functions. So it's fairly painless.

Core Text allows you work with it on a variety of levels. The simplest way lets you take a text string and a rectangle, and with a few lines of code, have the text rendered for you. If you want more fine-grained control, it's possible to reach in and tweak the rendering a bit as well, but most of the time, the high-level functionality is all you'll need. You'll access this through an opaque type called CTFramesetter and its associated functions. You create a CTFramesetter by passing a special kind of string called an *attributed string* to the CTFramesetterCreateWithAttributedString() function, then create another Core Text object called a CTFrame by passing the CTFramesetter and a CGPath (containing just a rectangle) to the CTFramesetterCreateFrame() function, and finally render the result with a call to the CTFrameDraw() function. Figure 5–2 shows how these different pieces fit together.

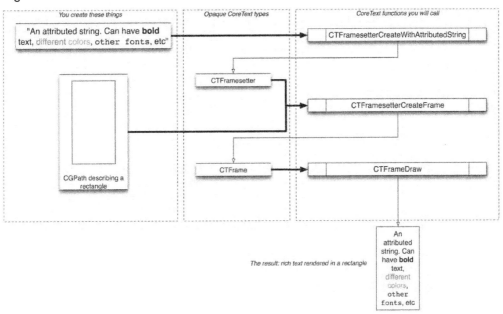

Figure 5–2. *The basic Core Text workflow*

An attributed string consists of a string and some metadata describing formatting attributes for portions of the string. For instance, you might want to render text where some words are underlined, bold, or in a different font or color. Attributed strings give you a concrete way to represent this sort of thing. In iOS, attributed strings are represented by the Objective-C class NSAttributedString and the C type CFAttributedStringRef. These are toll-free bridged to one another, so you can use them interchangeably.

TOLL-FREE BRIDGING FROM ONE FOUNDATION TO ANOTHER

In both iOS and Mac OS X, there are some kinds of entities that are said to be *toll-free bridged* to one another. This typically refers to an Objective-C class and an opaque C type. In a nutshell, this means that the types are equivalent, and that any function or method that accepts one of them will work just as well with the other (though you may need to do some manual casting to satisfy the compiler). Many of the types that are used in the Core Foundation C library, such as `CFString`, `CFArray`, and so on, are toll-free bridged to a similarly named counterpart in Objective-C's Foundation framework.

The Core Foundation types are all opaque types, which means that each of them is really a pointer to a structure whose contents you, as a user of the API, shouldn't be concerned with. As a way of highlighting the fact that you're dealing with references rather than with the structures themselves, the opaque types defined in Core Foundation have the suffix `Ref` on the end of each type name. The following lines illustrate the concept of passing bridged types around.

```
NSString *objcString;  // assume this exists.
CFStringRef cfString;  // this too.

functionThatWantsCFString(cfString);                 // this is fine,
functionThatWantsCFString((CFStringRef)objcString); // and so is this!

[objcString length];           // this returns an integer,
[(NSString *)cfString length]; // and so does this!
```

The opaque types created by Core Foundation abide by the same memory management rules as Objective-C objects do: You're required to release anything that you create or retain. However, whenever you create these objects from C functions instead of Objective-C methods, you should always manage them using functions like `CFRetain()` and `CFRelease()`, instead of the `retain` and `release` methods. This is partly to be stylistically consistent, but also because some of them may not actually be Objective-C objects at all.

As an example, let's look at some code that creates an `NSAttributedString` from an `NSString`, and assigns a bold attribute to a part of the string.

```
NSString *myString = @"A dingo stole my baby!";
NSMutableAttributedString *attrString =
  [[[NSMutableAttributedString alloc] initWithString:myString] autorelease];
[attrString addAttribute:(NSString *)(kCTForegroundColorAttributeName)
                   value:(id)[UIColor redColor].CGColor
                   range:NSMakeRange(0, [myString length])];
```

The specified attribute name, `kCTForegroundColorAttributeName`, defines which attribute of the text we're setting, and then we pass in a value to set for that attribute and the range of the text to cover. In this case, we're just making it all red, but you can do whatever you like. The *Core Text String Attributes Reference*, included with the SDK, contains a list of all the attributes that apply, their meanings, and the type of values expected for each. In addition to color, you can set fonts, paragraph styles, and more.

Once you've created an attributed string, all you really need to do is create a `CTFramesetter`, use that to generate `CTFrame`, and tell it to draw itself.

```
CTFramesetterRef framesetter =
  CTFramesetterCreateWithAttributedString((CFAttributedStringRef)attrString);
```

```
CTFrameRef frame = CTFramesetterCreateFrame(framesetter,
                                    CFRangeMake(0, [attrString length]),
                                    myCGPath, // the rect to draw into
                                    NULL);
CTFrameDraw(frame, graphicsContext);  // needs a graphics context to draw into
```

This code is taken out of context, and will need some help before it will really do anything. The next section will provide some context for it, in the form of a new Text tool for Dudel.

Preparing Dudel for a New Tool

We're going to be adding a few files to Dudel, and making changes to a few others, so now might be a good time to make a copy of your Dudel project directory. That way, you can work with the copy, and still have your previous version for reference in case something goes wrong. If you would prefer to start working from a clean slate, you can take a fresh copy of the completed app from Chapter 4, and use it as the basis for what we're doing here.

Preparing the Controller Interface

Let's start off, as before, by dealing with the interface for our controller class. We're going to have a new button for the Text tool, so DudelViewController will get a new instance variable to point at that, as well as a new action method for the button to call. Additionally, we'll add a new font property, which the Text tool will access to figure out which font to use to draw its text. For now, we're not going to provide any GUI for the user to actually set the font—that will come later, in Chapter 6. The updated DudelViewController.h looks like this (the lines shown in bold text are the new parts):

```
// DudelViewController.h

#import <UIKit/UIKit.h>
#import <MessageUI/MessageUI.h>

#import "Tool.h"
#import "DudelView.h"

@interface DudelViewController : UIViewController <ToolDelegate, DudelViewDelegate,
MFMailComposeViewControllerDelegate> {
    id <Tool> currentTool;
    IBOutlet DudelView *dudelView;
    IBOutlet UIBarButtonItem *textButton;
    IBOutlet UIBarButtonItem *freehandButton;
    IBOutlet UIBarButtonItem *ellipseButton;
    IBOutlet UIBarButtonItem *rectangleButton;
    IBOutlet UIBarButtonItem *lineButton;
    IBOutlet UIBarButtonItem *dotButton;
    UIColor *strokeColor;
    UIColor *fillColor;
    CGFloat strokeWidth;
    UIFont *font;
```

```
}

@property (retain, nonatomic) id <Tool> currentTool;
@property (retain, nonatomic) UIColor *strokeColor;
@property (retain, nonatomic) UIColor *fillColor;
@property (assign, nonatomic) CGFloat strokeWidth;
@property (retain, nonatomic) UIFont *font;

- (IBAction)touchTextItem:(id)sender;
- (IBAction)touchFreehandItem:(id)sender;
- (IBAction)touchEllipseItem:(id)sender;
- (IBAction)touchRectangleItem:(id)sender;
- (IBAction)touchLineItem:(id)sender;
- (IBAction)touchDotItem:(id)sender;
- (IBAction)touchSendPdfEmailItem:(id)sender;

@end
```

Setting Up the GUI

We'll also need a pair of images, normal and highlighted, for the Text tool button. Either grab these from the book's code archive or make something on your own, similar to what's shown in Table 5-1.

Table 5-1. *New Buttons for the Text Tool*

Filename	Image
button_text.png	T
button_text_selected.png	T

Add those to your project alongside the other button images, and then open *DudelViewController.xib* in Interface Builder. Make sure you can see toolbar at the bottom of the Dudel View window. Drag a new UIBarButtonItem from the Library to the toolbar, placing it to the right of the other tools, but to the left of the flexible space. Use the attribute inspector to set its Image to *button_text.png* and set its Style to Plain. Figure 5–3 shows the end result.

Figure 5–3. *Placement of the new Text tool*

Now control-drag from the new button to the File's Owner in the main *.nib* window, and select the `touchTextItem:` action from the menu that appears. Then control-drag from the File's Owner back to the button, and select the `textButton` outlet from the menu. That's all the GUI configuration we need to do, so you can save your work and go back to Xcode.

Implementing Changes to the Controller Class

Let's return to `DudelViewController`, and make the implementation changes to match the new things in the interface. Open *DudelViewController.m*, and start off by adding the following near the top of the file, so that the controller will get access to the new `TextTool` class we'll soon create:

```
#import "TextTool.h"
```

We also have the new font property to synthesize. Add it to the existing line:

```
@synthesize currentTool, fillColor, strokeColor, strokeWidth, font;
```

Next, we want to make sure we have a default value for the font, so add a line to `viewDidLoad`, like this:

```
- (void)viewDidLoad {
  [super viewDidLoad];
  self.currentTool = [DotTool sharedDotTool];
  [dotButton setImage:[UIImage imageNamed:@"button_dot_selected.png"]];
  self.fillColor = [UIColor colorWithWhite:0.0 alpha:0.25];
  self.strokeColor = [UIColor blackColor];
  self.font = [UIFont systemFontOfSize:24.0];
}
```

Now let's update the `deselectAllToolButtons` method so that it knows about the new button:

```
- (void)deselectAllToolButtons {
  [textButton setImage:[UIImage imageNamed:@"button_text.png"]];
  [freehandButton setImage:[UIImage imageNamed:@"button_bezier.png"]];
  [ellipseButton setImage:[UIImage imageNamed:@"button_ellipse.png"]];
  [rectangleButton setImage:[UIImage imageNamed:@"button_rectangle.png"]];
  [lineButton setImage:[UIImage imageNamed:@"button_line.png"]];
  [dotButton setImage:[UIImage imageNamed:@"button_dot.png"]];
}
```

Finally, implement the method that the new button will call:

```
- (IBAction)touchTextItem:(id)sender {
  self.currentTool = [TextTool sharedTextTool];
  [self deselectAllToolButtons];
  [textButton setImage:[UIImage imageNamed:@"button_text_selected.png"]];
}
```

Those are all the changes our controller class needs in order to handle the new tool. Next, let's update the `ToolDelegate` protocol to match the new bit of functionality in the controller. Our new Text tool will want to get the currently selected font from the controller, which it knows of only as an object conforming to the `ToolDelegate` protocol. Edit the *Tool.h file,* and add a line to the `ToolDelegate` section at the bottom:

```
@protocol ToolDelegate
- (void)addDrawable:(id <Drawable>)d;
- (UIView *)viewForUseWithTool:(id <Tool>)t;
- (UIColor *)strokeColor;
- (UIColor *)fillColor;
- (UIFont *)font;
@end
```

Creating the Text Tool

With that in place, we can now create the `TextTool` class itself. This class is a lot like the `RectangleTool` class, but with an extra twist: When the user finishes drawing a rectangle, this tool switches into text-editing mode by placing a `UITextView` at the location where the rectangle was drawn. It's set up as the first responder so that the keyboard will appear, and users can enter their text. It also shows a gray shade over the rest of the screen, to give the users some focus so they can see where they're typing, as shown in Figure 5–4.

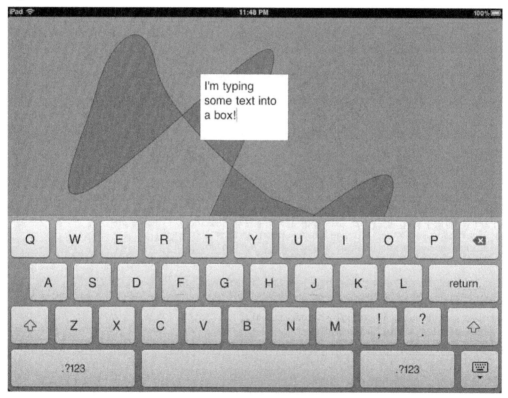

Figure 5–4. *The text field's so bright; you gotta show shade.*

When the user presses the bottom-right keyboard button to dismiss the keyboard, or taps anywhere else in the drawing area, the text entry is considered complete. At that point, the tool creates an instance of a new class called TextDrawingInfo (which we haven't created yet). That will be another class that implements the Drawable protocol (like the PathDrawingInfo class from the Chapter 4), and can therefore be added to the list of things that DudelView needs to draw.

Declaring the Text Tool Interface

Create a new class called TextTool, and start defining it by putting this code into *TextTool.h*:

```
//  TextTool.h
#import <Foundation/Foundation.h>
#import "Tool.h"

@interface TextTool : NSObject <Tool, UITextViewDelegate> {
  id <ToolDelegate> delegate;
  NSMutableArray *trackingTouches;
  NSMutableArray *startPoints;
  UIBezierPath *completedPath;
  CGFloat viewSlideDistance;
}
@property (retain, nonatomic) UIBezierPath *completedPath;
+ (TextTool*)sharedTextTool;
@end
```

Most of what's declared here is pretty similar to what our other tools had. The one new addition is the viewSlideDistance, which we'll use to determine how far to shift the view in case it's being covered up by the on-screen keyboard (more on that in a page or two).

Implementing TextTool

The file containing the implementation, *TextTool.m*, is a bit more complicated than the tools we created in Chapter 4, so I'll interject some additional information at the tricky spots as we go through it. Start off with some #imports:

```
//  TextTool.m

#import "TextTool.h"
#import "TextDrawingInfo.h"

#import "SynthesizeSingleton.h"
```

After the rectangle is drawn, we'll create a temporary view, which will need to be cleaned up later. Instead of using an instance variable for this, we're going to assign a tag number for later retrieval.

```
#define SHADE_TAG 10000
```

Later on, we'll check the distance between the drawn rectangle's start and end points to see if we think it's big enough to contain any text. This function will help us out.

```
static CGFloat distanceBetween(const CGPoint p1, const CGPoint p2) {
  // Pythagoras in the house!
  return sqrt(pow(p1.x-p2.x, 2) + pow(p1.y-p2.y, 2));
}

@implementation TextTool
@synthesize delegate, completedPath;
SYNTHESIZE_SINGLETON_FOR_CLASS(TextTool);
- init {
  if ((self = [super init])) {
    trackingTouches = [[NSMutableArray array] retain];
    startPoints = [[NSMutableArray array] retain];
  }
  return self;
}
- (void)activate {
}
- (void)deactivate {
  [trackingTouches removeAllObjects];
  [startPoints removeAllObjects];
  self.completedPath = nil;
}
- (void)touchesBegan:(NSSet *)touches withEvent:(UIEvent *)event {
  UIView *touchedView = [delegate viewForUseWithTool:self];
  [touchedView endEditing:YES];
```

Unlike the Rectangle tool introduced in Chapter 4, this tool should allow the user to drag out only one rectangle at a time. If we let it do more, how would we know which one should get the text? So here, instead of dealing with all the touches, we just ask for any one of them.

```
  UITouch *touch = [[event allTouches] anyObject];
```

Remember the touch, and its original start point, for future reference.

```
  [trackingTouches addObject:touch];
  CGPoint location = [touch locationInView:touchedView];
  [startPoints addObject:[NSValue valueWithCGPoint:location]];
}
- (void)touchesCancelled:(NSSet *)touches withEvent:(UIEvent *)event {
}
- (void)touchesEnded:(NSSet *)touches withEvent:(UIEvent *)event {
  UIView *touchedView = [delegate viewForUseWithTool:self];
  for (UITouch *touch in [event allTouches]) {
    NSUInteger touchIndex = [trackingTouches indexOfObject:touch];
```

We continue with the rest only if we actually remember the start of this touch. We might be seeing a simultaneous touch that we ignored earlier.

```
    if (touchIndex != NSNotFound) {
      CGPoint startPoint = [[startPoints objectAtIndex:touchIndex] CGPointValue];
      CGPoint endPoint = [touch locationInView:touchedView];
      [trackingTouches removeObjectAtIndex:touchIndex];
      [startPoints removeObjectAtIndex:touchIndex];
```

Detect short taps that are too small to contain any text. These are probably accidents.

```
      if (distanceBetween(startPoint, endPoint) < 5.0) return;
```

Make a rectangle that stretches from the start point to the current point, and wrap that in a path.

```
CGRect rect = CGRectMake(startPoint.x, startPoint.y,
                         endPoint.x - startPoint.x, endPoint.y - startPoint.y);
self.completedPath = [UIBezierPath bezierPathWithRect:rect];
```

Draw a shaded area over the entire view, so that the users can easily see where to focus their attention.

```
UIView *backgroundShade = [[[UIView alloc] initWithFrame:touchedView.bounds]
                           autorelease];
backgroundShade.backgroundColor = [UIColor colorWithWhite:0.0 alpha:0.5];
backgroundShade.tag = SHADE_TAG;
backgroundShade.userInteractionEnabled = NO;
[touchedView addSubview:backgroundShade];
```

Now comes the fun part. We make a temporary UITextView for the actual text input, and set ourselves up to receive notifications when that input begins and ends.

```
UITextView *textView = [[[UITextView alloc] initWithFrame:rect] autorelease];
[[NSNotificationCenter defaultCenter] addObserver:self
                                  selector:@selector(keyboardWillShow:)
                                      name:UIKeyboardWillShowNotification
                                    object:nil];
[[NSNotificationCenter defaultCenter] addObserver:self
                                  selector:@selector(keyboardWillHide:)
                                      name:UIKeyboardWillHideNotification
                                    object:nil];
```

Anyone dealing with text input on the iPhone has probably had to tackle the problem of displaying content that may be obscured by the on-screen keyboard. Here in Dudel, we're going to have the same problem, since users can easily drag a text rectangle in the lower half of the screen.

The following code determines how far the main view needs to be shifted to account for the current rectangle, based on the current orientation and the size of the on-screen keyboard. This value is stored in the viewSlideDistance variable. It will be used later when the keyboard slides into place, and again when it slides back out. Although a user can still create a text rectangle so tall that it will be partly obscured, by doing the following, we're at least making a solid effort and covering the most common cases.

```
CGFloat keyboardHeight = 0;
UIInterfaceOrientation orientation =
  ((UIViewController*)delegate).interfaceOrientation;
if (UIInterfaceOrientationIsPortrait(orientation)) {
  keyboardHeight = 264;
} else {
  keyboardHeight = 352;
}
CGRect viewBounds = touchedView.bounds;
CGFloat rectMaxY = rect.origin.y + rect.size.height;
CGFloat availableHeight = viewBounds.size.height - keyboardHeight;
if (rectMaxY > availableHeight) {
  // calculate a slide distance so that the dragged box is centered vertically
  viewSlideDistance = rectMaxY - availableHeight;
} else {
```

```
              viewSlideDistance = 0;
          }


          textView.delegate = self;
          [touchedView addSubview:textView];
```

This next part is a bit of a trick. Due to a bug in UITextView, just telling it to become the first responder doesn't actually make it happen. The users typically must tap it once on their own to make the keyboard pop up. Toggling the editable flag is a work-around that makes the keyboard actually appear.

```
          textView.editable = NO;
          textView.editable = YES;
          [touchedView becomeFirstResponder];
      }
  }
}
- (void)touchesMoved:(NSSet *)touches withEvent:(UIEvent *)event {
}
- (void)drawTemporary {
  if (self.completedPath) {
    [delegate.strokeColor setStroke];
    [self.completedPath stroke];
  } else {
    UIView *touchedView = [delegate viewForUseWithTool:self];
    for (int i = 0; i<[trackingTouches count]; i++) {
      UITouch *touch = [trackingTouches objectAtIndex:i];
      CGPoint startPoint = [[startPoints objectAtIndex:i] CGPointValue];
      CGPoint endPoint = [touch locationInView:touchedView];
      CGRect rect = CGRectMake(startPoint.x, startPoint.y, endPoint.x - startPoint.x,
                              endPoint.y - startPoint.y);
      UIBezierPath *path = [UIBezierPath bezierPathWithRect:rect];
      [delegate.strokeColor setStroke];
      [path stroke];
    }
  }
}
- (void)dealloc {
  self.completedPath = nil;
  [trackingTouches release];
  [startPoints release];
  self.delegate = nil;
  [super dealloc];
}
```

These are the methods that are triggered by the hiding and showing of the keyboard. When the keyboard slides into place, it covers up the lower portion of the display. Here, we handle this by shifting things a bit if the rectangle we're operating on is covered up.

```
- (void)keyboardWillShow:(NSNotification *)aNotification {
  UIInterfaceOrientation orientation =
    ((UIViewController*)delegate).interfaceOrientation;
  [UIView beginAnimations:@"viewSlideUp" context:NULL];
  UIView *view = [delegate viewForUseWithTool:self];
  CGRect frame = [view frame];
  switch (orientation) {
```

```
      case UIInterfaceOrientationLandscapeLeft:
        frame.origin.x -= viewSlideDistance;
        break;
      case UIInterfaceOrientationLandscapeRight:
        frame.origin.x += viewSlideDistance;
        break;
      case UIInterfaceOrientationPortrait:
        frame.origin.y -= viewSlideDistance;
        break;
      case UIInterfaceOrientationPortraitUpsideDown:
        frame.origin.y += viewSlideDistance;
        break;
      default:
        break;
    }
    [view setFrame:frame];
    [UIView commitAnimations];
}
- (void)keyboardWillHide:(NSNotification *)aNotification {
    UIInterfaceOrientation orientation =
      ((UIViewController*)delegate).interfaceOrientation;
    [UIView beginAnimations:@"viewSlideDown" context:NULL];
    UIView *view = [delegate viewForUseWithTool:self];
    CGRect frame = [view frame];
    switch (orientation) {
      case UIInterfaceOrientationLandscapeLeft:
        frame.origin.x += viewSlideDistance;
        break;
      case UIInterfaceOrientationLandscapeRight:
        frame.origin.x -= viewSlideDistance;
        break;
      case UIInterfaceOrientationPortrait:
        frame.origin.y += viewSlideDistance;
        break;
      case UIInterfaceOrientationPortraitUpsideDown:
        frame.origin.y -= viewSlideDistance;
        break;
      default:
        break;
    }
    [view setFrame:frame];
    [UIView commitAnimations];
}
```

This method, declared in the UITextViewDelegate protocol, is called when the user taps outside the textView or dismisses the keyboard. Here, we create the TextDrawingInfo object (which we'll define shortly) that contains the entered text, along with the current font and color choices. Then we get rid of the temporary views we created earlier.

```
- (void)textViewDidEndEditing:(UITextView *)textView {
    NSLog(@"textViewDidEndEditing");
    TextDrawingInfo *info = [TextDrawingInfo textDrawingInfoWithPath:completedPath
                                          text:textView.text
                                   strokeColor:delegate.strokeColor
                                          font:delegate.font];

    [delegate addDrawable:info];
    self.completedPath = nil;
```

```
    UIView *superView = [textView superview];
    [[superView viewWithTag:SHADE_TAG] removeFromSuperview];
    [textView resignFirstResponder];
    [textView removeFromSuperview];
    [[NSNotificationCenter defaultCenter] removeObserver:self];
}
@end
```

So that's the Text tool. It's fairly complex, but that's actually a good thing! All the intricacies of entering text are in one place, and the rest of our architecture requires minimal changes in order to deal with it. You've already seen the few changes that DudelViewController needed, and the DudelView class itself requires no changes at all! All that's left now is to define the TextDrawingInfo class.

Creating a New Drawable Class

Once again, create a new class in Xcode, and name it TextDrawingInfo. The code for this is pretty similar to the PathDrawingInfo class from Chapter 4, but here we're keeping track of a slightly different set of details and providing a different set of methods for creating new instances. *TextDrawingInfo.h* looks like this:

```
//  TextDrawingInfo.h
#import <Foundation/Foundation.h>
#import "Drawable.h"
@interface TextDrawingInfo : NSObject <Drawable> {
  UIBezierPath *path;
  UIColor *strokeColor;
  UIFont *font;
  NSString *text;
}
@property (retain, nonatomic) UIBezierPath *path;
@property (retain, nonatomic) UIColor *strokeColor;
@property (retain, nonatomic) UIFont *font;
@property (copy, nonatomic) NSString *text;
- (id)initWithPath:(UIBezierPath*)p text:(NSString*)t strokeColor:(UIColor*)s
font:(UIFont*)f;
+ (id)textDrawingInfoWithPath:(UIBezierPath *)p text:t strokeColor:(UIColor *)s
font:(UIFont *)f;
@end
```

As for the implementation, *TextDrawingInfo.m* is pretty straightforward. The only interesting method is the draw method. Here's the whole thing:

```
//  TextDrawingInfo.m
#import "TextDrawingInfo.h"
#import <CoreText/CoreText.h>

@implementation TextDrawingInfo
@synthesize path, strokeColor, font, text;
- initWithPath:(UIBezierPath*)p text:(NSString*)t strokeColor:(UIColor*)s
font:(UIFont*)f {
  if ((self = [self init])) {
    path = [p retain];
    strokeColor = [s retain];
    font = [f retain];
```

```
    text = [t copy];
  }
  return self;
}
+ (id)textDrawingInfoWithPath:(UIBezierPath *)p text:t strokeColor:(UIColor *)s
font:(UIFont *)f {
  return [[[self alloc] initWithPath:p text:t strokeColor:s font:f] autorelease];
}
- (void)dealloc {
  self.path = nil;
  self.strokeColor = nil;
  self.font = nil;
  self.text = nil;
  [super dealloc];
}
- (void)draw {
  CGContextRef context = UIGraphicsGetCurrentContext();

  NSMutableAttributedString *attrString =
    [[[NSMutableAttributedString alloc] initWithString:self.text] autorelease];
  [attrString addAttribute:(NSString *)(kCTForegroundColorAttributeName)
                    value:(id)self.strokeColor.CGColor
                    range:NSMakeRange(0, [self.text length])];
  CTFramesetterRef framesetter =
    CTFramesetterCreateWithAttributedString((CFAttributedStringRef)attrString);

  CTFrameRef frame = CTFramesetterCreateFrame(framesetter,
                                     CFRangeMake(0, [attrString length]),
                                     self.path.CGPath, NULL);
  CFRelease(framesetter);
  if (frame) {
    CGContextSaveGState(context);

    // Core Text wants to draw our text upside down! This flips it the
    // right way.
    CGContextTranslateCTM(context, 0, path.bounds.origin.y);
    CGContextScaleCTM(context, 1, -1);
    CGContextTranslateCTM(context, 0, -(path.bounds.origin.y +
path.bounds.size.height));

    CTFrameDraw(frame, context);
    CGContextRestoreGState(context);
    CFRelease(frame);
  }
}
@end
```

You may recognize some pieces of the draw method. They're very similar to the example shown earlier in this chapter. We create an attributed string and set its color, use it to create a CTFramesetterRef, and then use that to create a CTFrameRef. Here, we've added a check to make sure the CTFrameRef is created and also a few CGContext function calls. These are here for a specific reason: On the Mac OS X platform, the y axis is flipped (relative to the way it's done on iOS) for normal drawing. Core Text, which comes from Mac OS X, expects that flipped axis, which means that when it draws in an iOS context, the results are upside down! The translate/scale/translate triad in the preceding code makes sure that the text appears right side up.

Before this will compile, we need to add the Core Text framework to the Xcode project. Right-click the Frameworks folder, select **Add ➤ Existing Frameworks...** from the context menu, select *CoreText.framework* from the list that appears, and then click the Add button.

Now that everything is in place, you should be able to build and run Dudel in the simulator, and use the new Text tool to add text to your drawings. The masterpiece on display in Figure 5–5 just scratches the surface of what can be done here.

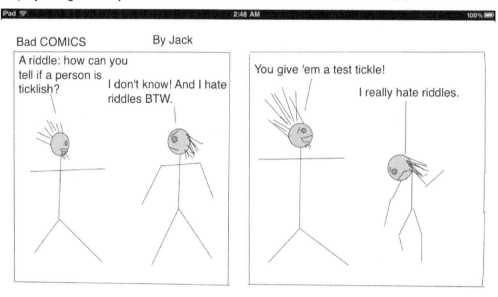

Figure 5–5. *This is the only joke I can consistently remember, people—seriously.*

Rendering Multiple Styles

So, we now have a tool for drawing text, but we still haven't reached the core of what's interesting about Core Text: rendering multiple styles. At this point, lacking a standard GUI widget that gives us anything like a WYSIWYG display while editing the text, there's no really nice way to enter rich text as you can in a word processor, with buttons to change fonts or set colors.

Fortunately for me, I know that you're a computer programmer, and chances are you're already familiar with a way of marking text attributes that isn't as nice, but *is* applicable to a wide range of problems: HTML! Let's extend our text-rendering algorithm to include a very basic parsing of the text that the user enters, looking for embedded tags that we can use to assign attributes to the text.

I'm going to show you a very simple approach that uses an NSScanner object to scan through the entire text string, searching for just a single kind of tag: <font> (and its matching end tag). It will use the specified values to add attributes to the text. What we're doing here is just barely what I would call "parsing," and will probably make you cringe if your computer science education is less rusty than mine. I'm also well aware that the font tag has been deprecated for years, but it's sure an easy way to do quick-'n-dirty markup compared to using CSS! And it works well for our purposes here.

Edit the beginning of the draw method of TextDrawingInfo as shown here, removing the crossed-out lines and replacing them with the bold line:

```
- (void)draw {
  CGContextRef context = UIGraphicsGetCurrentContext();

  //NSMutableAttributedString *attrString = [[[NSMutableAttributedString alloc]
initWithString:self.text] autorelease];
  //[attrString addAttribute:(NSString *)(kCTForegroundColorAttributeName)
value:(id)self.strokeColor.CGColor range:NSMakeRange(0, [self.text length])];
  NSAttributedString *attrString = [self attributedStringFromMarkup:self.text];
  CTFramesetterRef framesetter =
    CTFramesetterCreateWithAttributedString((CFAttributedStringRef)attrString);
```

Now we need to define the attributedStringFromMarkup: method in the same class (anywhere above the draw method should be fine). This uses NSScanner to look for the tags it knows about, and makes one big NSMutableAttributedString out of a number of smaller NSAttributedStrings generated between tags. Here, you also see a little usage of CTFontRef, which is Core Text's own way of referring to fonts.

```
- (NSAttributedString *)attributedStringFromMarkup:(NSString *)markup {
  NSMutableAttributedString *attrString =
    [[[NSMutableAttributedString alloc] initWithString:@""] autorelease];
  NSString *nextTextChunk = nil;
  NSScanner *markupScanner = [NSScanner scannerWithString:markup];
  CGFloat fontSize = 0.0;
  NSString *fontFace = nil;
  UIColor *fontColor = nil;
  while (![markupScanner isAtEnd]) {
    [markupScanner scanUpToString:@"<" intoString:&nextTextChunk];
    [markupScanner scanString:@"<" intoString:NULL];
    if ([nextTextChunk length] > 0) {
      CTFontRef currentFont =
        CTFontCreateWithName((CFStringRef)(fontFace ? fontFace : self.font.fontName),
                             (fontSize != 0.0 ? fontSize : self.font.pointSize),
                             NULL);
      UIColor *color = fontColor ? fontColor : self.strokeColor;
      NSDictionary *attrs = [NSDictionary dictionaryWithObjectsAndKeys:
                            (id)color.CGColor, kCTForegroundColorAttributeName,
                            (id)currentFont, kCTFontAttributeName,
                            nil];
      NSAttributedString *newPiece = [[[NSAttributedString alloc]
        initWithString:nextTextChunk attributes:attrs] autorelease];
      [attrString appendAttributedString:newPiece];
```

```
      CFRelease(currentFont);
    }
    NSString *elementData = nil;
    [markupScanner scanUpToString:@">" intoString:&elementData];
    [markupScanner scanString:@">" intoString:NULL];
    if (elementData) {
      if ([elementData length] > 3 &&
        [[elementData substringToIndex:4] isEqual:@"font"]) {
        fontFace = fontFaceNameFromString(elementData);
        fontSize = fontSizeFromString(elementData);
        fontColor = fontColorFromString(elementData);
      } else if ([elementData length] > 4 &&
        [[elementData substringToIndex:5] isEqual:@"/font"]) {
        // reset all values
        fontSize = 0.0;
        fontFace = nil;
        fontColor = nil;
      }
    }
  }
  return attrString;
}
```

This method, in turn, offloads the parsing of the font element attributes to the following three functions. Put these directly above the attributedStringFromMarkup: method. (Although it may seem wrong, putting them inside the @implementation block is totally fine.)

```
static NSString *fontFaceNameFromString(NSString *attrData) {
  NSScanner *attributeDataScanner = [NSScanner scannerWithString:attrData];
  NSString *faceName = nil;
  if ([attributeDataScanner scanUpToString:@"face=\"" intoString:NULL]) {
    [attributeDataScanner scanString:@"face=\"" intoString:NULL];
    if ([attributeDataScanner scanUpToString:@"\"" intoString:&faceName]) {
      return faceName;
    }
  }
  return nil;
}
static CGFloat fontSizeFromString(NSString *attrData) {
  NSScanner *attributeDataScanner = [NSScanner scannerWithString:attrData];
  NSString *sizeString = nil;
  if ([attributeDataScanner scanUpToString:@"size=\"" intoString:NULL]) {
    [attributeDataScanner scanString:@"size=\"" intoString:NULL];
    if ([attributeDataScanner scanUpToString:@"\"" intoString:&sizeString]) {
      return [sizeString floatValue];
    }
  }
  return 0.0;
}
static UIColor *fontColorFromString(NSString *attrData) {
  return nil;
}
```

You'll notice that the third method, fontColorFromString(), isn't shown in a completed form here. In the interests of time and space, and not wandering too far afield from our main topic, let's leave that as an exercise for the reader, shall we?

With this in place, we now have a way to define some characteristics of the text we enter! Build and run Dudel, and create some new objects using the Text tool to try it out. Here are some suggestions for putting it through its paces:

- Create a paragraph with some `<font size="64">really big text</font>` and then more normal-sized text.

- Try sticking some `<font face="Courier">Courier into the mix</font>` to see how multiple fonts are rendered

Mix and match these however you like. Our parser is far from perfect, and throwing something like nested font tags at it will probably confuse it, but at least it's something!

The Lessons of Core Text

In this chapter, you learned how to use Core Text to render text, including some styled text. You also saw how this works in the context of a real application, and how you can leverage different components to achieve a decent user experience, by using a tried-and-tested input control (UITextView) to let the user enter text that's displayed in a different way by your own component. Understanding when to use the components included in Cocoa Touch, and how to make them work together with your own components, is really important for building larger, more complex applications.

In Chapter 6, you'll see how to give the user a whole lot more functionality than simple buttons in a toolbar will allow. This is possible through the use of the new UIPopoverController class.

Chapter 6

Popovers

Up until recently, the iOS user interface paradigm supported showing only a limited amount of material on the screen at any point in time. In a Cocoa Touch application, there's typically one view controller in focus at a time, and that view controller is in charge of the whole screen (or most of it). The notable exceptions are classes like UINavigationController and UITabBarController, which don't display any interesting content on their own, but instead help developers organize other view controllers.

On the small screen of the iPhone and the iPod touch, this makes a lot of sense. Instead of a profusion of tiny widgets fighting for space on the screen, iOS users have gotten used to being able to focus on one thing at a time, with new views sliding into place when on-screen objects or controls are used. This paradigm is so widely used that even controls that would take up just a small space on a desktop computer, such as a popup list, fill the iPhone's screen when you activate them. On the iPad, however, this behavior isn't always suitable. Sometimes, you need to display a little GUI in order to choose an option, such as from a popup list. Filling the larger iPad screen with a simple list of items would feel both unnatural and wasteful of that nice screen real estate!

The new UIPopoverController class in iOS 3.2 lets you display an auxiliary view that floats in front of the other on-screen content, without filling the entire screen. Like the UINavigationController and UITabBarController, UIPopoverController doesn't display any interesting content on its own. Instead, it serves an organizational role and acts as a container for your own view controllers.

In this chapter, you'll learn how to use UIPopoverController in a variety of ways. We'll add popover views to Dudel for setting fonts, stroke width, and colors.

Popover Preparations

So far, Dudel serves as a nice demo of a few features, but it's extremely limited in comparison to the vector-drawing applications that have been around for decades. One of the main features it lacks is the ability to change the properties of what you're drawing. Right now, you're stuck with the line width, stroke and fill colors, and font that the app gives you from the outset. It's time to change all that!

In this chapter, we're going to create GUIs that let users change all those attributes, giving users much more control over their creations. Each of these attributes requires a little different approach to setting them, and therefore a different sort of GUI:

- Selecting a font will occur through a simple list that displays the name of each font, rendered in that font itself.

- The font's size will be set using a slider in a popup, with a preview showing a piece of text rendered at the chosen size.

- A popup with a slider will let you set the line width, again with a built-in preview.

- Another popup will let you choose the fill and stroke colors from a predefined grid of colors.

The idea is for you to learn several ways that popovers can be used in a real application, starting with the simplest type and working up to more complicated examples.

Before we proceed, let's clarify a point about the concept of a selected object, and the context to which the attributes you set will be applied. Most vector-drawing applications include some sort of selector tool that lets you click an object you've drawn, which then becomes highlighted and editable in some way. Any changes you make to color settings, line width, and so on are typically applied immediately to the selected object. In Dudel, however, we have none of that. There's never a selected object, and therefore never any visible item to which your attribute settings are applied. Instead, the settings are remembered in a central spot (the DudelViewController class), where they will be used for the *next* thing you draw.

The Basic GUI

Before you begin making any changes, make a copy of your entire project directory. Or, if you haven't been following along in earlier chapters, grab a fresh copy of the completed Chapter 5 project from the book's source code archive and work from there.

Let's start off by making some modifications to the main GUI in DudelViewController. We're going add a set of new UIBarButtonItems at the bottom of the screen for the popovers, each with a new icon. Unlike the icons for the tools we created earlier, these don't need to have any sort or highlighting state, so just a single icon for each is fine. Table 6-1 shows the icons you'll need for this chapter. You'll find these in the Chapter 6 project from the book' source code archive, or use your own creations if you prefer. Add these images, using the filenames listed in Table 6-1, to your project.

Table 6–1. *New Buttons for the Popovers*

Filename	Image
button_strokewidth.png	
button_strokecolor.png	
button_fillcolor.png	
button_fontname.png	
button_fontsize.png	

Now let's add action methods to our controller class's interface for connecting these buttons. Open *DudelViewController.h*, and somewhere near the end of the file, but before the @end line, add the following lines:

```
- (IBAction)popoverFontName:(id)sender;
- (IBAction)popoverFontSize:(id)sender;
- (IBAction)popoverStrokeWidth:(id)sender;
- (IBAction)popoverStrokeColor:(id)sender;
- (IBAction)popoverFillColor:(id)sender;
```

Then, just to keep our code in a compilable state, switch over to *DudelViewController.m* and insert some empty implementations for those methods inside the @implementation DudelViewController section:

```
- (IBAction)popoverFontName:(id)sender {
}
- (IBAction)popoverFontSize:(id)sender {
}
- (IBAction)popoverStrokeWidth:(id)sender {
}
- (IBAction)popoverStrokeColor:(id)sender {
}
- (IBAction)popoverFillColor:(id)sender {
}
```

We'll go back and fill in the implementations of those methods a little later, but first we want to hook up the GUI. Save your work, and then open *DudelViewController.xib* in Interface Builder. We'll add the new buttons as a group, between the group of tools on the left and the e-mail action on the right, as shown in Figure 6–1.

Figure 6–1. *Positioning the settings buttons*

First, duplicate the flexible space object in place, by selecting it and pressing ⌘D. That will give you a location to put more buttons. Then use the Library to find a UIBarButtonItem and drag it out between the two flexible spaces. Next, open the attribute inspector. Set the new item's Style to Plain, and set its image to *button_strokewidth.png*. This gives us the basic template for how all five buttons will appear. While the new item is still selected, press ⌘D four times to make a row of five identical items.

Now we need to add the actions and images to the buttons. Select the leftmost item, control-drag to the File's Owner icon in the main *.nib* window, and click popoverStrokeWidth: in the list of actions that appears. Then go along the rest of the row, configuring each item's action and connecting it to the appropriate image. The second item should get the *popover_strokecolor.png* image and be connected to popoverStrokeColor:. The third should use *popover_fillcolor.png* and popoverFillColor:. The last two items are for choosing a font name and font size, and I'll bet that by now, you can figure out which images and actions to use for them.

Popover Considerations

One of the main uses for popovers is to present a list of selectable items, not unlike the menus available in Mac OS X and other desktop operating systems. When using menus in a Mac OS X application, the system takes care of things such as making sure that only one menu is shown at a time and making the menu disappear when an item is selected. But the popover in iOS is a different beast.

A popover won't automatically disappear when the user selects something inside it, and opening one popover doesn't remove any previously opened popover from the screen. This means that you could easily wind up with multiple popovers on the screen at once, overlapping each other.

The only time the system automatically closes a popover is when you touch some part of the screen outside the popover (except, notably, touching an item in a UIToolbar, which leaves the popover just as it is). The rest of the time, you'll need to dismiss the popover yourself any time a user action warrants it.

However, this apparent lack of automation actually gives you some amount of flexibility compared to what's typically possible with a menu. A popover can, for instance, contain interactive controls, such as sliders or check boxes, to let the user quickly try out different possibilities and see the results instantly. That wouldn't be possible if the popover went away as soon as someone clicked it. Similarly, allowing multiple popovers to be displayed simultaneously may be useful in situations where you want to let the user quickly change multiple settings or attributes. For example, in a word processing app, you might want to let the user open two popovers: one for selecting from a list of fonts, and one for toggling attributes (bold, italics, underline, and so on).

> **NOTE:** Apple recommends against displaying multiple popovers at once, in order to avoid "confusing" your users, so think twice before going that route.

In Dudel, we're going to allow for only one popover at a time by keeping an instance variable in DudelViewController that points at the current popover, and taking steps to make sure that it's properly managed. Start off by editing *DudelViewController.h*, adding the following code shown in bold. In addition to adding the instance variable (and its matching property declaration), here we're also adding UIPopoverControllerDelegate to the list of protocols this class implements.

```
@interface DudelViewController : UIViewController <ToolDelegate, DudelViewDelegate,
MFMailComposeViewControllerDelegate, UIPopoverControllerDelegate> {
    id <Tool> currentTool;
    IBOutlet DudelView *dudelView;
    IBOutlet UIBarButtonItem *textButton;
    IBOutlet UIBarButtonItem *freehandButton;
    IBOutlet UIBarButtonItem *ellipseButton;
    IBOutlet UIBarButtonItem *rectangleButton;
    IBOutlet UIBarButtonItem *lineButton;
    IBOutlet UIBarButtonItem *dotButton;
    UIColor *strokeColor;
    UIColor *fillColor;
    UIFont *font;
    CGFloat strokeWidth;
    UIPopoverController *currentPopover;
}

@property (retain, nonatomic) id <Tool> currentTool;
@property (retain, nonatomic) UIColor *strokeColor;
@property (retain, nonatomic) UIColor *fillColor;
@property (retain, nonatomic) UIFont *font;
@property (assign, nonatomic) CGFloat strokeWidth;
@property (retain, nonatomic) UIPopoverController *currentPopover;
```

Follow up by switching over to *DudelViewController.m* to synthesize the currentPopover property, and clean it up in the dealloc method.

```
@synthesize currentTool, fillColor, strokeColor, font, strokeWidth, currentPopover;

- (void)dealloc {
    self.currentTool = nil;
    self.fillColor = nil;
    self.strokeColor = nil;
    self.currentPopover = nil;
    [super dealloc];
}
```

One tricky aspect of dealing with popovers has to do with cleanup after a popover has been dismissed. If the user clicked outside the popover, causing it to be automatically dismissed, then a method will be called in the UIPopoverController's delegate. But if you dismiss the popup from within code, that method *isn't* called. We'll handle this discrepancy by just making the delegate method call our own cleanup method, handleDismissedPopoverController:, which we'll be careful to call every time we dismiss a popup manually.

```
- (void)handleDismissedPopoverController:(UIPopoverController*)popoverController {
    self.currentPopover = nil;
}
- (void)popoverControllerDidDismissPopover:(UIPopoverController *)popoverController {
    [self handleDismissedPopoverController:popoverController];
}
```

As you can see, our current cleanup method doesn't do much cleanup yet, but that will change!

The main thing we're going to need to do in our cleanup method, besides clearing our currentPopover instance variable, is to get whatever values we need from the popover's displayed controller. In Dudel, we'll implement this by checking for the specific classes we're using for the view controllers. So the handleDismissedPopoverController: method will end up containing a series of if/else blocks, like this:

```
// just for explanatory purposes, not for copy-and-paste!
if ([popoverController.contentViewController isMemberOfClass:[SomeController class]]) {
    // now we know which view controller we're dealing with
    SomeController *sc = (SomeController *)popoverController.contentViewController;
    // retrieve some values from the controller, to see what the user selected/adjusted
    self.something = sc.something;
    ...
} else if (...)
```

Yes, I agree that this sort of if/else pileup is distasteful. But it's the simplest solution in this case, and our project is small enough that it's not introducing too much painful ugliness.

The Font Name Popover

The first popover we're going to create is for choosing the font used by the Text tool. We'll simply display a list of all available font names on the device; specifying the size will be the job of our next popover. What we need here is a view controller that will let us display a list of selectable items, and this list may be larger than the screen itself, so it should be scrollable—sounds like a job for a UITableView!

Add a new class to your project, and use the assistant that comes up to specify that you want a Cocoa Touch class, specifically a UIViewController subclass. If you've ever created a UIViewController subclass for iPhone in the past—and I suspect you have—this should look pretty familiar. The main difference is the inclusion of a new Targeted for iPad check box. If that's checked, Xcode will use a slightly different template for creating your class. Go ahead and make sure that's turned on, along with the

UITableViewController subclass check box, but not the XIB check box, as shown in Figure 6–2. Click Next, and then enter FontListController as the name of your new class.

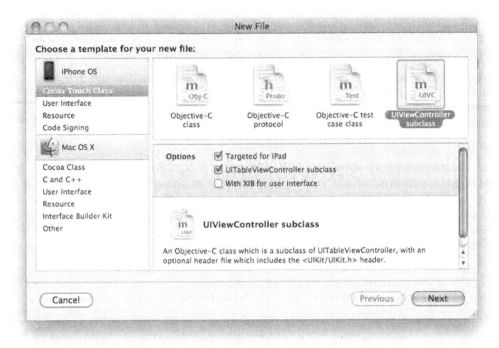

Figure 6–2. *Creating a new controller class*

The Simplest Popover You'll Ever Create

Thanks to the power and flexibility of UITableView, creating this class is going to be a breeze. All we need to do is add a few instance variables for hanging onto a list of fonts as well as the current selection, and fill in a few short methods in the controller class.

Start with *FontListController.h*, adding the instance variables and matching properties as shown in the following code. We're also defining a string constant, which will be used to let the main view controller know that the user has selected something.

```
#import <UIKit/UIKit.h>
// we'll use a notification with this name, to let the main
// view controller know that something was selected here.
#define FontListControllerDidSelect @"FontListControllerDidSelect"
@interface FontListController : UITableViewController {
  NSArray *fonts;
  NSString *selectedFontName;
  UIPopoverController *container;
}
@property (retain, nonatomic) NSArray *fonts;
@property (copy, nonatomic) NSString *selectedFontName;
```

```
@property (assign, nonatomic) UIPopoverController *container;
@end
```

As you can see, we also created an instance variable for pointing to the UIPopoverController that acts as the container for an instance of this class. FontListController doesn't have any use for this itself, but it will be used later when DudelViewController needs to close the containing UIPopoverController.

Now switch over to *FontListController.m*, where we have a series of small changes to make to the default template. Apart from the changes shown here, you can leave the rest of the autogenerated class as is. First, synthesize all the declared properties by adding this line inside the @implementation FontListController section:

```
@synthesize fonts, selectedFontName, container;
```

Then uncomment the viewDidLoad method, remove most of the code in there (except for the call to [super viewDidLoad]), and add the bold lines shown here to its body:

```
- (void)viewDidLoad {
  [super viewDidLoad];
  NSArray *familyNames = [UIFont familyNames];
  NSMutableArray *fontNames = [NSMutableArray array];
  for (NSString *family in familyNames) {
    [fontNames addObjectsFromArray:[UIFont fontNamesForFamilyName:family]];
  }
  self.fonts = [fontNames sortedArrayUsingSelector:@selector(compare:)];
}
```

In a nutshell, this goes through an array of strings containing font family names, gets all the fonts that belong to each family, and adds them to an array. Finally, it puts them in alphabetical order and saves the sorted array in the fonts instance variable.

Next, uncomment the viewWillAppear: method, and add the bold lines shown here:

```
- (void)viewWillAppear:(BOOL)animated {
  [super viewWillAppear:animated];
  NSInteger fontIndex = [self.fonts indexOfObject:self.selectedFontName];
  if (fontIndex != NSNotFound) {
    NSIndexPath *indexPath = [NSIndexPath indexPathForRow:fontIndex inSection:0];
    [self.tableView scrollToRowAtIndexPath:indexPath
        atScrollPosition:UITableViewScrollPositionMiddle animated:NO];
  }
}
```

This code tries to find the location of the selected font in the array of fonts, and scrolls the table view to make it visible. This works under the assumption that the code that initializes this class (which we'll add to DudelViewController soon) also sets the selectedFontName property. The check against NSNotFound makes sure that we don't crash in case that value hasn't been set or is set to something invalid (a font name that isn't in our list).

Next, we fill in the blanks for the basic UITableViewDatasource methods that every UITableViewController subclass must implement:

```
- (NSInteger)numberOfSectionsInTableView:(UITableView *)tableView {
```

```
    // Return the number of sections.
    return 1;
}

- (NSInteger)tableView:(UITableView *)tableView numberOfRowsInSection:(NSInteger)section
{
    // Return the number of rows in the section.
    return [fonts count];
}

// Customize the appearance of table view cells.
- (UITableViewCell *)tableView:(UITableView *)tableView
cellForRowAtIndexPath:(NSIndexPath *)indexPath {

  static NSString *CellIdentifier = @"Cell";

  UITableViewCell *cell = [tableView dequeueReusableCellWithIdentifier:CellIdentifier];
  if (cell == nil) {
    cell = [[[UITableViewCell alloc] initWithStyle:UITableViewCellStyleDefault
reuseIdentifier:CellIdentifier] autorelease];
  }

  // Configure the cell...
  NSString *fontName = [fonts objectAtIndex:indexPath.row];
  cell.textLabel.text = fontName;
  cell.textLabel.font = [UIFont fontWithName:fontName size:17.0];
  if ([self.selectedFontName isEqual:fontName]) {
    cell.accessoryType = UITableViewCellAccessoryCheckmark;
  } else {
    cell.accessoryType = UITableViewCellAccessoryNone;
  }
  return cell;
}
```

The first two methods are self-explanatory, and the last one isn't much more complicated. It just sees which font name is at the specified index, and uses that name both as the display value and to look up a font. That way, each font name is displayed in its own font! It also sets a check box on the cell if (and only if) the current font name matches the selected font, so the user can see the current selection while scrolling through the list.

Next, we're going to implement the method that's called when the user selects a row. The idea is to make a note of which font the user selected, update the display of the affected rows (so the check box appears in the correct cell) to give the user some immediate feedback, and then post a notification so that whoever is listening, such as DudelViewController, will get a chance to do something. This method already exists in the template code, but contains some commented-out example code that isn't relevant here. Delete that, and add the code shown in bold:

```
- (void)tableView:(UITableView *)tableView didSelectRowAtIndexPath:(NSIndexPath
*)indexPath {
  // determine two affected table columns: the one that was selected before,
  // and the one that's selected now.
  NSInteger previousFontIndex = [self.fonts indexOfObject:self.selectedFontName];
```

```
  // don't do any updating etc. if the user touched the already-selected row
  if (previousFontIndex != indexPath.row) {
    NSArray *indexPaths = nil;
    if (previousFontIndex!= NSNotFound) {
      NSIndexPath *previousHighlightedIndexPath = [NSIndexPath
        indexPathForRow:previousFontIndex inSection:0];
      indexPaths = [NSArray arrayWithObjects:indexPath, previousHighlightedIndexPath,
nil];
    } else {
      indexPaths = [NSArray arrayWithObjects:indexPath, nil];
    }

    // notice the new selection
    self.selectedFontName = [self.fonts objectAtIndex:indexPath.row];

    // then reload
    [self.tableView reloadRowsAtIndexPaths:indexPaths
      withRowAnimation:UITableViewRowAnimationFade];
    [[NSNotificationCenter defaultCenter]
postNotificationName:FontListControllerDidSelect
      object:self];
  }
}
```

Finally, we need to add a bit of cleanup, so that the list of font names doesn't hang around forever:

```
- (void)viewDidUnload {
  // relinquish ownership of anything that can be re-created in viewDidLoad or on
demand.
  // For example: self.myOutlet = nil;
  self.fonts = nil;
}

- (void)dealloc {
  self.fonts = nil;
  self.selectedFontName = nil;
  [super dealloc];
}
```

That should be all we need for the FontListController class itself. At this point, you should try to build your app, just to make sure no syntax errors have snuck in, but you won't see any difference when you run the app just yet. Our next step here will be enabling DudelViewController to use our new class.

The Back End

Now it's time to implement the portions of DudelViewController that will fire up the FontListController, dismiss its popover when the user makes a selection, and grab the selected value. Start with an import:

```
#import "FontListController.h"
```

Then fill in this previously empty method:

```
- (IBAction)popoverFontName:(id)sender {
  FontListController *flc = [[[FontListController alloc]
    initWithStyle:UITableViewStylePlain] autorelease];
  flc.selectedFontName = self.font.fontName;
  [self setupNewPopoverControllerForViewController:flc];
  flc.container = self.currentPopover;
  [[NSNotificationCenter defaultCenter] addObserver:self
    selector:@selector(fontListControllerDidSelect:)
    name:FontListControllerDidSelect
    object:flc];
  [self.currentPopover presentPopoverFromBarButtonItem:sender
    permittedArrowDirections:UIPopoverArrowDirectionAny
    animated:YES];
}
```

This method creates and configures a FontListController instance. Part of the configuration involves calling a method named setupNewPopoverControllerForViewController: (which we're going to create in just a minute). It also sets us up as an observer for a notification, which will tell us that the user selected something, and then displays a popover.

What's not really clear here is the final line, which contains self.currentPopover. We haven't set that, have we? Well, the following auxiliary method does! Insert this method somewhere above all the popover action methods:

```
- (void)setupNewPopoverControllerForViewController:(UIViewController *)vc {
  if (self.currentPopover) {
    [self.currentPopover dismissPopoverAnimated:YES];
    [self handleDismissedPopoverController:self.currentPopover];
  }
  self.currentPopover = [[[UIPopoverController alloc] initWithContentViewController:vc]
    autorelease];
  self.currentPopover.delegate = self;
}
```

We'll use this method every time we're going to present a popover. By doing so, we save a few lines in each popover action method, and also ensure that we're doing things the same way each time. Now, I'm not going to pretend that this separate method sprang from my forehead in one piece. The fact is that I had this code, or something very much like it, inside each action method as I was working on this chapter. Eventually, I realized that there was a sizable chunk that was identical in each method, and refactored it into a method on its own.

> **TIP**: Any time you find yourself doing cut-and-paste coding, consider chunking things off into separate methods, because someone is probably going to revisit your code someday. The mind you save may be your own.

So now we have code in place to fire up the popover, but we still need to handle the user selecting something. Begin by creating a method to be called when the notification we're observing is triggered:

```
- (void)fontListControllerDidSelect:(NSNotification *)notification {
    FontListController *flc = [notification object];
    UIPopoverController *popoverController = flc.container;
    [popoverController dismissPopoverAnimated:YES];
    [self handleDismissedPopoverController:popoverController];
    self.currentPopover = nil;
}
```

Here, you see the reason for putting the container property in FontListController. After the user makes a selection, FontListController shoots off a notification. DudelViewController picks it up, and uses the container property to dismiss the popover. This method also calls the main handler for all our popovers, which you should now revise to this:

```
- (void)handleDismissedPopoverController:(UIPopoverController*)popoverController {
    if ([popoverController.contentViewController isMemberOfClass:
        [FontListController class]]) {
      // this is the font list, grab the new selection
      FontListController *flc = (FontListController *)
        popoverController.contentViewController;
      self.font = [UIFont fontWithName:flc.selectedFontName size:self.font.pointSize];
    }
    self.currentPopover = nil;
}
```

This is where the selection in the popover finally ends up having an effect. The font is now set according to what the user picked.

You should now be able to build and run the app, and then touch the font list button in the toolbar to see something like the popup shown in Figure 6–3.

Try selecting a different font, and then using the Text tool to create some text. Neat! You now have the full complement of fonts included with the iPad at your disposal. You're still stuck with just one size, so let's tackle that next.

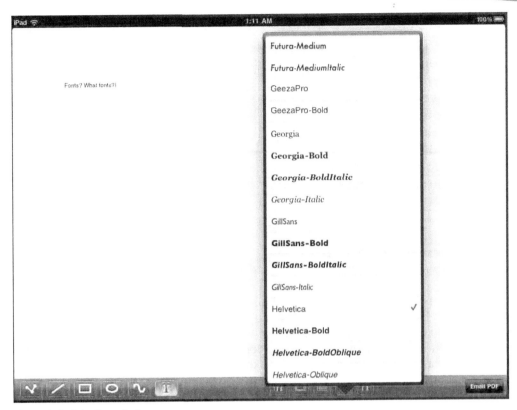

Figure 6–3. *Selecting a font*

The Font Size Popover

To keep the font selector simple, we'll have the size selection as a separate operation, in its own popover. The GUI for the font size selector will consist of a slider, a label showing the slider's value, and a text view showing a preview of the chosen font at the chosen size. As the user operates the slider, the preview immediately reflects the slider's value. Figure 6–4 shows the GUI in action.

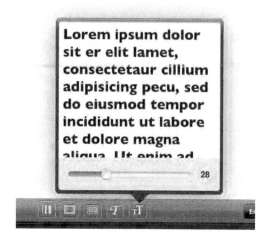

Figure 6–4. *Setting the font size, with live preview*

Unlike the font list, the font size popover shouldn't go away as soon as the user touches it—that would be a pretty surprising response from touching a slider. That means that the interaction between DudelViewController and this new popover will be a little simpler than it was for the font list, since the font size popover will never need to be explicitly dismissed in our code. We'll rely on the system to dismiss it when the user clicks outside it.

Creating the GUI

In Xcode, use the New File Assistant to make a new Cocoa Touch class. Select UIViewController as its superclass, and configure the check boxes to target iPad and create an *.xib* file, but to *not* make it a subclass of UITableViewController. Name the new class FontSizeController.

Start by editing *FontSizeController.h*, which will contain outlets for each GUI object we need to interact with, an instance variable containing the current chosen font, and an action method for the slider to call. Here's the entire content of the file:

```
// FontSizeController.h
#import <UIKit/UIKit.h>
@interface FontSizeController : UIViewController {
  IBOutlet UITextView *textView;
  IBOutlet UISlider *slider;
  IBOutlet UILabel *label;
  UIFont *font;
}
@property (retain, nonatomic) UIFont *font;
- (void)takeIntValueFrom:(id)sender;
@end
```

Now open *FontSizeController.xib* in Interface Builder. The first thing you'll notice is that the default view contained within is the size of the entire iPad screen. That's way too big for our purposes! It's also showing a black status bar at the top, as if it were a full-screen view.

Select the view, and use the attribute inspector to set the Status Bar value to Unspecified. Then use the size inspector to set its size to 320 by 320. You actually need to do these two steps in that order, since if the Status Bar value is set to Black, Interface Builder wants to treat that view as a full-screen view, and won't let you change its size.

> **NOTE:** Apple's documentation says that the minimum width for a popover is 320 pixels.

Now use the Library to grab a UITextView, a UISlider, and a UILabel, and put them each into the view, laid out something like what you saw in Figure 6–4. In my version, I've broken up the monotony of the white background by setting the main view's background color to light gray. You can skip this step if you like, or use a different background color.

Next, connect each outlet from File's Owner to one of the GUI objects by control-clicking that icon, dragging to a GUI object, and selecting the appropriate outlet from the list that appears. Then connect the slider's target and action by control-clicking the slider, dragging to File's Owner, and selecting the takeIntValueFrom: method.

Select the UITextView you created earlier. This contains some "Lorem ipsum" text by default, which is fine for our purposes, so leave that bit alone. However, we don't want users interacting with this text view, so use the attribute inspector to turn off the Editable check box, as well as all of the check box options that affect scrolling behavior.

Finally select the slider, and set its minimum and maximum values to 1 and 96, respectively. The GUI is now complete! Save your work, and go back to Xcode.

Making It Work

Now it's time for the FontListController implementation, which is shown here in an abbreviated form after deleting extra comments and unneeded overrides from the template:

```
//  FontSizeController.m
#import "FontSizeController.h"
@implementation FontSizeController
@synthesize font;
// Implement viewDidLoad to do additional setup after loading the view, typically from a
nib.
- (void)viewDidLoad {
  [super viewDidLoad];
  textView.font = self.font;
  NSInteger i = self.font.pointSize;
  label.text = [NSString stringWithFormat:@"%d", i];
  slider.value = i;
}
```

```
- (BOOL)shouldAutorotateToInterfaceOrientation:
    (UIInterfaceOrientation)interfaceOrientation {
    // Overridden to allow any orientation.
    return YES;
}
- (void)dealloc {
    self.font = nil;
    [super dealloc];
}
- (void)takeIntValueFrom:(id)sender {
    NSInteger size = ((UISlider *)sender).value;
    self.font = [self.font fontWithSize:size];
    textView.font = self.font;
    label.text = [NSString stringWithFormat:@"%d", size];
}
@end
```

As you can see, this class is quite simple. It basically just responds to the user dragging the slider by modifying the font property and updating the display.

Now all that's left to do is integrate this new class with the view controller. Switch back to *DudelViewController.m*, where we have a few changes to make. Add this near the top:

```
#import "FontSizeController.h"
```

Then update the handleDismissedPopoverController: method like this:

```
- (void)handleDismissedPopoverCo2ntroller:(UIPopoverController*)popoverController {
    if ([popoverController.contentViewController isMemberOfClass:
        [FontListController class]]) {
        // this is the font list, grab the new selection
        FontListController *flc = (FontListController *)
            popoverController.contentViewController;
        self.font = [UIFont fontWithName:flc.selectedFontName size:self.font.pointSize];
    } else if ([popoverController.contentViewController isMemberOfClass:
        [FontSizeController class]]) {
        FontSizeController *fsc = (FontSizeController *)
            popoverController.contentViewController;
        self.font = fsc.font;
    }
    self.currentPopover = nil;
}
```

After that, we just need to fill in the popoverFontSize: method, like this:

```
- (IBAction)popoverFontSize:(id)sender {
    FontSizeController *fsc = [[[FontSizeController alloc] initWithNibName:nil bundle:nil]
        autorelease];
    fsc.font = self.font;
    [self setupNewPopoverControllerForViewController:fsc];
    self.currentPopover.popoverContentSize = fsc.view.frame.size;
    [self.currentPopover presentPopoverFromBarButtonItem:sender
        permittedArrowDirections:UIPopoverArrowDirectionAny animated:YES];
}
```

The one new thing we're doing in this method is setting the popoverContentSize property on the currentPopover. If we didn't do this, the popup would automatically fill the maximum height of the screen.

With that in place, we're finished with the font size selection popup. Build and run the app, and you should see something like Figure 6–5. Notice that since this popover knows about the complete UIFont object that is currently set, not just the size, we can display the font preview with the correct font and size.

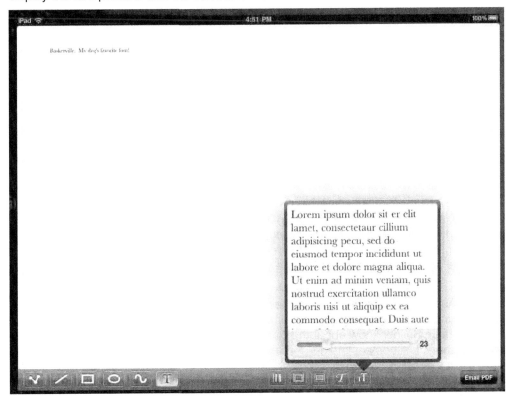

Figure 6–5. *Setting a font size*

Now we have pretty good control over the fonts we're using for the Text tool. This is still far from a word processor or page layout app, but it's a pretty decent start, especially considering how little code we've written!

The Stroke Width Popover

Next up is the popover for setting the stroke width. This one is pretty similar to the one for font size. We'll give the user a slider to drag back and forth for setting the width, as well as a preview. This time, the preview will draw a few lines and curves in a

UIBezierPath just like the ones the user can make, clearly showing the result of the user's selection.

Paving the Way

Start by creating yet another UIViewController subclass, using the New File Assistant. Just like FontSizeController, this one should *not* be a subclass of UITableViewController, but it *should* have an *.xib* file and be targeted for iPad. Name it StrokeWidthController. After Xcode creates it, open *StrokeWidthController.h* and give it the following content:

```
//  StrokeWidthController.h
#import <UIKit/UIKit.h>
@class StrokeDemoView;
@interface StrokeWidthController : UIViewController {
  IBOutlet UISlider *slider;
  IBOutlet UILabel *label;
  IBOutlet StrokeDemoView *strokeDemoView;
  CGFloat strokeWidth;
}
@property (assign, nonatomic) CGFloat strokeWidth;
- (void)takeIntValueFrom:(id)sender;
@end
```

This class is pretty similar to FontSizeController. The main differences are that here, we're keeping track of a simple floating-point value for the width, and we're also referencing a new class we're about to create, called StrokeDemoView, which we'll use to display the preview of the selected stroke width.

Before we create the GUI, we also need to create the StrokeDemoView class. Using the New File Assistant once again, make a new UIView subclass and name it StrokeDemoView. Just creating the class in our project is all we need to do in order to make Interface Builder know about the class and let us use it in the GUI. We'll go back and fill in the actual content later.

Creating the GUI

To begin, open *StrokeWidthController.xib* in Interface Builder. Once again, you'll see that the UIView it contains is meant to take up an entire screen, which isn't what we want here either. Use the attribute inspector to set the view's Status Bar to Unspecified, and then use the size inspector to make its size 320 by 320.

Now use the Library to find the three classes that are needed for our GUI: UISlider, UILabel, and StrokeDemoView. Drag each of them to the view, laying them out as shown in Figure 6–6.

Figure 6–6. *Creating the GUI for StrokeWidthController*

You can't really tell from the figure, but the large, white rectangle filling most of the view is an instance of StrokeDemoView. For best results with our preview-drawing code, make this view 320 by 257, since the StrokeDemoView is going to have hard-coded locations for the lines and curves it draws. Here, I've once again given the entire view a light-gray background, to make the control area stand out from the preview a bit. Use the attribute inspector to give the slider a reasonable range by setting its minimum value to 1 and its maximum value to 20.

Make all the connections described in the header file, by control-dragging from File's Owner to each of the GUI components and making the connection, then control-dragging from the slider back to File's Owner and selecting the takeIntValueFrom: action. Now the basic GUI configuration is complete, so let's return to Xcode and make it work!

Previewing the Stroke Width with a Custom View

Now we're going to define the StrokeDemoView class. This class will be pretty simple. It defines a property called strokeWidth, which determines how it draws its path. Our controller will set this each time the user moves the slider. *StrokeDemoView.h* looks like this:

```
//  StrokeDemoView.h
#import <UIKit/UIKit.h>
@interface StrokeDemoView : UIView {
  CGFloat strokeWidth;
  UIBezierPath *drawPath;
}
@property (assign, nonatomic) CGFloat strokeWidth;
@end
```

The implementation is also pretty simple. It defines the path to draw when it's initialized, and implements the setStrokeWidth: method in order to mark itself as "dirty" by calling [self setNeedsDisplay], so the view is scheduled for redrawing. The drawRect: method simply draws the path. Here's the whole thing:

```
//  StrokeDemoView.m
#import "StrokeDemoView.h"
@implementation StrokeDemoView
@synthesize strokeWidth;
- (void)setStrokeWidth:(CGFloat)f {
  strokeWidth = f;
  drawPath.lineWidth = f;
  [self setNeedsDisplay];
}
- (id)initWithCoder:(NSCoder *)aDecoder {
  if ((self = [super initWithCoder:aDecoder])) {
    drawPath = [[UIBezierPath bezierPathWithRect:CGRectMake(10, 10, 145, 100)] retain];
    [drawPath appendPath:
      [UIBezierPath bezierPathWithOvalInRect:CGRectMake(165, 10, 145, 100)]];

    [drawPath moveToPoint:CGPointMake(10, 120)];
    [drawPath addLineToPoint:CGPointMake(310, 120)];

    [drawPath moveToPoint:CGPointMake(110, 140)];
    [drawPath addLineToPoint:CGPointMake(310, 200)];

    [drawPath moveToPoint:CGPointMake(100, 180)];
    [drawPath addLineToPoint:CGPointMake(310, 140)];

    [drawPath moveToPoint:CGPointMake(90, 200)];
    [drawPath addCurveToPoint:CGPointMake(300, 230)
              controlPoint1:CGPointMake(0, 0)
              controlPoint2:CGPointMake(-100, 300)];
  }
  return self;
}
- (void)dealloc {
  [drawPath dealloc];
  [super dealloc];
}
- (void)drawRect:(CGRect)rect {
  [[UIColor blackColor] setStroke];
  [drawPath stroke];
}
@end
```

Note that since this class is instantiated only from within an *.xib* file, and never directly in code, we implement initWithCoder: and not initWithFrame:. If we wanted to also be able to instantiate this class in code, we would need to implement the latter as well in order to create the path.

Implementing the Controller

Now that we have a working StrokeDemoView, our next move is to go back and implement StrokeWidthController. This class is quite simple, and quite similar to the FontSizeController we built earlier. Here's the entire content of *StrokeWidthController.m*:

```
//  StrokeWidthController.m
#import "StrokeWidthController.h"
#import "StrokeDemoView.h"
@implementation StrokeWidthController
@synthesize strokeWidth;
- (void)viewDidLoad {
  [super viewDidLoad];
  NSInteger i = self.strokeWidth;
  strokeDemoView.strokeWidth = i;
  label.text = [NSString stringWithFormat:@"%d", i];
  slider.value = i;
}
-
(BOOL)shouldAutorotateToInterfaceOrientation:(UIInterfaceOrientation)interfaceOrientatio
n {
    // Overriden to allow any orientation.
    return YES;
}
- (void)takeIntValueFrom:(id)sender {
  NSInteger i = ((UISlider *)sender).value;
  self.strokeWidth = i;
  strokeDemoView.strokeWidth = self.strokeWidth;
  label.text = [NSString stringWithFormat:@"%d", i];
  slider.value = self.strokeWidth;
}
@end
```

Making it Work

Now all we need to do is update our main controller to make it aware of the new popover. Open *DudelViewController.m*, and start with an import:

```
#import "StrokeWidthController.h"
```

Once again, we update the handleDismissedPopoverController: method, this time grabbing the new stroke width after completion:

```
- (void)handleDismissedPopoverController:(UIPopoverController*)popoverController {
  if ([popoverController.contentViewController isMemberOfClass:
    [FontListController class]]) {
    // this is the font list, grab the new selection
    FontListController *flc = (FontListController *)
      popoverController.contentViewController;
    self.font = [UIFont fontWithName:flc.selectedFontName size:self.font.pointSize];
  } else if ([popoverController.contentViewController isMemberOfClass:
    [FontSizeController class]]) {
    FontSizeController *fsc = (FontSizeController *)
      popoverController.contentViewController;
```

```
    self.font = fsc.font;
  } else if ([popoverController.contentViewController isMemberOfClass:
    [StrokeWidthController class]]) {
    StrokeWidthController *swc = (StrokeWidthController *)
      popoverController.contentViewController;
    self.strokeWidth = swc.strokeWidth;
  }
  self.currentPopover = nil;
}
```

And finally, we implement the action that sets it in motion:

```
- (IBAction)popoverStrokeWidth:(id)sender {
  StrokeWidthController *swc = [[[StrokeWidthController alloc] initWithNibName:nil
    bundle:nil] autorelease];
  swc.strokeWidth = self.strokeWidth;
  [self setupNewPopoverControllerForViewController:swc];
  self.currentPopover.popoverContentSize = swc.view.frame.size;
  [self.currentPopover presentPopoverFromBarButtonItem:sender
    permittedArrowDirections:UIPopoverArrowDirectionAny animated:YES];
}
```

Build and run the app, and try out the new popover. Now you can finally see what that UIBezierPath we defined in the StrokeDemoView class looks like! Figure 6–7 shows the stroke width popover in action.

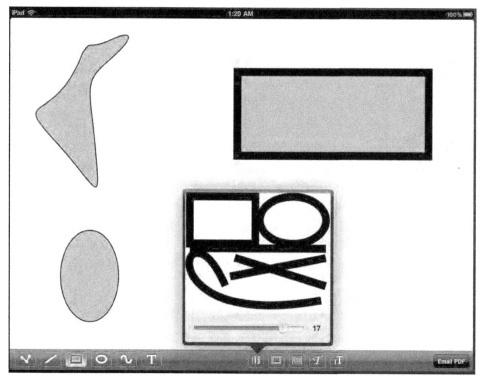

Figure 6–7. *Setting a stroke width*

Drag the slider back and forth, and the stroke width changes. As we discussed, there's no concept of an active selection in Dudel, so changing this affects only the stroke width of the next graphic you draw, leaving the existing graphics unchanged.

The Dual-Action Color Popover

We're down to just two popovers left to implement, and they're both actually the same. What we need is a simple color picker that lets the user set colors for either stroke or fill, depending on which button is clicked.

> **NOTE:** We wouldn't need to implement a color selector popover if iOS included some sort of color picker (along the lines of Mac OS X's NSColorPanel, for instance), but it currently does not.

Recall that our implementation of DudelViewController works by checking each dismissed popover by class to see which one it was. So, we'll implement the color selector GUI in one class, but use two subclasses to create the popovers, so that we can tell which is which when it's dismissed.

To keep things simple, we're just going to let the user pick from a simple grid that shows 12 colors, as shown in Figure 6–12. An additional view at the top of the GUI will show the currently selected color.

Figure 6–8. *Our simple color picker (I know you're probably seeing this in black and white, so please take my word for it when I tell you that those are colors.)*

As for the user interaction, it seems natural that this popover should have a "touch-and-dismiss" policy, unlike the stroke width and font size popovers, which hang around to let users move the slider multiple times until they got it just right. For the color selector, we'll let the users drag their finger around the grid, always displaying the latest color in the view at the top, and dismiss the popover as soon as they release their finger.

Creating a Simple Color Grid

Let's start by making a view class that just knows how to display a grid of colors, and respond to touch events by sending notifications containing the touched color. Later, our view controller class will register as an observer for those notifications. Create a new UIView subclass called ColorGrid, and put the following code in *ColorGrid.h*:

```
// ColorGrid.h
#import <UIKit/UIKit.h>
// notification names
#define ColorGridTouchedOrDragged @"ColorGridTouchedOrDragged"
#define ColorGridTouchEnded @"ColorGridTouchEnded"
// key into the notification's userInfo dictionary
#define ColorGridLatestTouchedColor @"ColorGridLatestTouchedColor"
@interface ColorGrid : UIView {
  NSArray *colors;
  NSUInteger columnCount;
  NSUInteger rowCount;
}
@property (retain, nonatomic) NSArray *colors;
@property (nonatomic) NSUInteger columnCount;
@property (nonatomic) NSUInteger rowCount;
@end
```

This interface shows all the elements we'll need in order to use this class: a set of properties for specifying the colors, as well as the number of columns and rows to display, all of which need to be set in order for the view to draw properly. Here, we also define a pair of NSString constants that interested parties (such as our controller class) will use to register themselves as NSNotification observers, and another string that's used as a key into the userInfo dictionary passed along with the notification for retrieving the chosen color. It's a good idea to define strings that will be used in multiple spots this way, instead of putting the literal strings, quotes and all, in your code. With the defined version, Xcode will help autocomplete as you type, and the compiler will complain if you misspell it.

Now for the implementation. Switch to *ColorGrid.m*, and start things off with the basics:

```
// ColorGrid.m
#import "ColorGrid.h"
@implementation ColorGrid
@synthesize colors, columnCount, rowCount;
- (void)dealloc {
  self.colors = nil;
  [super dealloc];
}
```

Next up is the drawRect: method. This method relies on columnCount and rowCount being set to a nonzero value before being drawn. Those values determine the layout of the grid as a whole. The UIColor objects stored in the colors array will be used to fill rectangles in the grid, row by row. If there aren't enough colors in the array to fill the grid, the rest of the "cells" will be filled with white.

```
- (void)drawRect:(CGRect)rect {
  CGRect b = self.bounds;
```

```
      CGContextRef myContext = UIGraphicsGetCurrentContext();
      CGFloat columnWidth = b.size.width / columnCount;
      CGFloat rowHeight = b.size.height / rowCount;
      for (NSUInteger rowIndex = 0; rowIndex < rowCount; rowIndex++) {
        for (NSUInteger columnIndex = 0; columnIndex < columnCount; columnIndex++) {
          NSUInteger colorIndex = rowIndex * columnCount + columnIndex;
          UIColor *color = [self.colors count] > colorIndex ?
                              [self.colors objectAtIndex:colorIndex] :
                              [UIColor whiteColor];
          CGRect r = CGRectMake(b.origin.x + columnIndex * columnWidth,
                                b.origin.y + rowIndex * rowHeight,
                                columnWidth, rowHeight);
          CGContextSetFillColorWithColor(myContext, color.CGColor);
          CGContextFillRect(myContext, r);
        }
      }
    }
```

We also need to be able to determine the color shown at any given point, for the touch
methods to be able to report with a notification. Rather than putting that directly into the
touch methods, we split it off into a separate colorAtPoint: method that each of them
can use. This is basically the inverse of what's going on in the innermost loop of the
drawRect: method.

```
- (UIColor *)colorAtPoint:(CGPoint)point {
    if (!CGRectContainsPoint(self.bounds, point)) return nil;

    CGRect b = self.bounds;
    CGFloat columnWidth = b.size.width / columnCount;
    CGFloat rowHeight = b.size.height / rowCount;
    NSUInteger rowIndex = point.y / rowHeight;
    NSUInteger columnIndex = point.x / columnWidth;
    NSUInteger colorIndex = rowIndex * columnCount + columnIndex;
    return [self.colors count] > colorIndex ?
            [self.colors objectAtIndex:colorIndex] :
            nil;
}
```

Finally, we get to the touch methods themselves. This class responds to both initial
touches and drags in the same way, so touchesMoved: just calls touchesBegan:.
However, touchesEnded: uses a different notification name, so we'll let it have its own
code.

```
- (void)touchesBegan:(NSSet *)touches withEvent:(UIEvent *)event {
    CGPoint location = [[touches anyObject] locationInView:self];
    UIColor *color = [self colorAtPoint:location];
    if (color) {
      NSDictionary *userDict = [NSDictionary dictionaryWithObject:color
                                          forKey:ColorGridLatestTouchedColor];
      [[NSNotificationCenter defaultCenter] postNotificationName:ColorGridTouchedOrDragged
                                          object:self userInfo:userDict];
    }
}
- (void)touchesMoved:(NSSet *)touches withEvent:(UIEvent *)event {
    [self touchesBegan:touches withEvent:event];
}
- (void)touchesEnded:(NSSet *)touches withEvent:(UIEvent *)event {
```

```
    CGPoint location = [[touches anyObject] locationInView:self];
    UIColor *color = [self colorAtPoint:location];
    if (color) {
      NSDictionary *userDict = [NSDictionary dictionaryWithObject:color
                                    forKey:ColorGridLatestTouchedColor];
      [[NSNotificationCenter defaultCenter] postNotificationName:ColorGridTouchEnded
                                    object:self userInfo:userDict];
    }
  }
}
@end
```

Hooking Up the Grid

Now that we have a view class ready to go, we can create a view controller that makes
use of it. Use the New File Assistant to create a new UIViewController subclass, making
it include the creation of an .xib file, but *not* making it a UITableViewController
subclass. Name it SelectColorController, and give it the following interface in
SelectColorController.h:

```
//  StrokeColorController.h
#import <UIKit/UIKit.h>
@class ColorGrid;
// a notification name
#define ColorSelectionDone @"ColorSelectionDone"
@interface SelectColorController : UIViewController {
  IBOutlet ColorGrid *colorGrid;
  IBOutlet UIView *selectedColorSwatch;
  UIColor *selectedColor;
  UIPopoverController *container;
}
@property (retain, nonatomic) ColorGrid *colorGrid;
@property (retain, nonatomic) UIColor *selectedColor;
@property (assign, nonatomic) UIPopoverController *container;
@end
```

The GUI for this class will contain a ColorGrid instance, as well as a simple UIView for
displaying the selected color. We make the colorGrid an accessible property so that our
main controller, DudelViewController, can set its properties (rowCount, columnCount, and
colors) when setting things up. This class also has properties for the currently selected
color and the UIPopoverController that displays it. And, like the ColorGrid class, it will
communicate "upstream" to the DudelViewController indirectly, through the use of a
notification, whose name is defined here.

Now open *SelectColorController.xib* in Interface Builder. Once again, the default view is
meant to be full-screen, so use the attribute inspector to turn off the Status Bar by
setting it to Unspecified, and then the size inspector to make it 320 by 320. Use the
Library to get instances of UIView and ColorGrid, and lay them out as shown in Figure
6–9.

Figure 6–9. *The basic layout of our color picker in Interface Builder*

The upper view there is the UIView, and the lower one is the ColorGrid. You don't need to get too picky about the sizes of these views, since ColorGrid will adjust to whatever you throw at it, but it's good to have the ColorGrid reasonably large and both views centered in the parent view. Connect the outlets from File's Owner to the colorGrid and selectedColorSwatch views. The GUI is complete! Now we just need to make it work.

Here's the code for *SelectColorController.m*:

```
//
//  StrokeColorController.m
#import "SelectColorController.h"
#import "ColorGrid.h"
@implementation SelectColorController
@synthesize colorGrid, selectedColor, container;
- (void)viewDidLoad {
  [super viewDidLoad];
  [[NSNotificationCenter defaultCenter] addObserver:self
    selector:@selector(colorGridTouchedOrDragged:)
    name:ColorGridTouchedOrDragged object:colorGrid];
  [[NSNotificationCenter defaultCenter] addObserver:self
    selector:@selector(colorGridTouchEnded:)
    name:ColorGridTouchEnded object:colorGrid];
  selectedColorSwatch.backgroundColor = self.selectedColor;
}
- (BOOL)shouldAutorotateToInterfaceOrientation:(UIInterfaceOrientation)orientation {
    // Overriden to allow any orientation.
    return YES;
}
- (void)viewDidUnload {
  [super viewDidUnload];
  [[NSNotificationCenter defaultCenter] removeObserver:self];
}
- (void)dealloc {
  [[NSNotificationCenter defaultCenter] removeObserver:self];
  self.colorGrid = nil;
```

```
    [super dealloc];
}
- (void)colorGridTouchedOrDragged:(NSNotification *)notification {
    NSDictionary *userDict = [notification userInfo];
    self.selectedColor = [userDict objectForKey:ColorGridLatestTouchedColor];
    selectedColorSwatch.backgroundColor = self.selectedColor;
}
- (void)colorGridTouchEnded:(NSNotification *)notification {
    NSDictionary *userDict = [notification userInfo];
    self.selectedColor = [userDict objectForKey:ColorGridLatestTouchedColor];
    selectedColorSwatch.backgroundColor = self.selectedColor;
    [[NSNotificationCenter defaultCenter] postNotificationName:ColorSelectionDone
      object:self];
}
@end
```

This should be pretty straightforward. We register methods to listen for activity from the ColorGrid, each of which grabs the latest touched color from the notification object. If the touch ended, we send out yet another notification, so that our main controller gets the message that a color has been set.

Serving Two Masters

Before we use this new controller from DudelViewController, we need to make two subclasses of the SelectColorController class, since DudelViewController uses the class of the currently active popover controller to determine exactly which controller it's dealing with.

> **NOTE:** Purists may object to the creation of subclasses that don't have any behavior or data of their own, but then again, purists object to a lot of things. Being reality-based, we'll do it this way, both because it's simple and because it lets DudelViewController deal with all the popovers as consistently as possible.

Use the New File Assistant to create a new class. The assistant doesn't know about the SelectColorController class, so we need to use NSObject as the superclass and change it later. Name the class StrokeColorController, and give its .h and .m files the following contents:

```
//  StrokeColorController.h
#import <Foundation/Foundation.h>
#import "SelectColorController.h"
@interface StrokeColorController : SelectColorController {}
@end

//  StrokeColorController.m
#import "StrokeColorController.h"
@implementation StrokeColorController
@end
```

Create another new class named FillColorController, and define it like this:

```
// FillColorController.h
#import "SelectColorController.h"
@interface FillColorController : SelectColorController {}
@end

// FillColorController.m
#import "FillColorController.h"
@implementation FillColorController
@end
```

Now let's add support for both of these to DudelViewController in one fell swoop. Open *DudelViewController.m*, and start off adding these includes:

```
#import "StrokeColorController.h"
#import "FillColorController.h"
#import "ColorGrid.h"
```

Next, let's look at the code that will launch each of the font selectors. The two action methods are very similar, so instead of repeating a lot of code, we put most of it into a separate method, shown here:

```
// both of the color popover action methods call this method.
- (void)doPopoverSelectColorController:(SelectColorController*)scc sender:(id)sender {
    [self setupNewPopoverControllerForViewController:scc];
    scc.container = self.currentPopover;
    self.currentPopover.popoverContentSize = scc.view.frame.size;

    // these have to be set after the view is already loaded (which happened
    // a couple of lines ago, thanks to scc.view...)
    scc.colorGrid.columnCount = 3;
    scc.colorGrid.rowCount = 4;
    scc.colorGrid.colors = [NSArray arrayWithObjects:
                            [UIColor redColor],
                            [UIColor greenColor],
                            [UIColor blueColor],
                            [UIColor cyanColor],
                            [UIColor yellowColor],
                            [UIColor magentaColor],
                            [UIColor orangeColor],
                            [UIColor purpleColor],
                            [UIColor brownColor],
                            [UIColor whiteColor],
                            [UIColor lightGrayColor],
                            [UIColor blackColor],
                            nil];
    [[NSNotificationCenter defaultCenter] addObserver:self
        selector:@selector(colorSelectionDone:) name:ColorSelectionDone object:scc];

    [self.currentPopover presentPopoverFromBarButtonItem:sender
        permittedArrowDirections:UIPopoverArrowDirectionAny animated:YES];
}
- (IBAction)popoverStrokeColor:(id)sender {
    StrokeColorController *scc = [[[StrokeColorController alloc]
        initWithNibName:@"SelectColorController" bundle:nil] autorelease];
    scc.selectedColor = self.strokeColor;
```

```
    [self doPopoverSelectColorController:scc sender:sender];
}
- (IBAction)popoverFillColor:(id)sender {
  FillColorController *fcc = [[[FillColorController alloc]
    initWithNibName:@"SelectColorController" bundle:nil] autorelease];
  fcc.selectedColor = self.fillColor;
  [self doPopoverSelectColorController:fcc sender:sender];
}
```

In each of those cases, our main controller is set up to listen for notifications from the color selector. Here's the method that will handle the notifications:

```
- (void)colorSelectionDone:(NSNotification *)notification {
  SelectColorController *object = [notification object];
  UIPopoverController *popoverController = object.container;
  [popoverController dismissPopoverAnimated:YES];
  [self handleDismissedPopoverController:popoverController];
}
```

Finally, we take care of the main popover dismissal handler. Add the bold lines to the following method, which will make us notice new values in the color selectors:

```
- (void)handleDismissedPopoverController:(UIPopoverController*)popoverController {
  if ([popoverController.contentViewController isMemberOfClass:
    [FontListController class]]) {
    // this is the font list, grab the new selection
    FontListController *flc = (FontListController *)
      popoverController.contentViewController;
    self.font = [UIFont fontWithName:flc.selectedFontName size:self.font.pointSize];
  } else if ([popoverController.contentViewController isMemberOfClass:
    [FontSizeController class]]) {
    FontSizeController *fsc = (FontSizeController *)
      popoverController.contentViewController;
    self.font = fsc.font;
  } else if ([popoverController.contentViewController isMemberOfClass:
    [StrokeWidthController class]]) {
    StrokeWidthController *swc = (StrokeWidthController *)
      popoverController.contentViewController;
    self.strokeWidth = swc.strokeWidth;
  } else if ([popoverController.contentViewController isMemberOfClass:
    [StrokeColorController class]]) {
    StrokeColorController *scc = (StrokeColorController *)
      popoverController.contentViewController;
    self.strokeColor = scc.selectedColor;
  } else if ([popoverController.contentViewController isMemberOfClass:
    [FillColorController class]]) {
    FillColorController *fcc = (FillColorController *)
      popoverController.contentViewController;
    self.fillColor = fcc.selectedColor;
  }
  self.currentPopover = nil;
}
```

You should now be able to build and run your app, and use the new color popovers to define stroke and fill colors for all of the tools.

With this functionality in place, we have all we need for a bare-bones vector-drawing app. No one's going to mistake this for Adobe Illustrator, but it's easy and functional enough for people to use for simple creations. Figure 6–10 shows an example of what you can create with Dudel.

Figure 6–10. *Drawing with Dudel (Dave Wooldridge's creation)*

Your Popover-Fu Is Strong

You've now seen a wide range of views presented as popovers. The examples in this chapter demonstrated some of the various ways you can deal with the popover interface, such as choosing whether to let the popover stick around while the user works with controls, and how to pass changes upstream using notifications. These techniques are already used by a wide variety of iPad apps. Adding them to your own apps will let your users access application features in ways that are similar to the menus, palettes, and inspectors of desktop applications, while still keeping your interface free from clutter.

With that, we wrap up the basic features of Dudel. We'll continue adding more to Dudel throughout the book, but now it's time to take a side trip and dig into the new possibilities for displaying video and using external screens. Chapter 7 covers video and display options for iPad apps.

Chapter 7

Video and Display Output

In older versions of iOS, displaying video was an all-or-nothing proposition. The `MPMoviePlayerController` included as part of the Media Player framework allowed you to display video that took over the whole screen, and that was it! There was no system-supported way to display video in any other way—for example, as a small video displayed within a web page.

Starting with iOS 3.2 for the iPad, the `MPMoviePlayerController` has changed a bit. Now, instead of taking over the screen, the default behavior is to display its video directly on the screen. In this chapter, you'll see how this is accomplished by creating an app that displays multiple videos on the screen simultaneously (with some limitations).

Also new in iOS 3.2 for the iPad is the ability for third-party developers to display content on an external screen connected through an adapter to the iPad's dock connector. While this sort of thing was possible in previous versions of iPhone OS, it required the use of private APIs, which meant that you couldn't actually ship software that made use of an external screen through the App Store. That privilege was exclusively Apple's! This has changed with iOS 3.2. In this chapter, you'll learn how to handle an external screen with ease.

Displaying Multiple Videos

Let's start by looking at how to display multiple videos on the screen using `MPMoviePlayerController`. If you haven't used this class in previous iPhone projects, you may not aware that it's not what you think of as a typical view controller in Cocoa Touch; in fact, it doesn't inherit from `UIViewController`. In MVC terms, it's a controller in the sense that it serves as an intermediary between a video file or stream (the model) and the on-screen view, but it doesn't fit into the UIKit scheme of shuffling view controllers around as users navigate the app. However, a new class included in iOS 3.2 fits that purpose perfectly—the similarly named `MPMoviePlayerViewController`.

The `MPMoviePlayerViewController` works just like any other `UIViewController` subclass. You create one (specifying its contents using the `initWithContentURL:` method), and push it onto a view controller navigation stack, just like any other view controller. This usage is so simple that we're not going to give it any more ink here. Instead, we'll focus on MPMoviePlayerController, and demonstrate how to display content from several of these controllers at once. We're going to create an app that shows a table view, with each row displaying a video.

Creating the Video App Project

In Xcode, create a new view-based application, targeted for iPad only, and name it VideoToy. This will create a few items, including the VideoToyAppDelegate and VideoAppViewController classes.

Before we start working on the code, take a few minutes to find some video clips that you can use in this project. Any sort of iPhone-friendly video will do nicely. If you don't already have some *.mp4* or *.m4u* files on your computer, you can find some on the Internet. An easy way is to browse the iTunes U section of iTunes and download videos from there. Then drag a few into your project.

Specifying Your Video Files

Now let's get started on the code. We're going to make a single change to *VideoAppDelegate.m* to specify the names of the video files we're using. We're passing this list along to the VideoAppViewController instance.

```
- (BOOL)application:(UIApplication *)application
  didFinishLaunchingWithOptions:(NSDictionary *)launchOptions {
  [window addSubview:viewController.view];
  [window makeKeyAndVisible];

  viewController.urlPaths = [NSMutableArray arrayWithObjects:
      [[NSBundle mainBundle] pathForResource:@"looking_for_my_leopard"
        ofType:@"mp4"],
      [[NSBundle mainBundle] pathForResource:@"knight_rider_season2intro"
        ofType:@"mp4"],
      [[NSBundle mainBundle] pathForResource:@"muppets" ofType:@"mp4"],
      [[NSBundle mainBundle] pathForResource:@"opengl" ofType:@"mp4"],
      nil];
  [viewController.tableView reloadData];
  return YES;
}
```

This code references a few properties that don't yet exist in VideoToyViewController, but don't worry. We're going to turn VideoToyViewController into a UITableViewController subclass that holds onto a list of video files to display.

The GUI will be created entirely from the table view delegate and dataSource methods, so we have no need for the *VideoToyViewController.xib* that was created along with the project. Delete *VideoToyViewController.xib* from the project. Then open *MainWindow.xib* so we can remove the reference it contains to that *.xib* file. Select the VideoToyViewController object, open the attribute inspector, and clear out the Nib Name field.

Next, make the following changes to *VideoToyViewController.h*:

```
// VideoToyViewController.h
#import <UIKit/UIKit.h>
#import <MediaPlayer/MediaPlayer.h>
@class VideoCell;
@interface VideoToyViewController : UITableViewController {
  NSMutableArray *urlPaths;
  IBOutlet VideoCell *videoCell;
}
@property (retain, nonatomic) NSMutableArray *urlPaths;
@end
```

Here, we change the superclass, declare the urlPaths property that we referenced earlier in the app delegate, and also lay the foundation for a more detailed part of the GUI by creating the videoCell instance variable. If you're wondering why we declared videoCell as an IBOutlet, when this class isn't loading its GUI from a *.xib* file, then good for you—you're really paying attention here! That will be explained in just a minute, so hang in there.

Switch over to *VideoToyViewController.m*, and add an import near the top:

```
// VideoToyViewController.m
#import "VideoCell.h"
```

Now add these methods to define the basic properties of the table view that will be displayed:

```
- (CGFloat)tableView:(UITableView *)tableView
  heightForRowAtIndexPath:(NSIndexPath *)indexPath {
  return [VideoCell rowHeight];
}
- (NSInteger)numberOfSectionsInTableView:(UITableView *)tableView {
  return 1;
}
- (NSInteger)tableView:(UITableView *)tableView
  numberOfRowsInSection:(NSInteger)section {
  return [urlPaths count];
}
```

Using the videoCell Outlet to Load the GUI

Now for the slightly trickier spot and the explanation for the existence of the videoCell outlet. The following shows a good way to load a table view's cell content from a *.nib* file, rather than defining your layout entirely in code.

```
- (UITableViewCell *)tableView:(UITableView *)tableView
  cellForRowAtIndexPath:(NSIndexPath *)indexPath {
  VideoCell *cell = (VideoCell *)[tableView
    dequeueReusableCellWithIdentifier:[VideoCell reuseIdentifier]];
  if (!cell) {
    [[NSBundle mainBundle] loadNibNamed:@"VideoCell" owner:self
      options:nil];
    cell = videoCell;
    cell.selectionStyle = UITableViewCellSelectionStyleNone;
```

```
      [videoCell autorelease];
      videoCell = nil;
    }
  cell.urlPath = [urlPaths objectAtIndex:indexPath.row];
  return cell;
}
```

The first line tries to find a cell to reuse, as usual. If it doesn't find one, then instead of programmatically creating a cell, we load one from a *.nib* file. The trick is that we load this file with self as the File's Owner, which will have the side effect of setting the videoCell outlet to point to whatever the File's Owner proxy in the *.xib* file has its videoCell outlet pointing to.

Remember to add a little cleanup for the new urlPaths property:

```
- (void)dealloc {
  self.urlPaths = nil;
  [super dealloc];
}
```

Now use the New File Assistant to make a new UITableViewCell subclass called VideoCell. Open its *.h* file, and add the bold lines shown here:

```
//  VideoCell.h
#import <UIKit/UIKit.h>
#import <MediaPlayer/MediaPlayer.h>
@interface VideoCell : UITableViewCell {
  IBOutlet UIView *movieViewContainer;
  IBOutlet UILabel *urlLabel;
  NSString *urlPath;
  MPMoviePlayerController *mpc;
}
@property (retain, nonatomic) NSString *urlPath;
@property (retain, nonatomic) MPMoviePlayerController *mpc;
+ (NSString *)reuseIdentifier;
+ (CGFloat)rowHeight;
@end
```

Switch to *VideoCell.m*, and remove the initWithStyle:reuseIdentifier: method, since we won't be needing it. Then make the rest of the file look like this:

```
//  VideoCell.m
#import "VideoCell.h"
@implementation VideoCell
@synthesize urlPath, mpc;
+ (NSString *)reuseIdentifier {
  return @"VideoCell";
}
+ (CGFloat)rowHeight {
  return 200;
}
- (void)setupMpc {
  if (mpc) {
    // we've already got one of these, time to get rid of it
    [mpc.view removeFromSuperview];
    self.mpc = nil;
```

```
  }
  if (urlPath) {
    NSURL *url = [NSURL fileURLWithPath:self.urlPath];
    self.mpc = [[[MPMoviePlayerController alloc] initWithContentURL:url]
      autorelease];
    mpc.shouldAutoplay = NO;
    mpc.view.frame = movieViewContainer.bounds;
    [movieViewContainer addSubview:mpc.view];
  }
}
- (void)setUrlPath:(NSString *)p {
  if (![p isEqual:urlPath]) {
    [urlPath autorelease];
    urlPath = [p retain];
    if (urlPath && !mpc) {
      [self setupMpc];
    }
    urlLabel.text = urlPath;
  }
}
- (void)awakeFromNib {
  if (urlPath && !mpc) {
    [self setupMpc];
  }
  urlLabel.text = urlPath;
}
- (void)dealloc {
  self.urlPath = nil;
  self.mpc = nil;
  [super dealloc];
}
- (void)setSelected:(BOOL)selected animated:(BOOL)animated {
  [super setSelected:selected animated:animated];
  // Configure the view for the selected state
  [mpc play];
}
@end
```

In this code, we're referring to a UILabel and an MPMoviePlayerController within our
GUI, as well as a plain-old UIView. The MPMoviePlayerController that we create
exposes a property called view, which lets us access the view object it uses to render
the video. We don't know the class of this view—it's essentially a private class that the
Media Player framework doesn't expose to us. When the time comes, after the .nib file
has loaded and the urlPath has been set, we create an MPMoviePlayerController, grab
its view, and put it into our view hierarchy by making it a child of the empty UIView.

Creating the VideoCell User Interface

Now use the New File Assistant to create a new empty GUI file called VideoCell.xib.
Open the new file in Interface Builder, add a VideoCell instance from the Library, and
resize it to 768 by 200. Use the attribute inspector to set the identifier to VideoCell, just
as we did in code. Add a label on the left to display a URL, and use the attribute

inspector to configure it for 0 lines and character wrap. Also add a plain-old UIView on the right. Figure 7–1 shows the basic layout.

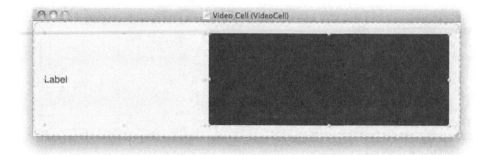

Figure 7–1. *Not exactly a polished user interface, but it's a start.*

Connect the outlets from VideoCell to the appropriate objects. Use the size inspector to configure the autosizing attribute of each of them so that they'll expand horizontally, while still remaining tied to their respective window edges when the cell is resized (such as when the iPad rotates). Finally, use the identity inspector to make File's Owner a VideoToyViewController, and connect its videoCell outlet to the one you just created.

Running the Video App

Now you should be able to build and run the app, and see the vertical list of video views. They will all be empty rectangles, except for the last one displayed, which will probably start playing on its own. Touching any other cell in the table view will activate the movie view in that row and start playing it. As you activate each video by tapping its row, you get a full set of video controls, including a button that switches to full-screen display.

You will also notice one of the main limitations of using multiple video views: only one of them can play at a time! Starting playback on an MPMoviePlayerController will simultaneously pause playback on any others that are running. Figure 7–2 shows the display after loading four videos and playing each of them a bit.

You now have the beginnings of a sort of video browser. This could be useful in a number of applications, letting you preview several videos in a list. That's fine, but what if you also wanted to display the video on an external screen? You'll be able to do that with a few adjustments, as described in the next section.

/var/mobile/Applications/38520CF0-CC51-410B-BCE6-ED931E09CFCC/VideoToy.app/looking_for_my_leopard.mp4

/var/mobile/Applications/38520CF0-CC51-410B-BCE6-ED931E09CFCC/VideoToy.app/knight_rider_season2intro.mp4

/var/mobile/Applications/38520CF0-CC51-410B-BCE6-ED931E09CFCC/VideoToy.app/muppets.mp4

/var/mobile/Applications/38520CF0-CC51-410B-BCE6-ED931E09CFCC/VideoToy.app/opengl.mp4

Figure 7–2. *Displaying a few of the videos floating around my hard drive.*

Outputting to an External Screen

The UIScreen class has been a part of iOS since the beginning. Its mainScreen class method gives you the screen of the device you're running on, which you can query for geometry information such as its bounds or frame.

In iOS 3.2, UIScreen gets a new class method, screens, which returns an array of all currently connected screens, including the iPad's own screen. This is the key to accessing an attached external screen. If it contains more than one item, all but the first are external screens. Also new in iOS 3.2 is the ability to ask any screen which resolutions it supports via the availableModes method, along with the currentMode method for determining and setting which resolution is in use.

You can move any of your content to an external screen simply by creating a new UIWindow object, adding your views to it, and setting its screen property to point to the external screen.

Extending the Video App to Handle an External Screen

When using an external screen, you need to consider how to properly handle when the user plugs in or unplugs a screen. To help with this, UIScreen defines a few notifications that let you know when a screen is connected or disconnected, so you can act accordingly.

In this section, we'll extend our VideoToy project so that if a screen is connected, the video you choose will play on it; if you disconnect the screen, the video will continue playing on the device. This will require a bit of extra bookkeeping on our part—we'll need to keep track of the currently selected video and its corresponding views, so that we can switch things around as the external screen comes and goes.

Start off by editing *VideoCell.h*, adding a few lines to define a delegate, a protocol the delegate should implement, and a property declaration for movieViewContainer so that we can reach it from other classes.

```
// VideoCell.h
#import <UIKit/UIKit.h>
#import <MediaPlayer/MediaPlayer.h>
@interface VideoCell : UITableViewCell {
  IBOutlet UIView *movieViewContainer;
  IBOutlet UILabel *urlLabel;
  NSString *urlPath;
  MPMoviePlayerController *mpc;
  id delegate;
}
@property (retain, nonatomic) UIView *movieViewContainer;
@property (retain, nonatomic) NSString *urlPath;
@property (retain, nonatomic) MPMoviePlayerController *mpc;
@property (assign, nonatomic) id delegate;
+ (NSString *)reuseIdentifier;
+ (CGFloat)rowHeight;
@end
@protocol VideoCellDelegate
- (void)videoCellStartedPlaying:(VideoCell *)cell;
@end
```

Now switch to *VideoCell.m*, and add synthesized accessors for movieViewContainer and delegate.

```
@synthesize urlPath, mpc, movieViewContainer, delegate;
```

Then free up one additional resource in dealloc:

```
- (void)dealloc {
  self.urlPath = nil;
  self.mpc = nil;
  self.movieViewContainer = nil;
  [super dealloc];
}
```

Next, implement the following change, to let the delegate know when the video has been selected. This way, the view can be shifted to the external screen (if it's connected).

```
- (void)setSelected:(BOOL)selected animated:(BOOL)animated {
  [super setSelected:selected animated:animated];
  if ([delegate respondsToSelector:@selector(videoCellStartedPlaying:)]) {
    [delegate videoCellStartedPlaying:self];
  }
  // Configure the view for the selected state
  [mpc play];
}
```

We really didn't do too much here. The most interesting part—handling a user selection that should put the video on the externalScreen—has been foisted off on a vaguely defined delegate object. Let's make that a bit more concrete, by having VideoToyViewController act as the delegate for VideoCell. This controller will now keep track of the selected VideoCell instance, as well as a UIWindow assigned to an external screen, if there is one.

Open *VideoToyViewController.h*, and make the changes shown here:

```
//  VideoToyViewController.h
#import <UIKit/UIKit.h>
#import <MediaPlayer/MediaPlayer.h>
@class VideoCell;
@interface VideoToyViewController : UITableViewController {
  NSMutableArray *urlPaths;
  IBOutlet VideoCell *videoCell;
  UIWindow *externalWindow;
  VideoCell *selectedCell;
}
@property (retain, nonatomic) NSMutableArray *urlPaths;
@property (retain, nonatomic) UIWindow *externalWindow;
@property (retain, nonatomic) VideoCell *selectedCell;
@end
```

Now it's time for *VideoToyViewController.m*, which is where the real work of managing the external screen happens. Synthesize the new properties, like this:

```
@synthesize urlPaths, externalWindow, selectedCell;
```

And make sure that resources are properly freed:

```
- (void)dealloc {
  self.urlPaths = nil;
  self.externalWindow = nil;
  self.selectedCell = nil;
  [super dealloc];
}
```

Next, move on to the viewDidLoad method. Here, we're going to first call the updateExternalWindow method (which we'll define in just a moment). We'll also set up notifications whenever an external screen is connected or disconnected. Both of these events will also call the updateExternalWindow method.

```
- (void)viewDidLoad {
  [super viewDidLoad];
  [self updateExternalWindow];
  [[NSNotificationCenter defaultCenter] addObserver:self
    selector:@selector(updateExternalWindow)
```

```
      name:UIScreenDidConnectNotification
      object:nil];
  [[NSNotificationCenter defaultCenter] addObserver:self
      selector:@selector(updateExternalWindow)
      name:UIScreenDidDisconnectNotification
      object:nil];
}
```

And now for the updateExternalWindow method itself. As you just saw, this method is
called when our view is loaded, as well as every time the external screen is connected or
disconnected. It's fairly complicated, since it is designed to handle the variety of
situations it may encounter and do the right thing. The comments in the code provide
more details.

```
- (void)updateExternalWindow {
  if ([[UIScreen screens] count] > 1) {
    //
    // An external screen is connected. Find the screen, put a
    // UIWindow on it.
    //
    UIScreen *externalScreen = [[UIScreen screens] lastObject];
    // Screen modes are sorted in order of increasing resolution.
    // Let's take the highest.
    UIScreenMode *highestScreenMode = [[externalScreen availableModes]
      lastObject];
    CGRect externalWindowFrame = CGRectMake(0, 0,
      [highestScreenMode size].width, [highestScreenMode size].height);
    self.externalWindow = [[[UIWindow alloc] initWithFrame:
      externalWindowFrame] autorelease];
    externalWindow.screen = externalScreen;
    [externalWindow.screen setCurrentMode:highestScreenMode];
    [externalWindow makeKeyAndVisible];
    if (selectedCell) {
      // A cell is selected. Move its view to the external window.
      [externalWindow addSubview:selectedCell.mpc.view];
      selectedCell.mpc.view.frame = externalWindow.bounds;
    }
  } else if ([[UIScreen screens] count] == 1) {
    //
    // No external screen is connected. Let's make sure we have no
    // dangling references
    // to anything off the main screen.
    //
    if ([[externalWindow subviews] count] > 0) {
      // externalWindow used to be attached to a screen which is no
      // longer there! Move its view back to where it came from.
      UIView *v = [[externalWindow subviews] lastObject];
      v.frame = selectedCell.movieViewContainer.bounds;
      [selectedCell.movieViewContainer addSubview:v];
    }
    self.externalWindow.screen = nil;
    self.externalWindow = nil;
  }
}
```

NOTE: The updateExternalWindow method could have been split into three methods: one for each of the notifications, and one for after the nib file loaded. In fact, the first version I wrote did just that. But I noticed there was some functional overlap, so I refactored a bit. To me, it seems that compressing it into one method brings it together a bit better.

The next thing to tackle is the creation of the VideoCell instances. Each needs to be told who its delegate is. Find the relevant section in tableView:cellForRowAtIndexPath:, and add the bold line shown here:

```
[[NSBundle mainBundle] loadNibNamed:@"VideoCell" owner:self
  options:nil];
cell = videoCell;
cell.selectionStyle = UITableViewCellSelectionStyleNone;
cell.delegate = self;
```

Implementing the VideoCell Delegate Method

Finally, let's implement the delegate method itself. As you may recall, this method is called whenever the user selects a VideoCell in the GUI. Here, we need to check whether an external screen is connected and whether another video is currently running. Yes, this method is even more complicated than the updateExternalWindow method, but it has a lot to do. Again, the code comments provide more explanation.

```
- (void)videoCellStartedPlaying:(VideoCell *)cell {
  if (selectedCell != cell) { // Skip everything if it's the same cell.
    if ([[UIScreen screens] count] > 1) {
      // Switching external from one video (or blank) to another
      UIScreen *externalScreen = [[UIScreen screens] lastObject];
      UIScreenMode *highestScreenMode = [[externalScreen availableModes]
        lastObject];
      CGRect externalWindowFrame = CGRectMake(0, 0,
        [highestScreenMode size].width, [highestScreenMode size].height);
      if ([[externalWindow subviews] count] > 0) {
        // There's already a movie there. Put its view back in the cell
        // it came from.
        UIView *v = [[externalWindow subviews] lastObject];
        v.frame = selectedCell.movieViewContainer.bounds;
        [selectedCell.movieViewContainer addSubview:v];
      }
      // We're done with the old movie and cell.
      self.selectedCell = cell;
      // Get rid of the old window and screens; create new ones.
      self.externalWindow = [[[UIWindow alloc] initWithFrame:
        externalWindowFrame] autorelease];
      externalWindow.screen = externalScreen;
      [externalWindow.screen setCurrentMode:highestScreenMode];
      [externalWindow makeKeyAndVisible];
      if (selectedCell) {
        // Move the selected cell's movie view to the external screen.
```

```
            [externalWindow addSubview:selectedCell.mpc.view];
            selectedCell.mpc.view.frame = externalWindow.bounds;
        }
    } else if ([[UIScreen screens] count] == 1) {
        // No external screen is connected.
        if ([[externalWindow subviews] count] > 0) {
            // We seem to have an old external window hanging around. Move
            // its view back to the cell it came from.
            UIView *v = [[externalWindow subviews] lastObject];
            v.frame = selectedCell.movieViewContainer.bounds;
            [selectedCell.movieViewContainer addSubview:v];
        }
        self.externalWindow.screen = nil;
        self.externalWindow = nil;
        // Keep track of the selected cell.
        self.selectedCell = cell;
    }
  }
}
```

Testing the External Screen Functionality

Now build and run the app, and then unplug your iPad from your computer. This will probably crash the app, but that's OK.

Start up the app again directly on the iPad. Now whip out your trusty iPad-VGA adapter, find a convenient monitor with a VGA input, and plug it in. If you do that while a video is playing, you'll see that the video jumps to the external monitor. Otherwise, start playing a video, and you'll see it appear there.

The code we wrote for this functionality is quite robust. You should be able to unplug and reattach the screen during playback, before starting playback, while switching songs, before launching the app, and so on. You'll find that "it just works."

Display Solutions

The app we've built in this chapter is not meant as any sort of commercial product. We've kept it bare-bones, just to focus on the new ways of dealing with video playback and with the new facility for putting views onto an external display. Both of these areas are pretty easy to implement. The most complicated thing we needed to do was to make sure our app keeps informed about external screen connections and disconnections, and behaves appropriately.

Now it's up to you to determine if any of your iPad apps could make use of video playback and/or an external screen, and apply what you've learned here to your own projects.

In the meantime, continue on to Chapter 8 to learn how to use the UIKit's new split view to let your iPad apps display both content and navigation at the same time.

Split Views and Modal Modes

With the iPhone's tiny screen, it's natural to build interfaces that focus on one small portion of your app at a time. Cocoa Touch includes specialized `UIViewController` subclasses to facilitate this, letting you organize different views into tabs or navigable trees. On the iPad, however, we have a whole lot more space, so it makes sense to make better use of it!

In this chapter, you'll learn about the `UISplitViewController`, which lets you move some of your application's navigation structure into a view that appears to the left of your main content or in a floating popover accessible via a button in a toolbar.

We'll also take a look at the new types of modal displays that can be used on the iPad, which give you added control over the way modal interactions are displayed and handled. To demonstrate these techniques, we'll continue to improve our Dudel app.

The Split View Concept

Up to this point, Dudel has been a fun toy, but it has at least one quite severe limitation: Apart from sending your drawing as e-mail, you have no way of saving what you've drawn. As soon as you quit the app, your work is gone! That's clearly not the way any iPhone or iPad app should work, so we're going to remedy that, and give the user a way to save any number of Dudel documents. We'll use a `UISplitViewController` to help us out here, so we can display an additional view controller that shows a list of all relevant files, letting the user switch between them easily.

The `UISplitViewController`, like the `UINavigationController` and `UITabBarController`, serves an organizational function. Rather than displaying any content on its own, it shows the view for an additional controller next to the main controller view in landscape mode, as shown in Figure 8–1.

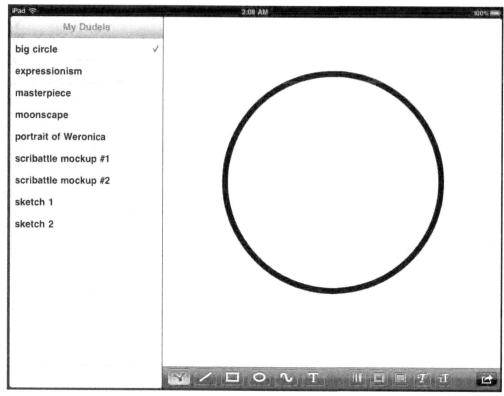

Figure 8–1. *Some inspiring Dudel art. Notice the list of available Dudel files on the left.*

NOTE: The use of the `UISplitViewController`, in combination with a toolbar at the bottom of the main view, is somewhat unorthodox. The `UISplitViewController` always creates the left-side view with a title row at the top ("My Dudels" here), and Apple's recommendation when using `UISplitViewController` is to put the main view's toolbar (if any) at the top as well. I didn't do this for Dudel, and it does give the screen a slightly lopsided appearance. But I think this adds character! Of course, you're free to move the main view's toolbar to the top if you wish, to bring it more in line with what Apple recommends. And when you use a `UISplitViewController` in your own apps, you should probably put your main view's toolbar at the top, unless you have a good reason not to (a better reason than my claims of adding character!).If you rotate the device to portrait mode, something interesting happens. The `UISplitViewController` switches gears, and no longer shows a list of files on the left. Instead, it gives a `UIBarButtonItem` to its delegate (a view controller of our own), which can then add it to a toolbar. That button item, when touched, brings up the same view that was shown on the left side in landscape mode, this time displayed using a `UIPopoverController`, as shown in Figure 8–2.

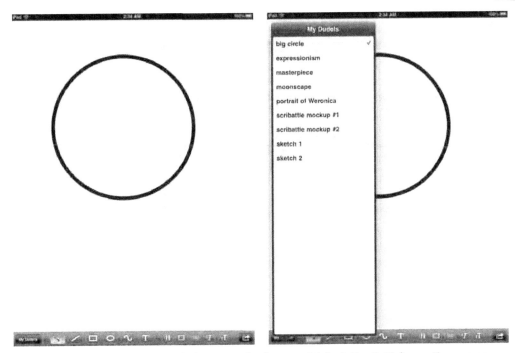

Figure 8–2. *In portrait mode, the file list is shown only when you click the button that brings up the popover.*

Unlike the popovers we set up in Chapter 6, this one will require no configuration on our part, since the UISplitViewController sets it up for us. However, we will still be required to dismiss the popover after the user makes a selection.

You might also notice in Figures 8-1 and 8-2 that the Email PDF button at the lower right has been swapped out for a generic action icon button. This will bring up a menu containing a handful of operations such as creating, renaming, and deleting files, which set up in this chapter.

The Basics of Saving and Loading

Before we can start thinking about showing a list of files, we need to add support for reading and writing files in the first place! Fortunately, the NSCoding protocol included in Cocoa Touch provides a solution that is easy to implement and perfectly adequate for our purposes.

The idea behind NSCoding is to add a couple of methods to each class that represents an object that needs to be saved: one method to save each of an object's instance variables to an archive, and another to populate an object's instance variables using values retrieved from an archive. When it's time to save, you just tell the root or top-level object to archive itself, and then when you want to load, you do the inverse. In our case, the top-level object is the NSArray containing the list of Drawable items. NSArray already implements the NSCoding protocol, but we need to do the same for our Drawable classes.

Confused? Let's start looking at some code that should clear this up.

Make a fresh copy of your Dudel project directory for this chapter's work, and open the Xcode project inside the new directory. Next, add the following lines to *PathDrawingInfo.m*:

```
- (void)encodeWithCoder:(NSCoder *)encoder {
    [encoder encodeObject:self.path forKey:@"path"];
    [encoder encodeObject:self.fillColor forKey:@"fillColor"];
    [encoder encodeObject:self.strokeColor forKey:@"strokeColor"];
}

- (id)initWithCoder:(NSCoder *)decoder {
    if ((self = [self init])) {
        self.path = [decoder decodeObjectForKey:@"path"];
        self.fillColor = [decoder decodeObjectForKey:@"fillColor"];
        self.strokeColor = [decoder decodeObjectForKey:@"strokeColor"];
    }
    return self;
}
```

Then add the following to *TextDrawingInfo.m*:

```
- (void)encodeWithCoder:(NSCoder *)encoder {
    [encoder encodeObject:self.path forKey:@"path"];
    [encoder encodeObject:self.strokeColor forKey:@"strokeColor"];
    [encoder encodeObject:self.font forKey:@"font"];
    [encoder encodeObject:self.text forKey:@"text"];
}

- (id)initWithCoder:(NSCoder *)decoder {
    if ((self = [self init])) {
        self.path = [decoder decodeObjectForKey:@"path"];
        self.strokeColor = [decoder decodeObjectForKey:@"strokeColor"];
        self.font = [decoder decodeObjectForKey:@"font"];
        self.text = [decoder decodeObjectForKey:@"text"];
    }
    return self;
}
```

Each of those methods receives an NSCoder object as an argument, which is primed to either receive values from our object or provide values for creating a new object, depending on which method we're talking about. All you do is set or retrieve values for all your instance variables, in a style similar to using an NSDictionary. That's all we need to do in the model classes, so move on to *DudelViewController.m*, where we'll add the machinery that starts these operations.

We'll start off by doing something quite simple. We'll add code that will make Dudel save the current state of the document it's working on when the user quits the app, and then reload that same document state when the app launches. For now, we'll just use a single file named *Untitled.dudeldoc* to save the user's work. Later in this chapter, we'll extend this to let the users name their own files.

Begin by adding the following utility method to the DudelViewController class. This method will save the current document (which is, in our running app, simply the contents of the DudelView's drawables array) to the specified filename, and return a Boolean value indicating whether or not the save was successful. Add a method declaration to the .h file, and the implementation itself to the .m file.

```
// DudelViewController.h
- (BOOL)saveCurrentToFile:(NSString *)filename;
```

```
// DudelViewController.m
- (BOOL)saveCurrentToFile:(NSString *)filename {
  return [NSKeyedArchiver archiveRootObject:dudelView.drawables toFile:filename];
}
```

Next, add the following method, which will do the inverse, attempting to read some object data from the specified file:

```
// DudelViewController.h
- (BOOL)loadFromFile:(NSString *)filename;
```

```
// DudelViewController.m
- (BOOL)loadFromFile:(NSString *)filename {
  id root = [NSKeyedUnarchiver unarchiveObjectWithFile:filename];
  if (root) {
    dudelView.drawables = root;
  }
  [dudelView setNeedsDisplay];
  return (root != nil);
}
```

The NSKeyedArchiver and NSKeyedUnarchiver classes used in these methods are both subclasses of NSCoder, the class that we treated somewhat like a dictionary in those earlier methods. These classes know how to open a file, and either write or read its contents (depending on which class and which method you're using). They save an existing object graph by traversing all its relationships to other objects, or create a new object graph from the data in the file.

Next, let's implement the code that will actually call these utility methods, inside the existing viewDidLoad method. The first new section comes up with a fully qualified file path, including a path to our app's documents directory, where our *Untitled.dudeldoc* file will reside, and calls the loadFromFile: method. The final section sets up this class as an observer of UIApplicationWillTerminateNotification, so that we can intervene when the app is about to exit.

```
// Implement viewDidLoad to do additional setup after loading the view, typically from a
nib.
- (void)viewDidLoad {
  [super viewDidLoad];
  self.currentTool = [PencilTool sharedPencilTool];
      [dotButton setImage:[UIImage imageNamed:@"button_cdots_selected.png"]];
  self.fillColor = [UIColor colorWithWhite:0.0 alpha:0.25];
  self.strokeColor = [UIColor blackColor];
  self.font = [UIFont systemFontOfSize:12.0];
  self.strokeWidth = 2.0;
```

```
// reload default document
NSArray *dirs = NSSearchPathForDirectoriesInDomains(NSDocumentDirectory,
    NSUserDomainMask, YES);
NSString *filename = [[dirs objectAtIndex:0]
    stringByAppendingPathComponent:@"Untitled.dudeldoc"];
[self loadFromFile:filename];

[[NSNotificationCenter defaultCenter] addObserver:self
    selector:@selector(applicationWillTerminate:)
    name:UIApplicationWillTerminateNotification
    object:[UIApplication sharedApplication]];
}
```

Now for the method that's actually triggered when the app is exiting. This method does the same work to determine the filename, and calls saveCurrentToFile: to ensure that the user's work isn't lost.

```
- (void)applicationWillTerminate:(NSNotification *)n {
  NSArray *dirs = NSSearchPathForDirectoriesInDomains(NSDocumentDirectory,
      NSUserDomainMask, YES);
  NSString *filename = [[dirs objectAtIndex:0]
      stringByAppendingPathComponent:@"Untitled.dudeldoc"];
  [self saveCurrentToFile:filename];
}
```

Note that the repetitive file-path creation is only temporary. A little later on, when we're ready to start thinking about handling multiple document files, we'll create a new class that will take care of the paths for us.

Now compile and run your app. The first time you run it, you won't notice anything different. You'll get a blank screen, where you can go ahead and doodle something. The fun part comes when you quit the app and then restart it. You'll find that your drawing is intact! This small change leads to a huge difference in how users perceive your app, since they're able to leave their work and come back to it at any time, in a seamless manner.

Document Management

The changes we made in the previous section gave us the basics for saving and loading a single file, but we'll need more than that! The iOS doesn't have anything like the Finder, so the only access our users will have to the drawings they make is what we provide for them in our app. That means we should offer at least the following capabilities:

- See a list of all Dudel documents
- Create a new document
- Rename a document
- Delete a document
- Keep track of which document was last used

Rather than putting the code for all that into one of our existing controller classes, we'll make a new class to manage the Dudel documents for us. This class will provide a single shared instance for all our other classes to use, and anyone who needs to access documents in any way will go through that shared instance.

Listing Files

Make a new class (a direct subclass of NSObject) and name it FileList. Here's the interface for *FileList.h*, which includes a notification name used to tell interested parties that the list of files has changed, properties for reading the list of all available documents and accessing the current document, and methods to do the other document-management operations:

```
// FileList.h

#import <Foundation/Foundation.h>

// notification name
#define FileListChanged @"FileListChanged"

@interface FileList : NSObject {
  NSMutableArray *allFiles;
  NSString *currentFile;
}

@property (nonatomic, readonly) NSArray *allFiles;
@property (nonatomic, copy) NSString *currentFile;

+ (FileList *)sharedFileList;

- (void)deleteCurrentFile;
- (void)renameFile:(NSString *)oldFilename to:(NSString *)newFilename;
- (void)renameCurrentFile:(NSString *)newFilename;
- (NSString *)createAndSelectNewUntitled;

@end
```

As for the implementation, FileList uses NSFileManager to do file operations, and NSUserDefaults to keep track of the current file. This is all fairly standard Objective-C activity.

```
// FileList.m
#import "FileList.h"
#import "SynthesizeSingleton.h"

// key for storing current filename in user defaults
#define DEFAULT_FILENAME_KEY @"defaultFilenameKey"

@implementation FileList
@synthesize allFiles;
@synthesize currentFile;

SYNTHESIZE_SINGLETON_FOR_CLASS(FileList)
```

```
- init {
  if (self = [super init]) {
    NSArray *dirs = NSSearchPathForDirectoriesInDomains(NSDocumentDirectory,
      NSUserDomainMask, YES);
    NSString *dirPath = [dirs objectAtIndex:0];
    NSArray *files = [[NSFileManager defaultManager] contentsOfDirectoryAtPath:dirPath
      error:NULL];
    NSArray *sortedFiles = [[files pathsMatchingExtensions:[NSArray
      arrayWithObject:@"dudeldoc"]] sortedArrayUsingSelector:@selector(compare:)];
    allFiles = [[NSMutableArray array] retain];
    // the filenames returned by pathsMatchingExtensions: don't include the whole
    // file path, so we add it to each file here.
    for (NSString *file in sortedFiles) {
      [allFiles addObject:[dirPath stringByAppendingPathComponent:file]];
    }
    currentFile = [[[NSUserDefaults standardUserDefaults]
      stringForKey:DEFAULT_FILENAME_KEY] retain];
    if ([allFiles count]==0) {
      // there are no documents, make one!
      [self createAndSelectNewUntitled];
    } else if (![allFiles containsObject:currentFile]) {
      // user defaults are suggesting a file that doesn't exist in our documents
      // directory, so just use the first file in the list.
      self.currentFile = [allFiles objectAtIndex:0];
    }
  }
  return self;
}
- (void)setCurrentFile:(NSString *)filename {
  if (![currentFile isEqual:filename]) {
    [currentFile release];
    currentFile = [filename copy];
    [[NSUserDefaults standardUserDefaults] setObject:currentFile
      forKey:DEFAULT_FILENAME_KEY];
    [[NSNotificationCenter defaultCenter] postNotificationName:FileListChanged
      object:self];
  }
}
- (void)deleteCurrentFile {
  if (self.currentFile) {
    NSUInteger filenameIndex = [self.allFiles indexOfObject:self.currentFile];
    NSError *error = nil;
    BOOL result = [[NSFileManager defaultManager] removeItemAtPath:self.currentFile
      error:&error];

    if (filenameIndex != NSNotFound) {
      [allFiles removeObjectAtIndex:filenameIndex];
      // now figure out which file to make current
      if ([self.allFiles count]==0) {
        [self createAndSelectNewUntitled];
      } else {
        if ([self.allFiles count]==filenameIndex) {
          filenameIndex--;
        }
        self.currentFile = [self.allFiles objectAtIndex:filenameIndex];
      }
    }
```

```
  }
  [[NSNotificationCenter defaultCenter] postNotificationName:FileListChanged
    object:self];
  }
}
- (void)renameFile:(NSString *)oldFilename to:(NSString *)newFilename {
  [[NSFileManager defaultManager] moveItemAtPath:oldFilename toPath:newFilename
    error:NULL];
  if ([self.currentFile isEqual:oldFilename]) {
    self.currentFile = newFilename;
  }
  int nameIndex = [self.allFiles indexOfObject:oldFilename];
  if (nameIndex != NSNotFound) {
    [allFiles replaceObjectAtIndex:nameIndex withObject:newFilename];
  }
  [[NSNotificationCenter defaultCenter] postNotificationName:FileListChanged
    object:self];
}
- (void)renameCurrentFile:(NSString *)newFilename {
  [self renameFile:self.currentFile to:newFilename];
}
- (NSString *)createAndSelectNewUntitled {
  NSString *defaultFilename = [NSString stringWithFormat:@"Dudel %@.dudeldoc",
    [NSDate date]];
  NSArray *dirs = NSSearchPathForDirectoriesInDomains(NSDocumentDirectory,
    NSUserDomainMask, YES);
  NSString *filename = [[dirs objectAtIndex:0] stringByAppendingPathComponent:
    defaultFilename];
  [[NSFileManager defaultManager] createFileAtPath:filename contents:nil
    attributes:nil];
  [allFiles addObject:filename];
    [allFiles sortUsingSelector:@selector(compare:)];
  self.currentFile = filename;
  [[NSNotificationCenter defaultCenter] postNotificationName:FileListChanged
    object:self];
  return self.currentFile;
}
@end
```

Adding a File List Controller

The FileList class will be used by both DudelViewController and our application
delegate, as well as one other class we haven't yet created: FileListViewController,
which will display a list of all the files and let the user select a file to change the current
selection. Create a new UIViewController subclass, and click the check boxes to make
it iPad-ready and a subclass of UITableViewController (but no .xib file). Then name it
FileListViewController. This is going to be a quite standard controller for a table view,
using FileList to see what it should be displaying. Here's the code for both the .h and
.m files (by now, the structure of a table view controller should look familiar to you):

```
// FileListController.h
#import <UIKit/UIKit.h>

// notification name
#define FileListControllerSelectedFile @"FileListControllerSelectedFile"
```

```objc
#define FileListControllerFilename @"FileListControllerFilename"

@interface FileListViewController : UITableViewController {
  NSString *currentDocumentFilename;
  NSArray *documents;
}
@property (nonatomic, copy) NSString *currentDocumentFilename;
@property (nonatomic, retain) NSArray *documents;
@end


// FileListController.m
#import "FileListViewController.h"
#import "FileList.h"

@implementation FileListViewController
@synthesize currentDocumentFilename, documents;
- (void)reloadData {
  self.currentDocumentFilename = [FileList sharedFileList].currentFile;
  self.documents = [FileList sharedFileList].allFiles;
  [self.tableView reloadData];
}
- (void)fileListChanged:(NSNotification *)n {
  [self reloadData];
}
- (void)viewDidLoad {
  [super viewDidLoad];
  [[NSNotificationCenter defaultCenter] addObserver:self
    selector:@selector(fileListChanged:) name:FileListChanged
    object:[FileList sharedFileList]];
}
- (void)viewWillAppear:(BOOL)animated {
  [super viewWillAppear:animated];
  [self reloadData];
}
- (BOOL)shouldAutorotateToInterfaceOrientation:(UIInterfaceOrientation)orientation {
  return YES;
}
- (NSInteger)numberOfSectionsInTableView:(UITableView *)tableView {
  return 1;
}
- (NSInteger)tableView:(UITableView *)tableView numberOfRowsInSection:(NSInteger)s {
  return [self.documents count];
}
- (UITableViewCell *)tableView:(UITableView *)tableView
  cellForRowAtIndexPath:(NSIndexPath *)indexPath {
  static NSString *CellIdentifier = @"Cell";
  UITableViewCell *cell = [tableView dequeueReusableCellWithIdentifier:
    CellIdentifier];
  if (cell == nil) {
    cell = [[[UITableViewCell alloc] initWithStyle:UITableViewCellStyleDefault
      reuseIdentifier:CellIdentifier] autorelease];
  }
  NSString *file = [self.documents objectAtIndex:indexPath.row];
  cell.textLabel.text = [[file lastPathComponent] stringByDeletingPathExtension];
  if ([file isEqual:self.currentDocumentFilename]) {
    cell.accessoryType = UITableViewCellAccessoryCheckmark;
  } else {
```

```
        cell.accessoryType = UITableViewCellAccessoryNone;
    }
    return cell;
}
- (void)tableView:(UITableView *)tv didSelectRowAtIndexPath:(NSIndexPath *)indexPath {
    NSDictionary *userInfo = [NSDictionary dictionaryWithObject:[documents
        objectAtIndex:indexPath.row] forKey:FileListControllerFilename];
    [[NSNotificationCenter defaultCenter]
        postNotificationName:FileListControllerSelectedFile object:self userInfo:userInfo];
    [self reloadData];
}
- (void)dealloc {
    [[NSNotificationCenter defaultCenter] removeObserver:self];
    self.currentDocumentFilename = nil;
    self.documents = nil;
    [super dealloc];
}
@end
```

The only interesting thing this class does is register for FileList's notification about
changes, so that the view can be updated automatically. Also, whenever the user
selects a row here, FileListViewController posts a notification to that effect. We'll use
that later in this chapter, to be able to update our main DudelViewController and
DudelView whenever that happens.

Changing the App Delegate

For the first time since we started on Dudel, it's time to make some changes to the app
delegate. Changes are required here because we're going to rearrange the top-level
view arrangement of our application. Inside the .xib file, we'll be making a
UISplitViewController the root view controller, with instances of
FileListViewController and DudelViewController as its "children" (up until now,
DudelViewController was the root view controller).

Before we edit the .xib file, let's make the necessary preparations to
DudelAppController.h (the app delegate), basically just adding a couple of outlets:

```
// DudelAppDelegate.h
#import <UIKit/UIKit.h>
@class DudelViewController;
@class FileListViewController;
@interface DudelAppDelegate : NSObject <UIApplicationDelegate> {
    UIWindow *window;
    DudelViewController *viewController;
    FileListViewController *fileListController;
    UISplitViewController *splitViewController;
}
@property (nonatomic, retain) IBOutlet UIWindow *window;
@property (nonatomic, retain) IBOutlet DudelViewController *viewController;
@property (nonatomic, retain) IBOutlet FileListViewController *fileListController;
@property (nonatomic, retain) IBOutlet UISplitViewController *splitViewController;
@end
```

Now open *MainWindow.xib* in Interface Builder. By default, the main *.xib* window shows you only the top-level structure of the items contained in the *.xib*, but we're going to need to fix the plumbing here a bit. First, switch to the column view by clicking the appropriate button, as shown in Figure 8–3.

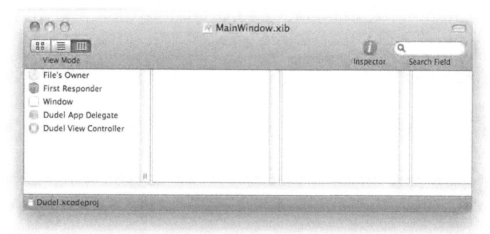

Figure 8–3. *The default contents of the MainWindow.xib file created with your project*

We're going to add a `UISplitViewController`, move the `DudelViewController` into it, and then add a `FileListController` to the mix. Start by finding a `UISplitViewController` in the Library and dragging it to the first column shown in the main window. Then click the new split view controller to see what's inside it, and click the navigation controller in there to see what it contains. You should see something like Figure 8–4.

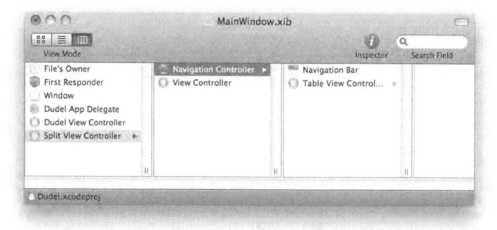

Figure 8–4. *We've put a split view in place. Now we just need to give it the correct contents.*

In the second column, the item labeled View Controller is where we want to have our `DudelViewController` now. And we want our `FileListViewController` to be in the item labeled Table View Controller in the third column.

This window does resemble a Finder window, so you might think you could just drag the Dudel view controller already at the top level into the split view controller, but that won't work. Instead, delete the top-level Dudel View Controller item, then click the Split View Controller item and select the view controller it contains. Open the identity inspector, and change its class to `DudelViewController`. Then click the Navigation Controller item, select the Table View Controller item it contains, and change its class to `FileListViewController`. You should now see something like Figure 8–5.

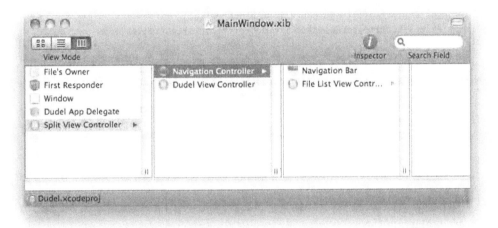

Figure 8–5. *A look at the completed reorganization*

Now all that's left here is to make some connections between objects in the *.xib* file. Connect each of `DudelAppDelegate`'s outlets to the appropriate view controllers in the nib file: `splitViewController`, `fileListController`, and `viewController`. Previously, the `viewController` outlet was connected to the old `DudelViewController`, but since we deleted that and are using a new one instead, you'll need to reconnect that outlet to the new `DudelViewController` inside the split view. Also, connect the `UISplitViewController`'s delegate outlet to the `DudelViewController`. This seems tricky, since the latter is contained inside the former, but as long as you're in column view, you shouldn't have a problem.

Save your work, and go back to Xcode, where it's time to finish the changes required for *DudelAppDelegate.m*. We're doing two main things here: switching out references to the top-level view controller and observing a notification from the `FileListViewController` class, so that whenever the user selects a file, we can set up the `DudelViewController` with the contents of the newly selected file.

```
//  DudelAppDelegate.m
#import "DudelAppDelegate.h"
#import "DudelViewController.h"
```

```
#import "FileListViewController.h"
#import "FileList.h"
@implementation DudelAppDelegate
@synthesize window;
@synthesize viewController;
@synthesize fileListController;
@synthesize splitViewController;
- (BOOL)application:(UIApplication *)application
didFinishLaunchingWithOptions:(NSDictionary *)launchOptions {
    // Override point for customization after app launch
    [window addSubview:viewController.view];
    [window addSubview:splitViewController.view];
    [window makeKeyAndVisible];
    [[NSNotificationCenter defaultCenter] addObserver:self
      selector:@selector(fileListControllerSelectedFile:)
      name:FileListControllerSelectedFile object:fileListController];
    return YES;
}
- (void)fileListControllerSelectedFile:(NSNotification *)n {
    NSString *oldFilename = [FileList sharedFileList].currentFile;
    [viewController saveCurrentToFile:oldFilename];
    NSString *filename = [[n userInfo] objectForKey:FileListControllerFilename];
    [FileList sharedFileList].currentFile = filename;
    [viewController loadFromFile:filename];
}
- (void)dealloc {
    [[NSNotificationCenter defaultCenter] removeObserver:self];
    [viewController release];
    [splitViewController release];
    [window release];
    [super dealloc];
}
@end
```

With that in place, we're getting very close to having a working split view up and running. Hang tight! The next step is to modify *DudelViewController.m*, removing the temporary "hack" we put in place for loading and saving a file to a single, hard-coded location. Start by importing the header for FileList somewhere at the top of the file:

```
#import "FileList.h"
```

Then, in both viewDidLoad and applicationWillTerminate:, make the following change. This eliminates the lengthy path construction, and instead just asks FileList for the current file.

```
NSArray *dirs = NSSearchPathForDirectoriesInDomains(NSDocumentDirectory,
    NSUserDomainMask, YES);
NSString *filename = [[dirs objectAtIndex:0]
    stringByAppendingPathComponent:@"Untitled.dudeldoc"];
NSString *filename = [FileList sharedFileList].currentFile;
```

We also need to add an outlet from DudelViewController to the toolbar in its display, so that we can add and remove toolbar items as the iPad rotates. Open *DudelViewController.h* and add the following line:

```
IBOutlet UIToolbar *toolbar;
```

To connect it, open *DudelViewController.xib* in Interface Builder, double-click to open the `DudelView` if it's not already open, then control-drag from the File's Owner icon to the toolbar at the bottom of the `DudelView`, and select `toolbar` from the pop-up menu.

One final step is necessary for the split view controller. I mentioned earlier that the actual split view is shown only in landscape mode, and that when switching to portrait mode, we instead get a `UIBarButtonItem` (which is set up to open a popover) passed to the `UISplitViewController`'s delegate (our `DudelViewController` instance). Likewise, another delegate method is called when switching to landscape mode, telling us that the `UIBarButtonItem` we were passed earlier is no longer valid. We'll implement these two methods, so that in the first method, we add the item to our toolbar, along with a flexible spacer so that it stands slightly removed from the tools. In the second method, we remove the two items.

```
- (void)splitViewController:(UISplitViewController*)svc
  willHideViewController:(UIViewController *)aViewController
  withBarButtonItem:(UIBarButtonItem*)barButtonItem
  forPopoverController:(UIPopoverController*)pc {
  // insert the new item and a spacer into the 33
  NSMutableArray *newItems = [[toolbar.items mutableCopy] autorelease];
  [newItems insertObject:barButtonItem atIndex:0];
  UIBarButtonItem *spacer = [[[UIBarButtonItem alloc]
    initWithBarButtonSystemItem:UIBarButtonSystemItemFlexibleSpace target:nil
    action:nil] autorelease];
  [newItems insertObject:spacer atIndex:1];
  [toolbar setItems:newItems animated:YES];
  // configure display of the button
  barButtonItem.title = @"My Dudels";
}
- (void)splitViewController:(UISplitViewController*)svc
  willShowViewController:(UIViewController *)aViewController
  invalidatingBarButtonItem:(UIBarButtonItem *)button {
  // remove the button, and the spacer that is beside it
  NSMutableArray *newItems = [[toolbar.items mutableCopy] autorelease];
  if ([newItems containsObject:button]) {
    [newItems removeObject:button];
    [newItems removeObjectAtIndex:0];
    [toolbar setItems:newItems animated:YES];
  }
}
```

We also need to implement a third delegate method, which is called when the popover created by the `UISplitViewController` is about to be displayed:

```
- (void)splitViewController:(UISplitViewController*)svc
  popoverController:(UIPopoverController*)pc
  willPresentViewController:(UIViewController *)aViewController {
  // we don't create this popover on our own, but we want to notice it so that
  // we can dismiss any other popovers, and also remove it later.
  if (self.currentPopover) {
    [self.currentPopover dismissPopoverAnimated:YES];
    [self handleDismissedPopoverController:self.currentPopover];
  }
  self.currentPopover = pc;
}
```

The point of this is mainly just to make sure that we're not showing multiple popovers, as we've done with all the other popovers.

At this point, you should now be able to build and run your app, and—finally!—see the split view in action. Rotate to landscape mode, and the file list appears on the left. Rotate to portrait mode, and the file list disappears, but in its place, there's a button at the left edge of the toolbar that brings up the file list in a popover.

That's great, but there's still a bit of a problem. The file list has only one item, which you can't rename or delete, and there's no way to make a new item! To remedy this, we need to add a few more things.

Creating and Deleting Files

All this time, we've had a button in the lower-right corner of our toolbar just for the purpose of sending our drawing as a PDF in an e-mail message. That's still a nice piece of functionality, but we can do more with that space—namely, replace it with a button that launches a small menu in another popover.

Let's start by creating yet another UIViewController subclass, once again a UITableViewController subclass with no *.xib* file, named ActionsMenuController. Like some of the other view controllers we've made, this one defines a notification name that's used when the user selects an item in the list it's going to display. It also defines an enumerated type that will show which of the menu items was selected. Here's the entire content of both the *.h* and *.m* files:

```
//  ActionsMenuController.h
#import <UIKit/UIKit.h>
#define ActionsMenuControllerDidSelect @"ActionsMenuControllerDidSelect"
typedef enum SelectedActionType {
  NoAction = -1,
  NewDocument,
  RenameDocument,
  DeleteDocument,
  EmailPdf,
  ShowAppInfo
} SelectedActionType;
@interface ActionsMenuController : UITableViewController {
  SelectedActionType selection;
  UIPopoverController *container;
}
@property (readonly) SelectedActionType selection;
@property (assign, nonatomic) UIPopoverController *container;
@end

//  ActionsMenuController.m
#import "ActionsMenuController.h"
@implementation ActionsMenuController
@synthesize selection, container;
- (void)viewWillAppear:(BOOL)animated {
  [super viewWillAppear:animated];
  selection = NoAction;
}
```

```objc
- (BOOL)shouldAutorotateToInterfaceOrientation:(UIInterfaceOrientation)orientation {
  return YES;
}
- (NSInteger)numberOfSectionsInTableView:(UITableView *)tableView {
return 1;
}
- (NSInteger)tableView:(UITableView *)tableView numberOfRowsInSection:(NSInteger)s {
return 5;
}
- (UITableViewCell *)tableView:(UITableView *)tableView
  cellForRowAtIndexPath:(NSIndexPath *)indexPath {
  static NSString *CellIdentifier = @"Cell";
  UITableViewCell *cell = [tableView dequeueReusableCellWithIdentifier:CellIdentifier];
  if (cell == nil) {
    cell = [[[UITableViewCell alloc] initWithStyle:UITableViewCellStyleDefault
      reuseIdentifier:CellIdentifier] autorelease];
  }
  switch (indexPath.row) {
    case NewDocument:
      cell.textLabel.text = @"New Dudel";
      break;
    case RenameDocument:
      cell.textLabel.text = @"Rename this Dudel";
      break;
    case DeleteDocument:
      cell.textLabel.text = @"Delete this Dudel";
      break;
    case ShowAppInfo:
      cell.textLabel.text = @"Dudel App Info";
      break;
    case EmailPdf:
      cell.textLabel.text = @"Send PDF via email";
      break;
    default:
      break;
  }
  return cell;
}
- (void)tableView:(UITableView *)tableView didSelectRowAtIndexPath:(NSIndexPath
*)indexPath {
  selection = indexPath.row;
  [[NSNotificationCenter defaultCenter]
    postNotificationName:ActionsMenuControllerDidSelect object:self];
}
@end
```

Switch over to DudelViewController, where we're going to make some slight changes:

Add this to the instance variables:

```objc
IBOutlet UIToolbar *toolbar;
```

Remove this action method:

```objc
- (IBAction)touchSendPdfEmailItem:(id)sender;
```

And add this action method:

```objc
- (IBAction)popoverActionsMenu:(id)sender;
```

Open *DudelViewController.xib* in Interface Builder, and select the button farthest to the right in the toolbar. Open the Inspector panel, clear out the Title field, and set the Identifier to Action. Then control-drag from the button to DudelViewController, and select the popoverActionsMenu: action. Now save your work, and go back to Xcode.

We'll need to make some changes to *DudelViewController.m* to match the header file's changes, and to handle this new menu controller. For starters, add this near the top:

```
#import "ActionsMenuController.h"
```

Then create the following methods:

```
- (IBAction)popoverActionsMenu:(id)sender {
  ActionsMenuController *amc = [[[ActionsMenuController alloc] initWithNibName:nil
    bundle:nil] autorelease];
  [self setupNewPopoverControllerForViewController:amc];
  amc.container = self.currentPopover;
  self.currentPopover.popoverContentSize = CGSizeMake(320, 44*5);
  [[NSNotificationCenter defaultCenter] addObserver:self
    selector:@selector(actionsMenuControllerDidSelect:)
    name:ActionsMenuControllerDidSelect object:amc];
  [self.currentPopover presentPopoverFromBarButtonItem:sender
    permittedArrowDirections:UIPopoverArrowDirectionAny animated:YES];
}
- (void)actionsMenuControllerDidSelect:(NSNotification *)notification {
 ActionsMenuController *amc = [notification object];
 UIPopoverController *popoverController = amc.container;
 [popoverController dismissPopoverAnimated:YES];
 [self handleDismissedPopoverController:popoverController];
 self.currentPopover = nil;
}
- (void)createDocument {
  [self saveCurrentToFile:[FileList sharedFileList].currentFile];
  [[FileList sharedFileList] createAndSelectNewUntitled];
  dudelView.drawables = [NSMutableArray array];
  [dudelView setNeedsDisplay];
}
- (void)deleteCurrentDocumentWithConfirmation {
  [[[[UIAlertView alloc] initWithTitle:@"Delete current Dudel" message:
  @"This will remove your current drawing completely. Are you sure you want to do that?"
  delegate:self cancelButtonTitle:@"Cancel" otherButtonTitles:@"Delete it!", nil]
  autorelease] show];
}
- (void)renameCurrentDocument {
  // hold on, we're not quite ready for this yet
}
- (void)showAppInfo {
  // not ready for this one, either!
}
// UIAlertView delegate method, called by the delete confirmation alert.
// we're only using one UIAlertView right now, so no need to check which
// one this is, just which button was pressed.
- (void)alertView:(UIAlertView *)alertView clickedButtonAtIndex:(NSInteger)buttonIndex {
  if (buttonIndex == 1) {
    [[FileList sharedFileList] deleteCurrentFile];
    [self loadFromFile:[FileList sharedFileList].currentFile];
  }
```

}

Then replace this:

- (IBAction)touchSendPdfEmailItem:(id)sender {

with this:

- (void)sendPdfEmail {

We need to add an additional check, which contains another bit of checking all its own, to our handleDismissedPopoverController: method, down near the end of the method (just before the return):

```
} else if ([popoverController.contentViewController
isMemberOfClass:[ActionsMenuController class]]) {
    ActionsMenuController *amc = (ActionsMenuController
*)popoverController.contentViewController;
    switch (amc.selection) {
      case NewDocument:
        [self createDocument];
        break;
      case RenameDocument:
        [self renameCurrentDocument];
        break;
      case DeleteDocument:
        [self deleteCurrentDocumentWithConfirmation];
        break;
      case EmailPdf:
        [self sendPdfEmail];
        break;
      case ShowAppInfo:
        [self showAppInfo];
        break;
      default:
        break;
    }
}
```

Now build and run your app, and try that on for size! You can now both create and delete Dudel documents, and switch between them. Each new document you create will be given a default name containing a timestamp, to ensure its uniqueness. All that's left to do now is to add the ability to rename the files you create here, and to display a brief info panel with another menu item. Both of these will be accomplished using modal displays.

Renaming Files

First, let's get the file renaming working. The idea here is that creating a new document should be instantaneous, with the default filename working as a placeholder until the time when the user decides to give it a name. At that point, the user can invoke this functionality through the menu.

Start by making a new UIViewController subclass. This one will *not* be a UITableViewController subclass, and it needs to have a matching *.xib* file, where we'll define a simple GUI for renaming a file. Name this controller class FileRenameViewController. Here's the content of the *FileRenameViewController.h* file:

```
//  FileRenameViewController.h
#import <UIKit/UIKit.h>
@protocol FileRenameViewControllerDelegate;
@interface FileRenameViewController : UIViewController {
  id <FileRenameViewControllerDelegate> delegate;
  NSString *originalFilename;
  NSString *changedFilename;
  IBOutlet UILabel *textLabel;
  IBOutlet UITextField *textField;
}
@property (nonatomic, retain) id <FileRenameViewControllerDelegate> delegate;
@property (nonatomic, copy) NSString *originalFilename;
@property (nonatomic, copy) NSString *changedFilename;
@end
@protocol FileRenameViewControllerDelegate
- (void)fileRenameViewController:(FileRenameViewController *)c
  didRename:(NSString *)oldFilename to:(NSString *)newFilename;
@end
```

One of the new features in iOS 3.2 is the ability to use presentation styles when displaying a modal view. In older versions of iOS, modal views always filled the screen, but here we're going to use a presentation style called UIModalPresentationFormSheet, which presents a 540-by-620 view, centered in the screen, with the rest of screen grayed out. This view slides in from the bottom of the screen, and since it doesn't cover the entire screen, it's slightly less jarring. Let's set it up now.

Open *FileRenameViewController.xib* in Interface Builder. Select the view, and use the attribute inspector to disable its status bar (as we've done for several other views in Dudel), which will let us resize the view. Use the size inspector to set its size to 540 by 620. Next, use the Library to find a UILabel and a UITextfield, dragging each of them into the view. Switch back to the attribute inspector, and set the font for each of those components to 24-point Helvetica. For the UILabel, also set its # Lines to 0, which will let it display text on multiple lines if necessary. Then make them each nearly fill the width of the view, and position them well above center (in order to leave space for the keyboard), something like what you see in Figure 8–6. For bonus points, use the attributes inspector to set the text field's placeholder text to **Entire Filename**.

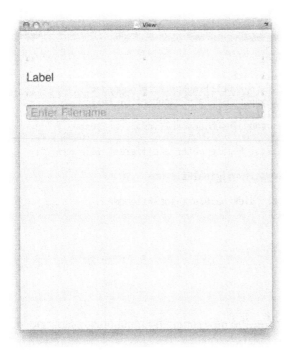

Figure 8–6. *Laying out GUI components for the FileRenameViewController. Notice the blue resize handles that extend nearly to the sides of the view.*

Now all we need to do is connect the `textField` and `textLabel` buttons from the File's Owner icon to the appropriate GUI components, and connect the text field's delegate outlet back to File's Owner. Save your *.xib*. This GUI is done!

Switch back to Xcode, and enter this code for *FileRenameViewController.m*:

```
//  FileRenameViewController.m
#import "FileRenameViewController.h"
#import "FileList.h"
@implementation FileRenameViewController
@synthesize delegate;
@synthesize originalFilename;
@synthesize changedFilename;
- (void)viewWillAppear:(BOOL)animated {
  [super viewWillAppear:animated];
  textField.text = [[originalFilename lastPathComponent] stringByDeletingPathExtension];
  textLabel.text = @"Please enter a new file name for the current Dudel.";
}
- (void)viewDidAppear:(BOOL)animated {
  [super viewDidAppear:animated];
  [textField becomeFirstResponder];
}
- (BOOL)shouldAutorotateToInterfaceOrientation:(UIInterfaceOrientation)orientation {
  return YES;
}
- (void)dealloc {
```

```
    self.delegate = nil;
    self.originalFilename = nil;
    self.changedFilename = nil;
    [super dealloc];
  }
- (void)textFieldDidEndEditing:(UITextField *)tf {
    NSString *dirPath = [originalFilename stringByDeletingLastPathComponent];
    self.changedFilename = [[dirPath stringByAppendingPathComponent:tf.text]
      stringByAppendingPathExtension:@"dudeldoc"];
    if ([[FileList sharedFileList].allFiles containsObject:self.changedFilename]) {
      textLabel.text =
        @"A file with that name already exists! Please enter a different file name.";
    } else {
      [[FileList sharedFileList] renameFile:self.originalFilename
        to:self.changedFilename];
      [delegate fileRenameViewController:self didRename:originalFilename
        to:changedFilename];
    }
  }
- (BOOL)textFieldShouldReturn:(UITextField *)tf {
    [tf endEditing:YES];
    return YES;
  }
@end
```

Now let's set up `DudelViewController` to use the new renaming mechanism. Starting in the header, add this:

```
#import "FileRenameViewController.h"
```

Then add a protocol to the list of protocols our controller implements:

```
@interface DudelViewController : UIViewController <ToolDelegate, DudelViewDelegate,
  MFMailComposeViewControllerDelegate, UIPopoverControllerDelegate,
  FileRenameViewControllerDelegate> {
```

Switch to the .m file, and fill in this method's body:

```
- (void)renameCurrentDocument {
  FileRenameViewController *controller = [[[FileRenameViewController alloc]
    initWithNibName:@"FileRenameViewController" bundle:nil] autorelease];
  controller.delegate = self;
  controller.modalPresentationStyle = UIModalPresentationFormSheet;
  controller.originalFilename = [FileList sharedFileList].currentFile;
  [self presentModalViewController:controller animated:YES];
}
```

Finally, implement the delegate method that gets called when the view's modal session is done:

```
- (void)fileRenameViewController:(FileRenameViewController *)c
  didRename:(NSString *)oldFilename to:(NSString *)newFilename {
  [self dismissModalViewControllerAnimated:YES];
}
```

Now build and run your app. You should be able to select a file in the list, and rename it using the **Rename this Dudel** menu item, as shown in Figure 8-7.

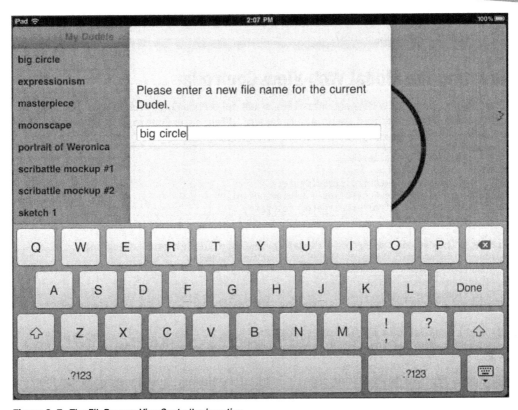

Figure 8–7. *The FileRenameViewController in action*

Implementing an About Panel in a Modal Way

The final feature we want in this chapter is to implement a sort of About panel, similar to what you can typically find in Mac OS X applications. iPhone applications don't often have these panels, but on the iPad, we have a little more space. In Dudel, we already have an action menu that's a good place to access such a feature, so off we go.

We'll present a `UIWebView` with information about Dudel and links at the bottom to get additional information. This web view will be presented modally, just like the file-renaming view.

As you may know, the Dudel application created during the writing of this book is actually available on the App Store as a free download. This is partly because while creating it, we found it was fun to use and worthy of making available to others. But we also figured that it could be a good way to promote the book itself!

The shipping version of Dudel includes an info screen that describes this book, tells the users that they can buy this book if they want to see how the app was made, and provides links to the Apress and Amazon web sites. In order to keep our promise to include full details on how to make this app, we're going to make the same info screen that could lead you to buying this book—if you didn't already have a copy, which you do. How self-referential is this?

Creating the Modal Web View Controller

Start by creating a new `UIViewController` class called `ModalWebViewController`, again with an *.xib* file and without being a subclass of `UITableViewController`. Give it the following interface declaration in *ModalWebViewController.h*:

```
//  ModalWebViewController.h
#import <UIKit/UIKit.h>
@protocol ModalWebViewControllerDelegate;
@interface ModalWebViewController : UIViewController {
  id <ModalWebViewControllerDelegate> delegate;
  UIWebView *webView;
}
@property (nonatomic, assign) id <ModalWebViewControllerDelegate> delegate;
@property (nonatomic, retain) IBOutlet UIWebView *webView;
- (IBAction)done;
- (IBAction)apressSite;
- (IBAction)amazonSite;

@end
@protocol ModalWebViewControllerDelegate
- (void)modalWebViewControllerDidFinish:(ModalWebViewController *)controller;
@end
```

Now open *ModalWebViewController.xib* in Interface Builder, and once again use the attribute inspector to disable the view's status bar. Then use the size inspector to set the view's size to 540 by 620. Use the Library to find a `UIToolbar` and put it at the bottom of the view, and then add a `UIWebView` to fill up the rest of the view. Now put five `UIBarButtonItems` into the toolbar. Use the attribute inspector to set the fourth button's identifier to **Flexible Space**, and the fifth item's identifier to **Done**. Then set the titles on the remaining three to **More Info**, **Buy the eBook**, and **Buy the Print Book**, respectively, as shown in Figure 8–8.

Figure 8–8. *The toolbar for our ModalWebViewController*

Control-drag to connect each of the four clickable buttons to the appropriate action methods in File's Owner: `apressSite`, `apressSite`, `amazonSite`, and `done`. (Yes, we're reusing the same method for both the More Info and Buy the eBook actions.)

Now control-drag from the File's Owner icon to the `UIWebView`, and connect the `webView` outlet. The GUI is complete. Save your work and switch back to Xcode to finish up this class. Here's the code for *ModalWebViewController.m*:

```objc
// ModalWebViewController.m
#import "ModalWebViewController.h"
@implementation ModalWebViewController
@synthesize delegate;
@synthesize webView;
- (void)viewDidLoad {
  // Load the bookInfo.html file into the UIWebView.
  NSString *path = [[NSBundle mainBundle] pathForResource:@"bookInfo" ofType:@"html"];
  NSURL *url = [NSURL fileURLWithPath:path];
  NSURLRequest *request = [NSURLRequest requestWithURL:url];
  [self.webView loadRequest:request];
  [super viewDidLoad];
}
- (IBAction)done {
  // The Done button was tapped, so close Modal Web View.
  [self.delegate modalWebViewControllerDidFinish:self];
}
- (IBAction)apressSite {
  // Go to the Apress.com book web page in Mobile Safari.
  NSURL *url = [NSURL URLWithString:@"http://www.apress.com/book/view/9781430230212"];
  [[UIApplication sharedApplication] openURL:url];
}
- (IBAction)amazonSite {
  // Go to the Amazon.com book web page in Mobile Safari.
  NSURL *url = [NSURL URLWithString:@"http://www.amazon.com/dp/1430230215/"];
  [[UIApplication sharedApplication] openURL:url];
}
- (BOOL)shouldAutorotateToInterfaceOrientation:(UIInterfaceOrientation)orientation {
  // Overridden to allow any orientation.
  return YES;
}
- (void)dealloc {
  [webView release];
  [super dealloc];
}
@end
```

Displaying a Web Page

Our modal web view controller code references an HTML page whose content should be displayed in the info panel. This is a standard HTML/CSS document, which displays some text and an image. That file is included in the source code archive for this book (along with the image file it references, *booktitle.png*). You can copy both files from the source code archive into your project, or just make a new empty *bookInfo.html* file in your Xcode project using the New File Assistant (pick Empty File from the Other section) and giving it something like the following content:

```html
<!DOCTYPE html PUBLIC "-//W3C//DTD XHTML 1.0 Transitional//EN"
"http://www.w3.org/TR/xhtml1/DTD/xhtml1-transitional.dtd">
<html xmlns="http://www.w3.org/1999/xhtml">
<head>
<meta name="viewport" content="width=540" />
<meta http-equiv="Content-Type" content="text/html; charset=UTF-8" />
<title>Beginning iPad Development for iPhone Developers: Mastering the iPad SDK</title>
<style type="text/css">
```

```
<!--
body {
  background: #000 url(booktitle.png) fixed bottom no-repeat;
  margin: 0px;
  font-family: Arial, Helvetica, sans-serif;
  font-size: 20px;
  color: #FC3;
}
a:link { color: #FFF; }
a:visited { color: #FFF; }
a:hover { color: #FFF; }
a:active { color: #FFF; }
.intro { padding: 30px; -align: center; }
-->
</style></head>
<body><div class="intro">Leverage your iPhone development skills to build apps for the
iPad. Learn how to utilize all of the new iPad SDK features from <b>Dudel</b> in your
own apps, plus so much more! This book includes the full source code for <b>Dudel</b>.
</p>
</body>
</html>
```

Integrating with the Dudel View Controller

Now let's deal with DudelViewController, where we'll tie up the loose ends needed to display this web view. Start with the *DudelViewController.h* file, adding this line:

```
#import "ModalWebViewController.h"
```

Also add one more protocol to the list for the DudelViewController class:

```
@interface DudelViewController : UIViewController <ToolDelegate, DudelViewDelegate,
  MFMailComposeViewControllerDelegate, UIPopoverControllerDelegate,
  FileRenameViewControllerDelegate, ModalWebViewControllerDelegate > {
```

Then switch to *DudelViewController.m* and fill out the following method, which was previously empty:

```
- (void)showAppInfo {
  // The About the Book button was tapped, so display the Modal Web View.
  ModalWebViewController *controller = [[[ModalWebViewController alloc]
    initWithNibName:@"ModalWebViewController" bundle:nil] autorelease];
  controller.delegate = self;
  // UIModalPresentationFormSheet has a fixed 540 pixel width and 620 pixel height.
  controller.modalPresentationStyle = UIModalPresentationFormSheet;
  [self presentModalViewController:controller animated:YES];
}
```

Finally, handle the removal of the modal web view by implementing the following delegate method to dismiss it:

```
- (void)modalWebViewControllerDidFinish:(ModalWebViewController *)controller {
  [self dismissModalViewControllerAnimated:YES];
}
```

Now you should be able to build and run the app, bring up the info panel through the action menu, and see something very much like the handsome page shown in Figure 8–9.

Figure 8–9. *The black ink used for this image alone is enough to print an entire book in a third-world country.*

Obviously, you'll be missing most of that if you didn't copy the image from the book's source code archive, but you get the idea.

Let's Split

We've covered a lot of ground in this chapter. You've seen how the UISplitViewController works and how to display a modal view without taking up the entire screen. You've also learned the basics of how to save and load documents in a way that can be somewhat simpler to use than Core Data (though for document types that are more complex than just a single array of items, you should really invest the time and effort to use Core Data instead). Along the way, you saw one possible approach to the issue of dealing with data files stored by your application, which is worth some consideration, since iOS doesn't provide any way for users to deal with them otherwise.

In the next chapter, we'll move on to another important aspect of apps. There, you'll learn some great new tricks that iOS 3.2 introduces for getting input from users.

Chapter 9

New Input Methods

You've already seen how iOS 3.2 provides several new techniques for displaying and arranging content, giving you more flexibility in presenting data to your users. But using iOS isn't a one-way street. Interactivity is crucial to the iPhone/iPad user experience.

Each major new release of iOS has provided new ways for users to interact with applications. iOS 3.2 is no exception, adding customizable menus for text editing, built-in gesture recognition for interpreting and handling sequences of touches, and new functionality for extending or even replacing the standard on-screen keyboard. This chapter explores each of these areas, demonstrating how to put them to use in a variety of applications. First, we'll look at how to add items to the little text-editing menu that pops up in response to a user pressing and hold a finger over a text-input object. Next, we'll deal with gesture recognition. Finally, you'll see how to customize the on-screen keyboard.

Menu Additions

Anyone who has edited text on an iOS device is probably familiar with the text-editing menu that appears at various times, hovering over the text area in response to user actions, as shown in Figure 9–1. This is a context-sensitive menu that displays only items relevant to the current selection (unlike menus in Mac OS X, where unavailable items are grayed out).

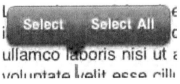

Figure 9–1. *The basic menu that's shown when no text is selected*

Starting with i OS 3.2, it's now possible for developers to tap into this functionality. You can set up a list of your own menu items that will be added to the menu, and also implement functionality to enable and disable your menu items on the fly, depending on the current selection or any other factors you want to take into account. (You can't do anything about the menu items that the system provides.)

The gateway for accessing all this functionality is the UIMenuController class. UIMenuController is a singleton class, whose single instance is used across all text views in your app. The idea is that you create one or more UIMenuItem instances (each of which specifies an action and a title), put them in an array, and pass them off to the UIMenuController instance. When it's time to display the menu, UIMenuController will use the responder chain to locate an object that implements the method for each menu item, and determine whether or not that item should be displayed.

To demonstrate this in action, we'll create a quick little test-bed app. This app won't really do anything apart from letting us edit a piece of text, and attach a menu item of our own design to the menu controller. The menu item will let users select a URL in their text and open that URL in Safari.

Start by creating a new view-based project in Xcode, targeted at iPad. I named my app TextMangler. The project that Xcode creates will have a TextManglerViewController class. Add the following instance variable to *TextManglerViewController.h*, between the two curly braces in the class declaration:

```
IBOutlet UITextView *textView;
```

Now open *TextManglerViewController.xib* in Interface Builder, and drag a UITextView object into the view, filling it completely. Then control-drag from the File's Owner icon to the text view and select textView from the small context menu that appears. This GUI is done, so save your work and go back to Xcode.

TextManglerViewController.m has a number of predefined methods that were put there when the project was created. You can leave all of those in place, and just add definitions for the few methods described here. Start by defining the viewDidLoad method, where we do our initialization. This code creates a menu item, and then passes it along to UIMenuController so that it can appear alongside the other menu items.

```
- (void)viewDidLoad {
  [super viewDidLoad];
  UIMenuItem *menuItem = [[[UIMenuItem alloc] init] autorelease];
  menuItem.title = @"Open URL in Safari";
  menuItem.action = @selector(openUrlInSafari:);
  [UIMenuController sharedMenuController].menuItems = [NSArray
    arrayWithObject:menuItem];
}
```

Note that in defining a UIMenuItem, we specify an action, but not a target. The target is determined dynamically by traversing the responder chain, sending each object in the chain the canPerformAction: method until one of them returns YES (or until there's nothing left in the responder chain to ask). Since this controller class will be in the responder chain, we'll implement the method here.

The canPerformAction: method first checks to make sure that the relevant action is being asked about, and then checks the text view's selected text to see if it's an URL that can be opened. If so, it returns YES. If it doesn't know what else to do with this query, it passes the call along by calling the superclass's implementation.

```
- (BOOL)canPerformAction:(SEL)action withSender:(id)sender {
  if (action == @selector(openUrlInSafari:)) {
    NSString *selectedText = [textView.text substringWithRange:textView.selectedRange];
    NSURL *url = [NSURL URLWithString:selectedText];
    return [[UIApplication sharedApplication] canOpenURL:url];
  }
  return [super canPerformAction:action withSender:sender];
}
```

> **NOTE:** You might think that you should explicitly return YES or NO here (depending on how you think about it) if you don't know what to do with the action in question, but you would be wrong. The canPerformAction: method is called for each and every menu item, so you would potentially be enabling (or disabling) all of them, not just yours!

Finally, here's the action method itself, which is called when the user selects the menu item we created.

```
- (void)openUrlInSafari:(id)sender {
  NSString *selectedText = [textView.text substringWithRange:textView.selectedRange];
  NSURL *url = [NSURL URLWithString:selectedText];
  [[UIApplication sharedApplication] openURL:url];
}
```

Build and run your app, and a big text view will fill the screen. Go ahead and play with it, pressing and holding somewhere, selecting some text, and so on. You'll see the same menu items as usual. Then type in a URL, such as http://apress.com, and select the text. Now you get the extra menu item, as shown in Figure 9–2. Touching it should launch Safari and bring up the page.

Figure 9–2. *Our new menu item has been added to the mix.*

Since UIMenuItemController is shared throughout your application, the menu items you add to it will be available in every UITextField and UITextView that the user sees. Since the menu items are enabled and disabled using the responder chain, you can decide the level of granularity you want. Use canPerformAction: to enable items in your app delegate if you want them to always be enabled, or in individual view controllers if you want more fine-grained control.

Gesture Recognition

Starting with iOS 3.2, UIViews can handle not only individual touch events, but they can also look for particular kinds of touch actions and let your code know when they occur. Some of this isn't entirely new. UIScrollView, for instance, has always known how to watch for pinch and drag gestures, which it uses for controlling zoom levels and panning the view. What's new is that you can now tell any UIView to watch for specific gestures and let you know when they occur.

To make this work, you first create an instance of the new UIGestureRecognizer class, or rather, an instance of one of its many subclasses:

- UILongPressGestureRecognizer
- UIPanGestureRecognizer
- UIPinchGestureRecognizer
- UIRotationGestureRecognizer
- UISwipeGestureRecognizer
- UITapGestureRecognizer

Each of those is fine-tuned to detect a particular user gesture, clearly indicated in the class name. Most of them have at least one property that allows you to set some configuration options or read a value back.

After creating a gesture recognizer, you just pass it to a view using the addGestureRecognizer: method. Then the method you specified when creating the gesture recognizer will be called whenever the user performs that gesture. Let's put this into action using Dudel.

Adding Undo to Dudel

One key feature that Dudel is missing is any sort of undo action. Each stroke you make in a drawing is a part of your drawing forever. We're going to remedy that by assigning a gesture to open a small popover containing a single item that lets us remove the most recently created Drawable object in dudelView's array. It's going to end up looking like Figure 9–3.

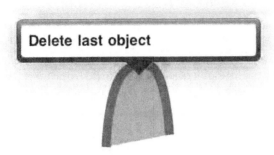

Figure 9–3. *A small menu that appears after a long touch. The arrow at the bottom edge of the popover points at the location of the touch, which in this case just happens to be the location of the last object.*

As you've done before, make a fresh copy of the Dudel project from the previous chapter, to contain your changes for this chapter. Then open the Xcode project in the new directory.

Let's start by making the view controller that will display a small pop-up menu in Dudel. Create a new UIViewController subclass, this time as a subclass of UITableViewController, without a matching *.xib* file, and name it DudelEditController. Here's the entire content of both the *.h* and *.m* files:

```
//  DudelEditController.h
#import <UIKit/UIKit.h>
#define DudelEditControllerDelete @"DudelEditControllerDelete"
@interface DudelEditController : UITableViewController {
  UIPopoverController *container;
}
@property (assign, nonatomic) UIPopoverController *container;
@end

//  DudelEditController.m
#import "DudelEditController.h"
@implementation DudelEditController
@synthesize container;
- (BOOL)shouldAutorotateToInterfaceOrientation:(UIInterfaceOrientation)orientation {
    // Override to allow orientations other than the default portrait orientation.
    return YES;
}
- (NSInteger)numberOfSectionsInTableView:(UITableView *)tableView {
    // Return the number of sections.
    return 1;
}
- (NSInteger)tableView:(UITableView *)tableView numberOfRowsInSection:(NSInteger)s {
    // Return the number of rows in the section.
    return 1;
}
- (UITableViewCell *)tableView:(UITableView *)tableView
    cellForRowAtIndexPath:(NSIndexPath *)indexPath {
  static NSString *CellIdentifier = @"Cell";
  UITableViewCell *cell = [tableView dequeueReusableCellWithIdentifier:CellIdentifier];
  if (cell == nil) {
```

```
    cell = [[[UITableViewCell alloc] initWithStyle:UITableViewCellStyleDefault
        reuseIdentifier:CellIdentifier] autorelease];
  }
  cell.textLabel.text = @"Delete last object";
  return cell;
}

- (void)tableView:(UITableView *)tableView didSelectRowAtIndexPath:(NSIndexPath *)ip {
  [[NSNotificationCenter defaultCenter] postNotificationName:DudelEditControllerDelete
    object:self];
}
@end
```

Now open *DudelViewController.m* and add this line near the top of the file:

```
#import "DudelEditController.h"
```

Then add these lines to the end of viewDidLoad:

```
UILongPressGestureRecognizer *longPress =
  [[[UILongPressGestureRecognizer alloc] initWithTarget:self
  action:@selector(handleLongPress:)] autorelease];
[dudelView addGestureRecognizer:longPress];
```

Next, implement the handleLongPress: method referenced earlier.

```
- (void)handleLongPress:(UIGestureRecognizer *)gr {
  if (gr.state == UIGestureRecognizerStateBegan) {
    DudelEditController *c = [[[DudelEditController alloc]
      initWithStyle:UITableViewStylePlain] autorelease];
    [self setupNewPopoverControllerForViewController:c];
    self.currentPopover.popoverContentSize = CGSizeMake(320, 44*1);
    c.container = self.currentPopover;
    [[NSNotificationCenter defaultCenter] addObserver:self
      selector:@selector(dudelEditControllerSelectedDelete:)
      name:DudelEditControllerDelete object:c];
    CGRect popoverRect = CGRectZero;
    popoverRect.origin = [gr locationInView:dudelView];
    [self.currentPopover presentPopoverFromRect:popoverRect inView:dudelView
      permittedArrowDirections:UIPopoverArrowDirectionAny animated:YES];
  }
}
```

Now it's time to implement the method that is called when the menu item is actually
selected.

```
- (void)dudelEditControllerSelectedDelete:(NSNotification *)n {
  DudelEditController *c = [n object];
  UIPopoverController *popoverController = c.container;
  [popoverController dismissPopoverAnimated:YES];
  [self handleDismissedPopoverController:popoverController];
  self.currentPopover = nil;
  if ([dudelView.drawables count] > 0) {
    [dudelView.drawables removeLastObject];
    [dudelView setNeedsDisplay];
  }
}
```

Build and run your app, do some doodling, and then press and hold anywhere on the screen until the popover appears. Select its one item, and watch as the last shape or stroke you made suddenly disappears! This is great, but now try to draw a couple more shapes using whatever tool you already had selected. You'll see that things get a little screwy. The screen doesn't seem to update properly while you drag, and the first shape you draw will disappear when you start drawing the next one. This is all due to the gesture activity leaving the chosen tool in an inconsistent state, which is easily remedied.

Resetting the Selected Tool's State

We need to make sure that when active touches are canceled (which happens when the gesture recognizer decides that a gesture is happening), the selected tool's state is reset so that it doesn't think it's still in the middle of tracking a drag.

Open the *.m* file for each of the tool classes (except FreehandTool), and add the following line to the touchesCancelled:withEvent: method:

```
- (void)touchesCancelled:(NSSet *)touches withEvent:(UIEvent *)event {
  // If you already had any other code here, leave it alone and add this:
  [self deactivate];
}
```

The FreehandTool class is the exception. It already implements this method. Here, just add a single line:

```
- (void)touchesCancelled:(NSSet *)touches withEvent:(UIEvent *)event {
  [self activate];
  isDragging = NO;
}
```

This one is a little different from the others. It calls the activate method instead of deactivate. That's due to a peculiarity in the creation of this class, where deactivate finishes the current drawing action—just what we want to avoid!

Now you should be able to build and run the app, and see everything behaving as it should.

We've used only UILongPressGestureRecognizer for this example, but the other gesture recognizers work similarly.

Keyboard Extensions and Replacements

Did you ever notice that when you're filling in a web-based form in Mobile Safari, a small row of additional buttons appears above the keyboard, containing buttons labeled Previous, Next, and so on? iOS 3.2 gives us a way to do that sort of thing, too, using the new inputAccessoryView property of UITextView and UITextField. You just put anything you like into a UIView (buttons, labels, sliders … you name it), and pass that view off to the text-input object in question.

As if that weren't enough, starting with OS 3.2 we can now replace the entire keyboard! The idea is similar to that for the accessory view. UIView has a new inputView property that you can set, using any UIView you like.

Adding a Keyboard Button in Dudel

To demonstrate how to extend the keyboard, we're going to add something that has been missing from the FileRenameViewController in Dudel: the ability to cancel the renaming operation. We'll do this by adding a Cancel button to the keyboard.

Open *FileRenameViewController.m*, and add the following method to set up the input accessory view:

```
- (void)viewDidLoad {
  [super viewDidLoad];
  UIView *inputAccessoryView = [[UIView alloc] initWithFrame:
    CGRectMake(0.0, 0.0, 768.0, 77.0)];
  inputAccessoryView.backgroundColor = [UIColor darkGrayColor];
  UIButton *cancelButton = [UIButton buttonWithType:
    UIButtonTypeRoundedRect];
  cancelButton.frame = CGRectMake(20.0, 20.0, 100.0, 37.0);
  [cancelButton setTitle: @"Cancel" forState:UIControlStateNormal];
  [cancelButton setTitleColor:[UIColor blackColor] forState:
    UIControlStateNormal];
  [cancelButton addTarget:self action:@selector(cancel:)
    forControlEvents:UIControlEventTouchUpInside];
  [inputAccessoryView addSubview:cancelButton];
  textField.inputAccessoryView = inputAccessoryView;
}
```

Also add the method that actually does the canceling:

```
- (void)cancel:(id)sender {
  [delegate fileRenameViewController:self didRename:originalFilename
    to:originalFilename];
}
```

Now build and run your app, bring up the file renaming view, and you'll see something like Figure 9-4.

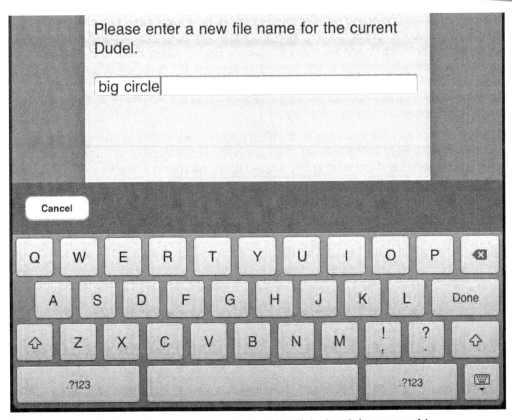

Figure 9–4. *Here's the Cancel button we've just added, making this keyboard view more useful.*

Replacing the Keyboard

In this section, we're going to implement a simple calculator that uses a normal UITextView object as an input field. Instead of letting the users enter any sort of text they want, we'll present an input view that contains buttons for numbers, as well as buttons for the calculator functions.

Our calculator will use Reverse Polish Notation (RPN). With RPN, the mathematical operators are shown after the numbers on which they should operate. For instance, 1 + 3 would be written as 1 3 + in RPN. In a longer sequence, the result of an operation can be used as input to the next operator. For example, 10 / 2 + 3 would be written as 10 2 / 3 + in RPN.

One consequence of this notation is that it eliminates the need for parentheses in expressions. RPN expressions are always evaluated left to right. To change the order of operations, you just need to shift the operators around. For example, (3 * 4) + 10 becomes 3 4 * 10 + in RPM, and 3 * (4 + 10) becomes 3 4 10 + *. When entering expressions like this in an RPN calculator, normally you press some sort of Enter key between entering numbers, as in 3 [Enter] 4 [Enter] 10 [+] [*].

Another consequence of using RPN is that creating a calculator app becomes really simple! At the core of the implementation lies a stack (in our case, an NSMutableArray will do nicely) onto which each number is pushed. Each mathematical operator uses the top item of the stack, along with the number currently in the text view, to perform an operation and leave the result in the text view. We don't need to worry about parsing parentheses or keeping track of pending operations that are waiting for a higher-precedence operation to take place first.

As a bonus, our app will make use of the iPad's screen real estate to show more than just the single number being entered. We'll show the entire stack of all numbers that have been entered and are waiting to be acted upon, as shown in Figure 9–5.

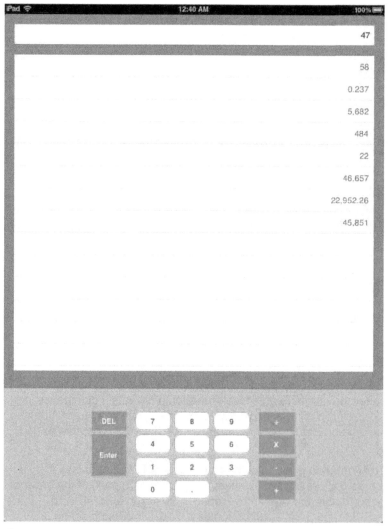

Figure 9–5. *An RPN calculator worthy of a strange name. The text area at the top is the editing area. Below that is the stack of entered numbers.*

In honor of this calculator's reverse Polish heritage, we're going to name it ClacHsilop. (Read it backward. If I have to explain it, that means it's not funny!)

Open Xcode, make a new view-based iPad project, and name it ClacHsilop. This class will have a single view controller, which will manage the text view and the table view in the display. For the text view, rather than just setting a property to specify the inputView, we're going to subclass UITextView and override the inputView method, returning a pointer to a view of our own.

Defining the InputView Class

Let's start by creating the new view. We'll subclass UITextView, and use Interface Builder to define the content for our inputView, laying out buttons the way we want, and connecting them to action methods in our UITextView subclass. Our text view class will also define a delegate protocol for passing along calculator command actions (+, −, and so on) to its delegate.

Use the New File Assistant to create a new Objective-C class, a subview of UIView (since UITextView isn't one of the choices), and name it InputView. The InputView class will a have a method that allows buttons in the inputView GUI to enter text directly (in our case, strings containing numeric digits), as well as a method that will let a button trigger a calculator action based on the sender's tag. Here's the complete source of the InputView class:

```
// InputView.h
#import <UIKit/UIKit.h>
typedef enum ActionTag {
  ActionEnter = 0,
  ActionDivide,
  ActionMultiply,
  ActionSubtract,
  ActionAdd
} ActionTag;
@protocol InputViewDelegate;
@interface InputView : UITextView {
  UIView *inputView;
  id <InputViewDelegate> ivDelegate;
}
- (IBAction)takeInputFromTitle:(id)sender;
- (IBAction)doDelete:(id)sender;
- (IBAction)doTaggedAction:(id)sender;
@end
@protocol InputViewDelegate
- (void)doTaggedAction:(ActionTag)tag forInputView:(InputView *)iv;
@end

// InputView.m
#import "InputView.h"
@implementation InputView
- (void)dealloc {
  [inputView release];
  [super dealloc];
}
```

```
- (UIView *)inputView {
  if (!inputView) {
    NSArray *objects = [[NSBundle mainBundle] loadNibNamed:@"RpnKeyboard" owner:self
      options:nil];
    inputView = [[objects objectAtIndex:0] retain];
  }
  return inputView;
}
- (IBAction)takeInputFromTitle:(id)sender {
  // remove the initial zero;
  if ([self.text isEqual:@"0"]) {
    self.text = @"";
  }
  self.text = [self.text stringByReplacingCharactersInRange:self.selectedRange
    withString:((UIButton *)sender).currentTitle];
}
- (IBAction)doDelete:(id)sender {
  NSRange r = self.selectedRange;
  if (r.length > 0) {
    // the user has highlighted some text, fall through to delete it
  } else {
    // there's just an insertion point
    if (r.location == 0) {
      // cursor is at the beginning, forget about it.
      return;
    } else {
      r.location -= 1;
      r.length = 1;
    }
  }
  self.text = [self.text stringByReplacingCharactersInRange:r withString:@""];
  r.length = 0;
  self.selectedRange = r;
}
- (IBAction)doTaggedAction:(id)sender {
  ActionTag tag = [sender tag];
  [ivDelegate doTaggedAction:tag forInputView:self];
}
@end
```

There are just a couple tricky parts here. The first is in the takeInputFromTitle: action, which is the one that all our numeric digit buttons will call. Like most handheld calculators, ours will display a 0 (zero) instead of an empty display when its value is zero. The small check for a 0 in that method makes that 0 go away when the user starts typing.

The other fussy bit is the doDelete: action, which will be called by the delete/backspace key on the keyboard. Since the user can always highlight a section of the number by touching it, as well as put the insertion cursor at the beginning of the number, we need to consider a few things there before deleting any text.

Creating the Keyboard Input View

Now let's create the GUI. Use the New File Assistant once again to make a new view .xib resource, naming it RpnKeyboard. Open the *RpnKeyboard.xib* file in Interface Builder, select the File's Owner proxy icon, and use the identity inspector to set its class to InputView.

The .xib should already contain a UIView, which you should now open. If you created the .xib file as an iPad resource (instead of an iPhone resource), it may be preconfigured for full-screen usage. In that case, use the attribute inspector to disable its status bar.

Now resize the view so that it can accommodate the buttons we need. The view will be resized to the correct iPad keyboard space before being displayed, so the exact size isn't too important—anything around 500 by 250 pixels should be just fine.

Use the attribute inspector to set the view's background color to light gray by clicking the color well for the background color, choosing the grayscale slider in the color picker that appears, and selecting 75%. This will help give your keyboard an appearance that's similar to the normal keyboard.

Now drag in a basic Round Rect Button from the Library, and then control-drag from it to the File's Owner icon, connecting it to the takeInputFromTitle: action. Then duplicate the button ten times with ⌘D, and arrange the buttons as shown in Figure 9–6, which also shows the titles you should set on each button. Let Interface Builder help you define spacing between these buttons. There should be a natural spot at which the buttons snap into place, 8 pixels apart from each other.

Figure 9–6. *The basic calculator-style numeric keypad*

Next, drag in another Round Rect Button from the Library, placing it to the right of the 9 button, and connect this one to the doTaggedAction: method in File's Owner. To make the function buttons stand out a bit from the numeric input buttons, use the attribute inspector to change this button's Type from Rounded Rect to Custom, and set its background color to something you like (I chose a slightly greenish blue). Duplicate this button three times, and put the buttons in a column to the right of the others, as shown in Figure 9–7. This figure also shows which mathematical symbol to use as the title for each button.

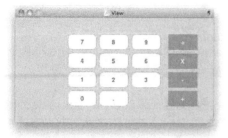

Figure 9–7. *Mathematical symbols*

Remember that the action method these buttons trigger looks at the sender's tag to see what it's supposed to do, so we're going to give each button a tag matching its function. Unfortunately, we can't use the tag names we defined as an enumerated type in InputView's header file (wouldn't that be sweet?). Instead, we need to use the corresponding integers: 1 for division, 2 for multiplication, 3 for subtraction, and 4 for addition. Open the attribute inspector, and then select one button at a time, setting each tag value in turn.

The final set of buttons will be the ones marked DEL and Enter on the left side. Select one of the buttons you just made on the right, duplicate it twice, and drag them both over to the left. Lay them out as shown in Figure 9–8, making the Enter button as tall as two normal buttons.

Figure 9–8. *The DEL and Enter buttons*

Change the Enter button's tag to 0 so that it activates the correct bit of functionality. Next, retarget the DEL button by control-dragging from the button to the File's Owner icon and selecting the doDelete: action. At this point, the DEL button will actually be misconfigured. A button click can trigger multiple action method calls, and setting a new connection doesn't delete any of the old ones. To fix this, open the connections inspector, where you can see the multiple actions that are configured for the DEL button. Delete the connection to doTaggedAction: so we don't have a DEL button doing crazy things.

I mentioned earlier that the view we create here will be resized automatically to the correct iPad keyboard size. Let's take control of how the resizing affects our buttons, making sure that the entire button group will remain a constant size and centered in the overall view.

Use the mouse to drag a rectangle across all 17 buttons, so that they're all highlighted, and then select **Layout ➤ Embed Objects In ➤ View** from the menu. With the new view selected, open the size inspector. To make sure this enclosing view remains centered, click to turn off all the red arrows and bars in the Autosizing section.

The special input view is now complete! Save your work, and then switch back to Xcode.

Creating the Calculator

We're now going to define our app's view controller, which does the actual work of being a calculator.

Open the *ClacHsilopViewController.h* file, and add the instance variables shown in the following listing. We also declare it to be a delegate of the InputView class.

```
//  ClacHsilopViewController.h
#import <UIKit/UIKit.h>
#import "InputView.h"
@interface ClacHsilopViewController : UIViewController <InputViewDelegate> {
  IBOutlet InputView *inputView;
  IBOutlet UITableView *stackTableView;
  NSNumberFormatter *decimalFormatter;
  NSMutableArray *stack;
}
@end
```

Before implementing that class, let's set up the GUI. Open *ClacHsilopViewController.xib* in Interface Builder. Select the main view and set its background color to a darker gray, just to make our other components stand out. Then use the Library to find an InputView, and drag it to the top of the view. Our table will eventually display the stack in a right-justified column, so right-justify the InputView as well, using the attribute inspector.

Next, drag out a UITableView, making it fill most of the view, as shown in Figure 9–9. The table doesn't need to extend to the bottom of the view, since the customized inputView will be appearing on top of it.

Connect the table view's dataSource and delegate outlets to the File's Owner proxy icon, as well as the InputView's ivDelegate outlet. Then connect the inputView and stackTableView outlets to the appropriate objects. Save your work now, and switch back to Xcode.

Figure 9–9. *Text and a table*

Open *ClacHsilopViewController.m*. This class will have two primary functions: presenting the contents of the stack in a table view and handling the actual calculator functionality in response to the user working the controls.

```
//  ClacHsilopViewController.m
#import "ClacHsilopViewController.h"
@implementation ClacHsilopViewController
- (void)viewDidLoad {
  [super viewDidLoad];
  stack = [[NSMutableArray alloc] init];
  decimalFormatter = [[NSNumberFormatter alloc] init];
  decimalFormatter.numberStyle = NSNumberFormatterDecimalStyle;
  [stackTableView reloadData];
  [inputView becomeFirstResponder];
}
- (BOOL)shouldAutorotateToInterfaceOrientation:(UIInterfaceOrientation)o {
  return YES;
}
- (void)dealloc {
  [stack release];
  [decimalFormatter release];
  [super dealloc];
}
- (NSInteger)numberOfSectionsInTableView:(UITableView *)tableView {
  return 1;
}
- (NSInteger)tableView:(UITableView *)tableView
  numberOfRowsInSection:(NSInteger)s {
```

```objc
  return [stack count];
}
- (UITableViewCell *)tableView:(UITableView *)tableView
    cellForRowAtIndexPath:(NSIndexPath *)indexPath {
  static NSString *CellIdentifier = @"Cell";
  UITableViewCell *cell = [tableView dequeueReusableCellWithIdentifier:
    CellIdentifier];
  if (cell == nil) {
    cell = [[[UITableViewCell alloc] initWithStyle:
      UITableViewCellStyleValue1
    reuseIdentifier:CellIdentifier] autorelease];
  }
  cell.detailTextLabel.text = [decimalFormatter stringFromNumber:[stack
    objectAtIndex:indexPath.row]];

  return cell;
}
- (void)handleError {
  // in case of an error, push the current number
  // onto the stack instead of just tossing it
  NSDecimalNumber *inputNumber = [NSDecimalNumber
    decimalNumberWithString:inputView.text];
  [stack insertObject:inputNumber atIndex:0];
  inputView.text = @"Error";
}
- (void)doEnter {
  NSDecimalNumber *inputNumber = [NSDecimalNumber
    decimalNumberWithString:inputView.text];
  [stack insertObject:inputNumber atIndex:0];
  [stackTableView reloadData];
  inputView.text = @"0";
}
- (void)doDecimalArithmetic:(SEL)method {
  if ([stack count] > 0) {
    NSDecimalNumber *inputNumber = [NSDecimalNumber
      decimalNumberWithString:inputView.text];
    NSDecimalNumber *stackNumber = [stack objectAtIndex:0];
    NSDecimalNumber *result = [stackNumber performSelector:method
      withObject:inputNumber];
    inputView.text = [decimalFormatter stringFromNumber:result];
    [stack removeObjectAtIndex:0];
  } else {
    [self handleError];
  }
  [stackTableView reloadData];
}
- (void)doTaggedAction:(ActionTag)tag forInputView:(InputView *)iv {
  switch (tag) {
    case ActionEnter:
      [self doEnter];
      break;
    case ActionDivide:
      [self doDecimalArithmetic:@selector(decimalNumberByDividingBy:)];
      break;
    case ActionMultiply:
      [self doDecimalArithmetic:
        @selector(decimalNumberByMultiplyingBy:)];
```

```
      break;
   case ActionSubtract:
      [self doDecimalArithmetic:@selector(decimalNumberBySubtracting:)];
      break;
   case ActionAdd:
      [self doDecimalArithmetic:@selector(decimalNumberByAdding:)];
      break;
   default:
      break;
   }
}
@end
```

That's it! With this code in place, you should now be able to build and run the app, see the GUI appear, and immediately have the RPN input keypad at your disposal.

That's All the Input You Need

In this chapter, you've learned about the great new input features included in iOS 3.2. While things like gesture recognition have been theoretically possible all along by tracking events, including an API for recognizing them will help developers add interactivity that they might have otherwise skipped. Adding items to the text-editing menu feels like a surprise, considering that the menu itself has been around for only about a year, but this could be a useful addition for some kinds of applications. Enhancing the keyboard has been a sore point for many iPhone developers for years, so the ability to extend or even completely redefine the keyboard as we wish is a welcome change indeed!

This concludes our coverage of the new GUI features in iOS 3.2. In Chapter 10, you'll learn about techniques for letting your app "play nice" with other apps by passing files and other kinds of data back and forth between them.

Working with Documents

For anyone with a background in programming desktop apps, the iPhone presents some unique challenges. Lacking anything like the Mac OS Finder or the Windows Explorer, the system does not provide a general-purpose technique for displaying a file or a collection of files. There has been no way to deal with files as discrete chunks of interchangeable data, and no way to determine if the device has any other installed apps that could have a use for your app's data. Furthermore, moving documents back and forth between the iPhone and the desktop has not been easy. Many developers have included a built-in web server in their apps for the sole purpose of letting a web browser on the desktop connect to an iPhone on the same Wi-Fi network and exchange files with it.

Starting with iOS 3.2 for the iPad, the support for working with files has improved greatly. Although there's still nothing like the Finder, apps can now declare their ability to open particular types of files. Additionally, each app that deals with a file of any kind can ask the system to display a list of other apps that can open that file, and pass the file directly to the app that the user chooses. Apple has also added basic document synchronization support, letting apps declare that particular documents should be shared with the desktop computer, where they'll show up in iTunes.

In this chapter, you'll learn how to use these new features so that your apps can play well with others. Once again, we'll be working with Dudel. You'll learn how to pass files to other apps, how to register a file type that an app can open, and how to deal with files that are passed in from other apps. You'll also learn how to use the new synchronization capabilities of iOS 3.2 (combined with iTunes) to copy files from your iPad to your computer, as well as the other way around.

Passing Files to Another Application

The new document-interaction features found in iOS 3.2 let apps work together in a whole new way, somewhat compensating for the operating system's lack of multitasking, or its inability to let you drag files or other objects from one app to another. With the new document-interaction facility, you can take the output of one app and pass it to another app, where the user might do some additional work on it, and then pass it along to yet another app.

Each iPhone app can register itself, via its *Info.plist* file, as being able to open particular types of files. The operating system itself keeps track of which apps are registered for which file types. All you need to do in order to pass a file to another app is call a single method that figures out the type of the file, determines which apps can open it, presents the user with a list of valid apps in a popover, and lets the user choose one. If the user chooses an app from the list, your app will exit, and the operating system will start the other app, passing along the file.

We'll implement this in Dudel by creating a PDF file and letting the user pass it off to another app. In order for this work, you'll first need to install an app from the App Store that will accept PDF files. I'm using GoodReader, which is an inexpensive, full-featured app for dealing with PDF and other image formats. But feel free to use any other PDF viewer you prefer. As long as it can open PDF files, it should work for our purposes.

> **NOTE:** All the examples used in this chapter involve communicating with other apps. Since the iPad Simulator lets you use only a small subset of the iPad's included apps (plus any apps you build and install yourself), you'll need to use an actual iPad connected to your computer to test the code in this chapter.

Adding a PDF-Sending Menu Action

Let's start by adding an item to the `ActionsMenuController` so that we have a way to activate the PDF-sending method. Add a line to the enumerated types declared in *ActionsMenuController.h*:

```
typedef enum SelectedActionType {
  NoAction = -1,
  NewDocument,
  RenameDocument,
  DeleteDocument,
  EmailPdf,
  OpenPdfElsewhere,
  ShowAppInfo
} SelectedActionType;
```

Then extend the implementation in *ActionsMenuController.m* to include one more row:

```
- (NSInteger)tableView:(UITableView *)tableView numberOfRowsInSection:
(NSInteger)section {
    // Return the number of rows in the section.
    return 5;
    return 6;
}
```

In the same file, make sure the `tableView:cellForRowAtIndexPath:` method provides a value for the new row as well. Add the following inside its large `switch` construct:

```
    case OpenPdfElsewhere:
      cell.textLabel.text = @"Open PDF in another app";
      break;
```

Now it's time to switch our attention to the DudelViewController, starting with a few changes to the interface in *DudelViewController.h*. First, add yet another protocol to the growing list of protocols that this class implements:

```
@interface DudelViewController : UIViewController <ToolDelegate, DudelViewDelegate,
MFMailComposeViewControllerDelegate, UIPopoverControllerDelegate,
ModalWebViewControllerDelegate, FileRenameViewControllerDelegate,
UIDocumentInteractionControllerDelegate> {
```

We're also going to need to have access to the menu bar item that brings up the action menu, so add the following instance variable:

```
IBOutlet UIBarButtonItem *actionsMenuButton;
```

Save your changes, and open *DudelViewController.xib* in Interface Builder. Open the view it contains, scroll to the bottom (if it's not already visible), and then control-drag from File's Owner to the relevant menu bar item and connect the actionsMenuButton outlet. Then save your changes.

Preparing a File for Sending

Switch back to Xcode and open *DudelViewController.m*, where we'll implement the rest of this functionality. Start off in handleDismissedPopoverController, adding this chunk to its switch construct:

```
case OpenPdfElsewhere:
  [self openPdfElsewhere];
  break;
```

Before we implement the openPdfElsewhere method, we need to refactor some work we did earlier. Back in Chapter 4, we added the sendPdfEmail method, which creates a PDF drawing context that writes into an NSMutableData object, does the drawing, and then uses the resulting data object as an attachment in an outbound e-mail message. In order to send a PDF representation of our document to another app, we need to do some of the same things. Rather than duplicating that functionality, let's break up the old method into two: one that generates the PDF data and another that sends the e-mail message. That way, our new method will be able to reuse the data-creation method, but then do its own thing with the data that's produced.

```
// Remove sendPdfEmail, and replace it with these two methods:
- (NSData *)pdfDataForCurrentDocument {
  // set up PDF rendering context
  NSMutableData *pdfData = [NSMutableData data];
  UIGraphicsBeginPDFContextToData(pdfData, dudelView.bounds, nil);
  UIGraphicsBeginPDFPage();

  // tell our view to draw
  [dudelView drawRect:dudelView.bounds];

  // remove PDF rendering context
  UIGraphicsEndPDFContext();
```

```
  return pdfData;
}
- (void)sendPdfEmail {
  NSData *pdfData = [self pdfDataForCurrentDocument];
  // send PDF data in mail message
  MFMailComposeViewController *mailComposer = [[[MFMailComposeViewController alloc]
init] autorelease];
  mailComposer.mailComposeDelegate = self;
  [mailComposer addAttachmentData:pdfData mimeType:@"application/pdf" fileName:@"Dudel
creation.pdf"];
  [self presentModalViewController:mailComposer animated:YES];
}
```

Invoking the Document Interaction Controller

Now we get to the interesting part. The openPdfElsewhere method takes the generated
PDF data, saves it to a temporary file, and passes it off to a newly created
UIDocumentInteractionController. This is a special-purpose controller that knows how
to see which installed apps can open a given file, based on their declared file-opening
abilities.

```
- (void)openPdfElsewhere {
  NSData *pdfData = [self pdfDataForCurrentDocument];
  NSString *filePath = [NSTemporaryDirectory() stringByAppendingPathComponent:@"Dudel
creation.pdf"];
  NSURL *fileURL = [NSURL fileURLWithPath:filePath];
  NSError *writeError = nil;
  [pdfData writeToURL:fileURL options:0 error:&writeError];
  if (writeError) {
    NSLog(@"Error writing file '%@' :\n%@", filePath, writeError);
    return;
  }
  UIDocumentInteractionController *docController =
  [UIDocumentInteractionController interactionControllerWithURL:fileURL];
  docController.delegate = self;
  BOOL result = [docController presentOpenInMenuFromBarButtonItem:actionsMenuButton
animated:YES];
}
```

Here, we call the presentOpenInMenuFromBarButtonItem method, which will bring up a
popover containing the names of all installed apps that can handle that file, as shown in
Figure 10–1. If no apps can handle the given file, you won't see this popover. But if one
or more apps will accept that file, the popover appears and waits for you to select an
app. In either case, this popover is taken care of by the
UIDocumentInteractionController itself, so we will never need to dismiss it or otherwise
deal with it.

Figure 10–1. *If any of the installed apps can open the file, a popover appears with a list.*

So, what happens when you select an app from the list? Basically, the current app will exit, and the chosen app will start up with some parameters telling it which file to open. Before the current app quits, the UIDocumentInteractionController will call some methods in its delegate (if the methods are implemented) that give you a chance to do some things. But at that stage, your app should really be prepared to just let go, so the chosen app can open as quickly and seamlessly as possible.

So that's all you need to do in order to send a file to another app. Most of the code we've added so far in this chapter has just been to facilitate a new item in our action menu. Passing a file to another app is basically just a matter of creating an instance of UIDocumentInteractionController and giving it the URL to your file. The rest is handled for you. So how do you go about receiving a file?

Receiving Files

As it turns out, receiving a file can be a bit trickier than sending one. The first step is to register your application as a suitable viewer/editor for the file type you want to have passed your way. This registration shouldn't be confused with anything like stuffing values into the Windows registry. In fact, this type of registration is completely passive. All you need to do is specify in your app's *Info.plist* (which is called *Dudel-Info.plist* in our case) which types of files it should open. The operating system itself will examine your declared type compatibilities and use that information to figure out where other apps may be able to send their data. The second step will be to implement a UIApplication delegate method that will let your app notice the URL of a file being sent its way at launch time and do something with it.

Registering As a Recipient

iOS, like its predecessor, Mac OS X, has a rather complex system of determining the type of data that's represented by a file or a data stream. Depending on whether the data is in a file, coming from a web server or a mail message, or being accessed in some other way, the operating system might use a filename extension, MIME type declaration, or a UTI to determine just what this hunk of data is and figure out which application should deal with it.

Everyone knows about filename extensions, and you probably have seen MIME type declarations in one place or another. But you may not be familiar with the UTI concept. The idea of UTI, introduced by Apple a few years ago, is to use a reverse domain name scheme (like the system used for naming Java packages or identifiers for iPhone apps) to identify data types.

Apple defines UITs for a large number of common data types, such as text and images, which all begin with the prefix `public` (such as `public.text`, `public.image`, and `public.png`). You should use `public` UTIs for describing your data whenever possible.

When you have your own data type, such as the format in which Dudel saves its document files, you should make up your own UTI. You can use some combination of the name of your company, the name of the primary application that uses the type, and the type name itself. In the case of our Dudel document files, we'll create a `com.rebisoft.dudeldoc` UTI. (Rebisoft is the name of the company through which Dudel is published on the App Store.)

Declaring a Data Type's Existence with UTI

To begin the registration, open *Dudel-Info.plist* in your Xcode project. By default, you'll be editing this file using a graphical editor that gives you an outline view of the property list document. For the changes we need to make, you're better off editing the XML directly. Right-click anywhere in the document view and select **Open As ➤ Plain Text File** from the context menu, forcing the editor to redisplay the property list's context as plain XML.

You'll see that the XML contains a `<plist>` tag, followed by a `<dict>` tag. To declare the existence of our new document type, insert the following chunk of XML immediately after the `<dict>` line, so that it ends up inside that element.

```
<key>UTExportedTypeDeclarations</key>
<array>
        <dict>
                <key>UTTypeConformsTo</key>
                <array>
                        <string>public.data</string>
                </array>
                <key>UTTypeDescription</key>
                <string>Dudel Document File</string>
                <key>UTTypeIdentifier</key>
                <string>com.rebisoft.dudeldoc</string>
                <key>UTTypeTagSpecification</key>
                <dict>
                        <key>public.filename-extension</key>
                        <string>dudeldoc</string>
                </dict>
        </dict>
</array>
```

Here, we first create a one-element array of dictionaries associated with the UTExportedTypeDeclarations key, which is used by the operating system to see which special data types our app knows about. We can declare one or more other UTIs to which our new type conforms.

The idea is that these types, like Objective-C classes, exist in a hierarchy. In this case, it's a multiple-inheritance hierarchy, since a type can have multiple parents. These parent types can be used by the operating system to determine which context a resource can be used in. In our case, we just declare public.data as a parent for our new type. This is about the most generic thing you can do. It basically just tells the operating system that our UTI exists and represents a chunk of data.

Note that the preceding XML doesn't say anything about our app. In fact, it's only there to declare the existence of our new data type, and establish a potential mapping between the filename extension we specified (*dudeldoc*) and the UTI (com.rebisoft.dudeldoc). With this bit of metadata at hand, the operating system can look at a *.dudeldoc* file and at least determine a UTI for it.

Declaring Data Type Ownership Using UTI

But what will the operating system do with that UTI? The idea is that it will find an app that declares, "Hey, I know how to open that file!" That's where another piece of XML comes in. Add the following to the *Dudel-Info.plist* file, directly below the previous XML you added.

```xml
<key>CFBundleDocumentTypes</key>
<array>
        <dict>
                <key>CFBundleTypeIconFiles</key>
                <array>
                        <string>Dudel_AppIcon_320x320.png</string>
                        <string>Dudel_AppIcon_64x64.png</string>
                </array>
                <key>CFBundleTypeName</key>
                <string>Dudel Document File</string>
                <key>CFBundleTypeRole</key>
                <string>Editor</string>
                <key>LSHandlerRank</key>
                <string>Owner</string>
                <key>LSItemContentTypes</key>
                <array>
                        <string>com.rebisoft.dudeldoc</string>
                </array>
        </dict>
</array>
```

Here, we have another single-entity array, this time declaring that our app knows how to open and edit documents of the com.rebisoft.dudeldoc type. It also specifies a couple of icons that the operating system can use to display a graphical representation of this type. The source archive for this book includes these two icons, which you should add to your Xcode project. This XML also defines a human-readable name for this document type.

Next are a couple of key/value pairs that give the operating system more information. The first says that Dudel is an `Editor` for this type, capable of making changes to it (as opposed to a `Viewer`, which can only display the file). The next definition says that our app should be considered the `Owner` for this data type. This means that if the system must choose between one of several apps capable of opening a *.dudeldoc* file, it will tend to pick Dudel first. These definitions are direct carryovers from Mac OS X, where they are commonly used by the Finder to figure out how to deal with files you double-click, for example. In iOS, there's still not a lot of concrete use for these settings. However, if your app is dealing with files, it's best to set these up, in case future versions of iOS make better use of this metadata.

Testing the File-Receiving Feature

Now that we've declared our UTIs, Dudel is nearly ready to have files sent to it. In fact, if you build and run Dudel on your iPad, as far as iPhone OS can tell, Dudel really seems ready. For example, if Mail encounters a *.dudeldoc* file in a mail message, it will try to open it in Dudel.

You can test this now by using your computer to e-mail yourself an empty document named *something.dudeldoc* and then viewing that e-mail on your iPad. You should see something like Figure 10–2, with Mail displaying an icon for the empty document. If you tap and hold on the document icon, you'll see a popover that gives you an option to open the file in Dudel. But don't try that just yet. We haven't implemented the method in our app delegate to handle the file. We'll do that next.

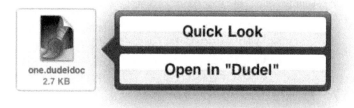

Figure 10–2. *About to open a Dudel document in Mail*

NOTE: As of this writing, using iOS 3.2, Mail's handling of custom UTIs seems a bit incomplete. A UTI declared with only `public.data` as its parent will sometimes show up in Mail, but other times it will not. If you're suffering from this problem, try making it declare `public.text` as the parent type. That will add another somewhat messy view to Mail (since it will want to try to preview the "text," which isn't text at all), but at least it will let you try out the workflow of sending and receiving documents.

Retrieving File Information from Launch Options

Now we need to write some code that will be run when our app is launched, making it check to see if it's being asked to open a file. We'll add code to the application:didFinishLaunchingWithOptions: method in DudelAppDelegate. If the app is being asked to open a file, it happens here, via one of the values in the launchOptions dictionary.

```
- (BOOL)application:(UIApplication *)application
didFinishLaunchingWithOptions:(NSDictionary *)launchOptions {
  // Override point for customization after app launch
  [window addSubview:splitViewController.view];
  [window makeKeyAndVisible];
  [[NSNotificationCenter defaultCenter] addObserver:self
    selector:@selector(fileListControllerSelectedFile:)
    name:FileListControllerSelectedFile object:fileListController];

  NSURL *openedUrl = [launchOptions
    objectForKey:UIApplicationLaunchOptionsURLKey];
  if (openedUrl) {
    if ([openedUrl isFileURL]) {
      // Handle the file that's passed in
      [[FileList sharedFileList] importAndSelectFromURL:openedUrl];
    }
  }
  return YES;
}
```

The URL that's passed in here points to a temporary location where the system is holding a copy of the file we sent. If we want to keep it, we need to make our own copy in the app's normal Documents directory. Instead of doing it right there in the app delegate, we pass that responsibility along to a class that has taken care of many other file-management issues for us: FileList. Add the following lines to *FileList.h* and *FileList.m* to make the magic happen.

```
// FileList.h
- (void)importAndSelectFromURL:(NSURL *)url;
// FileList.m
- (void)importAndSelectFromURL:(NSURL *)url {
  NSString *importFilePath = [url path];
  NSString *importFilename = [importFilePath lastPathComponent];
  NSArray *dirs =
    NSSearchPathForDirectoriesInDomains(NSDocumentDirectory,
    NSUserDomainMask, YES);
  NSString *dir = [dirs objectAtIndex:0];
  NSString *filename = importFilename;
  NSFileManager *fm = [NSFileManager defaultManager];
  if ([fm fileExistsAtPath:[dir
    stringByAppendingPathComponent:filename]]) {
    NSString *filenameWithoutExtension = [filename
      stringByDeletingPathExtension];
    NSString *extension = [filename pathExtension];
    BOOL filenameAlreadyInUse = YES;
    for (NSUInteger counter = 1; filenameAlreadyInUse; counter++) {
      filename = [NSString stringWithFormat:@"%@-%d.%@",
```

```
                    filenameWithoutExtension,
                    counter,
                    extension];
        filenameAlreadyInUse = [fm fileExistsAtPath:[dir
          stringByAppendingPathComponent:filename]];
      }
    }
    NSError *error = nil;
    [fm copyItemAtPath:importFilePath toPath:[dir
      stringByAppendingPathComponent:filename] error:&error];
    [allFiles addObject:filename];
    [allFiles sortUsingSelector:@selector(compare:)];
    self.currentFile = filename;
    [[NSNotificationCenter defaultCenter]
      postNotificationName:FileListChanged object:self];
}
```

This method basically just copies the file, but not before checking to make sure the
filename isn't already taken. If the name exists, it will come up with a new filename by
tacking on a number.

Sending a Dudeldoc File

Now we are ready to accept files sent to Dudel. But so far, there aren't any *.dudeldoc*
files anywhere outside Dudel's own documents directory, so no one else can send us
anything! Let's solve that by adding yet another item to our action menu to let us send a
.dudeldoc file as an e-mail attachment. This should be very familiar to you by now. Make
the additions and changes to the various files as follows:

```
// ActionsMenuController.h
typedef enum SelectedActionType {
  NoAction = -1,
  NewDocument,
  RenameDocument,
  DeleteDocument,
  EmailDudelDoc,
  EmailPdf,
  OpenPdfElsewhere,
  ShowAppInfo
} SelectedActionType;

// ActionsMenuController.m
- (NSInteger)tableView:(UITableView *)tableView numberOfRowsInSection:
  (NSInteger)section {
    // Return the number of rows in the section.
    return 6;
    return 7;
}
// Add this near the end of tableView:cellForRowAtIndexPath:
    case EmailDudelDoc:
      cell.textLabel.text = @"Send DudelDoc via email";
      break;

// DudelViewController.m
- (void)sendDudelDocEmail {
```

```
    NSString *filepath = [FileList sharedFileList].currentFile;

    [self saveCurrentToFile:filepath];
    NSData *fileData = [NSData dataWithContentsOfFile:filepath];
    MFMailComposeViewController *mailComposer =
      [[[MFMailComposeViewController alloc] init] autorelease];
    mailComposer.mailComposeDelegate = self;
    [mailComposer addAttachmentData:fileData
      mimeType:@"application/octet-stream"
      fileName:[filepath lastPathComponent]];
    [self presentModalViewController:mailComposer animated:YES];
}
// Add this near the end of handleDismissedPopoverController:
      case EmailDudelDoc:
        [self sendDudelDocEmail];
        break;
```

Now you should be able to test the entire workflow for handling Dudel documents. You can create a document, e-mail it to yourself, switch to Mail and see the attachment, and press and hold to see the popover that lets you send the file to Dudel. After you send the file, you can see it in your list with a new filename (in order to avoid overwriting the original file).

Desktop Synchronization

Another new piece of document-related functionality on the iPad is the ability to synchronize your app's files with the desktop. Starting with iOS 3.2, applications can register for desktop synchronization by adding the following key/value pair to their *Info.plist* file:

```
      <key>UIFileSharingEnabled</key>
      <true/>
```

That's all! Add this to *Dudel-Info.plist*, and build and run that on your iPad.

Now, while your iPad is still connected to your computer, go into iTunes on your computer, select your iPad in the navigation area on the left, and then click the Apps tab to bring it forward. You'll see all the installed apps as usual, but with one new twist: a new File Sharing section at the bottom of the window's content area. This section shows all the apps that have sharable document content, and Dudel is there! Select Dudel, and you can see everything in our Documents directory, as shown in Figure 10–3.

You can drag files out to the Finder to save them on your computer, and you can drag other files from your computer back in. You'll see whatever documents you've created in Dudel, and perhaps also a subdirectory called Inbox. (The Inbox directory is the place where the system puts files temporarily when your app is asked to open them. You should probably just leave it alone.)

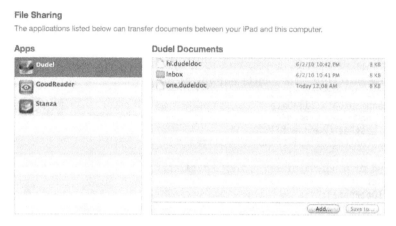

File Sharing

The applications listed below can transfer documents between your iPad and this computer.

Apps	Dudel Documents		
Dudel	hi.dudeldoc	6/2/10 10:42 PM	8 KB
GoodReader	Inbox	6/2/10 10:41 PM	8 KB
Stanza	one.dudeldoc	Today 12:08 AM	8 KB

Add...   Save to...

Figure 10–3. *The iTunes view of your Dudel document directory*

> **NOTE:** If the interface for accessing documents from your iPad seems uninspired to you, you're not alone. When Apple announced this technology initially, many of us were hoping for something better, like having the Documents directories from the iPad show up directly in the Finder, or even allowing you to automatically synchronize files between an iPad and a computer (instead of manually dragging them around as the current setup requires). However, the iPad is still a new product, and surely the software (both in the device and on the computer it links with) will evolve over time. Let's keep our fingers crossed for some improvements from Apple in this area.

Share and Share Alike

Now you've gotten a taste of the various document-management features that the iPad offers. What you've seen here only scratches the surface.

For instance, we've assumed that when importing a document whose filename already exists, we should just generate a new filename. However, you might want to make a suite of applications that are basically playing "hot potato" with a document, quickly passing it around to have different things done with it in each place. So, you might want to instead let a duplicate-named imported document just replace the old one. Or you may want to ask the user what to do each time it happens.

This way of dealing with documents opens a lot of possibilities for making apps that interoperate smoothly with one another. It will be interesting to see how this evolves.

Speaking of evolving, it's now time for you to head on to Chapter 11. There, you'll learn how to take an existing iPhone app and prepare it for the iPad, so that it can make the most of the new screen size and new GUI paradigms.

Chapter 11

From iPhone to iPad

Over the course of this book, you've gone through the creation of several apps made just for iPad. But if you're coming into this as an iPhone developer, chances are you already have one or more apps that you would like to bring over to the iPad. Yes, you could just run them on the iPad, but that's far from ideal. Both of the iPad's methods for displaying an iPhone app—either showing it at actual size in the middle of the screen or stretching the display to make it fill the entire iPad screen—are pretty disappointing for most applications.

In this chapter, you'll learn how to take an existing iPhone application and turn it into a first-class citizen on the iPad, making full use of the extra screen real estate, as well as the new user interface functionality available in the iPhone SDK. We'll start by creating a new iPhone application that includes drill-down navigation and a detail view, and then consider how to adapt it to the iPad. We'll walk through the steps to take in Xcode and Interface Builder, and reorganize the view controllers to make the application work more nicely on the big screen.

Introducing NavApp for iPhone

To demonstrate the process of preparing an iPhone app for the new world of the iPad, we're going to create a simple application called NavApp, which follows a typical iPhone app pattern. You pick an item from a table view, which leads you to another table view full of items. Pick one of those, and you see some sort of detail about the item you chose. This basic arrangement can be seen in standard iPhone and iPad apps such as Mail and Settings.

Figure 11–1 shows the basic flow of NavApp, starting with a top-level view and drilling down to the details. The functionality here is really bare-bones, in order to keep the project small. That way, we can focus on the techniques needed specifically for transforming an iPhone app into an iPad app. These techniques are applicable to any sort of app that should behave differently on the iPad than on the iPhone, particularly applications that make use of UINavigationController and should be updated to display the navigation views in a more iPad-friendly way (which is probably most of them).

Figure 11–1. *The views of NavApp, shown in sequence*

Creating the NavApp Project

Start by creating a new project in Xcode, and choose the Navigation-based Application template, which automatically forces you to target iPhone instead of iPad. Name your project NavApp and save it somewhere appropriate.

Xcode creates classes called RootViewController and NavAppAppDelegate for you, along with GUI layouts in *RootViewController.xib* and *MainWindow.xib*. If you've done much iPhone development in the past, you're familiar with this arrangement. The *MainWindow.xib* file, which is loaded when the app launches, contains a UINavigationViewController, which itself contains a RootViewController. The RootViewController will be presented as the initial view of the UINavigationViewController, and when the user selects an item, it will push the next view controller that should be displayed onto the UINavigationViewController.

We'll add a class that represents the next level of items that the user can drill down into, and then, a little later, another class that displays details about the user's selection. First, let's modify the classes that Xcode created for us, to make them do our bidding. As it turns out, the NavAppAppDelegate class created by Xcode is just fine, as is the *RootViewController.h* file, but we'll need to make some changes to *RootViewController.m*.

Enhancing the Root View Controller

First, import the header for the second-level view controller. We haven't created that class yet, but we'll get to it soon enough, so we may as well add it now:

```
#import "SecondLevelViewController.h"
```

Next, find the viewWillAppear: method. By default, it's commented out and doesn't really do anything. Remove the surrounding /* */ and give it the following content:

```
- (void)viewWillAppear:(BOOL)animated {
  [super viewWillAppear:animated];
  self.navigationItem.title = @"Too Many Choices";
}
```

Now make a small change so that our table view has some rows:

```
- (NSInteger)tableView:(UITableView *)tableView numberOfRowsInSection:(NSInteger)section
{
  return 0;
  return 5;
}
```

Next, add a few lines near the end of tableView:cellForRowAtIndexPath:, to give those rows some content:

```
  // Configure the cell.
  cell.textLabel.text = [NSString stringWithFormat:@"Item #%d",
    indexPath.row];
  cell.accessoryType = UITableViewCellAccessoryDisclosureIndicator;

  return cell;
```

Finally, remove the commented sample code from
tableView:didSelectRowAtIndexPath:, and give it the following content instead:

```
- (void)tableView:(UITableView *)tableView
  didSelectRowAtIndexPath:(NSIndexPath *)indexPath {
  SecondLevelViewController *detailViewController =
    [[SecondLevelViewController alloc] initWithStyle:
      UITableViewStylePlain];
  detailViewController.choice = [NSString stringWithFormat:@"Item #%d",
    indexPath.row];
  // Pass the selected object to the new view controller.
  [self.navigationController pushViewController:detailViewController
    animated:YES];
  [detailViewController release];
}
```

That's all we need to do for our RootViewController class.

Defining the Second Level View Controller

Now use the New File Assistant to create a new controller class called
SecondLevelViewController, making it a subclass of UITableViewController with no .xib
file. Like the RootViewController class, SecondLevelViewController requires just a few
changes to the Xcode-generated default to make it work the way we want.

Begin in the .h file, adding the choice instance variable and property to keep track of
which item the user chose at the root level:

```
@interface SecondLevelViewController : UITableViewController {
  NSString *choice;
}
@property (copy, nonatomic) NSString *choice;
@end
```

Now switch over to *SecondLevelViewController.m*, where we'll make a few changes, similar to those we made for RootViewController. Import the header for the detail class that we'll use to present the final choice:

```
#import "ChoiceViewController.h"
```

Then take care of the choice property by adding this line right after the @implementation line:

```
@synthesize choice;
```

Next, uncomment the viewWillAppear: method, and use it to set the title for the navigation bar.

```
- (void)viewWillAppear:(BOOL)animated {
  [super viewWillAppear:animated];
  self.navigationItem.title = self.choice;
}
```

Add the following details to give our table view a section and a few rows:

```
- (NSInteger)numberOfSectionsInTableView:(UITableView *)tableView {
  // Return the number of sections.
  return 1;
}
- (NSInteger)tableView:(UITableView *)tableView
  numberOfRowsInSection:(NSInteger)section {
  // Return the number of rows in the section.
  return 3;
}
```

Then fill in the end of the tableView:cellForRowAtIndexPath: method:

```
  // Configure the cell...
  cell.textLabel.text = [NSString stringWithFormat:@"Sub-Item #%d",
    indexPath.row];
  cell.accessoryType = UITableViewCellAccessoryDisclosureIndicator;
  return cell;
```

Now implement the tableView:didSelectRowAtIndexPath: method, to pass along the final selection to the detail view:

```
- (void)tableView:(UITableView *)tableView didSelectRowAtIndexPath:(NSIndexPath
*)indexPath {
  ChoiceViewController *detailViewController = [[ChoiceViewController
    alloc] initWithNibName:@"ChoiceViewController" bundle:nil];
  detailViewController.choice = [NSString stringWithFormat:
    @"%@, Sub-Item #%d", self.choice, indexPath.row];
  // Pass the selected object to the new view controller.
  [self.navigationController pushViewController:detailViewController
    animated:YES];
  [detailViewController release];
}
```

Finally, complete the handling of the choices property by clearing it in the dealloc method:

```
- (void)dealloc {
```

```
  self.choice = nil;
  [super dealloc];
}
```

That takes care of the SecondLevelViewController class.

Defining the Choice View Controller

The final class we need for this project is a UIViewController subclass, containing a *.xib* file, named ChoiceViewController. This class is very simple. We just need to add a couple of instance variables, implement a single method, and define the GUI in Interface Builder. Start by adding the bold lines here to the header file:

```
@interface ChoiceViewController : UIViewController {
  NSString *choice;
  IBOutlet UILabel *choiceLabel;
}
@property (copy, nonatomic) NSString *choice;
@end
```

Then switch to *ChoiceViewController.m*, and add the following directly after the @implementation line:

```
@synthesize choice;
```

Unlike the template-generated table view controller classes, ChoiceViewController doesn't have a commented-out viewWillAppear: method just waiting for us to fill in, so we'll need to give it one, as follows:

```
- (void)viewWillAppear:(BOOL)animated {
  [super viewWillAppear:animated];
  self.navigationItem.title = self.choice;
  choiceLabel.text = choice;
}
```

Finally, clear out the choices property in the dealloc method:

```
- (void)dealloc {
  self.choice = nil;
  [super dealloc];
}
```

The last step to complete this project is to set up the *ChoiceViewController.xib* file. Open it in Interface Builder, and use three UILabel objects from the Library window to create a GUI like the one shown in Figure 11–2.

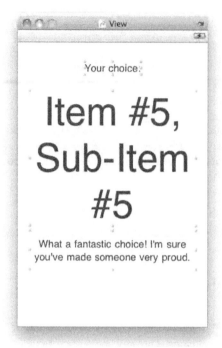

Figure 11–2. *The ChoiceViewController GUI layout. The little resizing controls show where the labels are placed.*

With the GUI in place, control-drag from the File's Owner icon to the central UILabel and connect the choiceLabel outlet to it. After doing that, save your work and go back to Xcode.

Now you're almost ready to build and run NavApp. Before that, though, you need to know about a nuance in Xcode that you may not have thought much about: the Overview popup in the Xcode toolbar, particularly the Active SDK section, where a number of SDK choices are made available.

Choosing the Active SDK

The Active SDK choice is actually dual-purpose. It controls both which SDK your app is built with (affecting which APIs are available to your app) and which SDK is used for launching the iPhone Simulator when you try things out on your machine. At the time of this writing, the latest public iPhone OS release for iPhone devices is 3.1.3; for iPad, it's 3.2.

To see what these settings do, first set the Active SDK to iPhone Simulator 3.1.3, and then hit the Build and Run button in the toolbar. Xcode will start the Simulator in iPhone mode and launch your application. You should now be able to navigate through the app as you would expect, making selections and seeing results in the final screen. Now quit your app.Back in Xcode, switch the Active SDK to iPhone Simulator 3.2. Then start your app, without first building, by selecting **Run ➤ Run** from the menu. Xcode will relaunch the simulator in iPad mode, and launch your app in the Simulator. But it won't work! You'll find that your app crashes immediately. This seems to be a problem inherent to the interaction between Xcode and the Simulator. Trying to run an app compiled for OS 3.1.3 in the Simulator running OS 3.2 just doesn't work.

However, the reverse is OK. You can build your app for OS 3.2 and still run it on OS 3.1.3, as long as you do some sort of runtime checks to make sure you're not using any OS 3.2 features. That's the suggested approach for creating universal apps that will run on both iPhone and iPad, and it's the direction we'll be taking with NavApp.

With iPhone Simulator 3.2 still selected, choose **Build ➤ Build and Run** from the menu. Your app will start up with the Simulator in iPad mode, and this time it will work, at least in a rudimentary way.

You'll have the sort of iPad experience that anyone with an iPad has probably had when running iPhone software that hasn't yet been updated for iPad. With a Cocoa Touch app such as this, your options are fairly uninteresting:

- You can display the app at actual size in the middle of the screen, ignoring most of the space available on the iPad.

- You can expand the app to fill the entire screen by doubling the number of pixels used. This misuses the nice big screen by just stretching all the GUI elements to grotesque proportions.

Fortunately, we can do better. Xcode gives us a way to upgrade an existing iPhone project to support iPad as well, automatically paving the way for our app to run on both iPhone and iPad by adding a new main *.xib* file, which is laid out to fit the iPad display, and configuring it to be loaded when the app is launched on an iPad.

Adding iPad to the Mix

Now we're ready to upgrade NavApp for the iPad. Before kicking off this process, make a backup copy of your project directory. This can be useful in case you want to compare your original app with the iPad-ready version that Xcode sets up.

Next, in the Groups & Files section of your Xcode project window, open the Targets section and select NavApp. Then select **Project ➤ Upgrade Current Target for iPad** from the menu. Xcode will present you with a modal sheet that asks whether you want to create a single universal application that will run on both iPhone and iPad, or create a second target for an iPad application in your project, leaving the original target intact. Select the One Universal application option, and then click OK.

Xcode now does a few simple things. It copies the *MainWindow.xib* file to *MainWindow-iPad.xib*, making a few changes to the file's contents, such as specifying the iPad's screen size. The new *.xib* file is added to the project, and a line is added to the *NavAppCompare-Info.plist* file, specifying that this new *.xib* file should be used when launching on the iPad. It also makes a few changes to your project, such as setting the base SDK to 3.2.

Taking the Upgraded NavApp for a Spin

Make sure that Simulator 3.2 is chosen as the Active SDK in Xcode, and then build and run the upgraded app. You should see NavApp spring to life, full size and at full resolution, in the Simulator. It will work just as it did in iPhone form, letting you drill down through the structure we laid out previously and displaying a similar result, as shown in Figure 11–3.

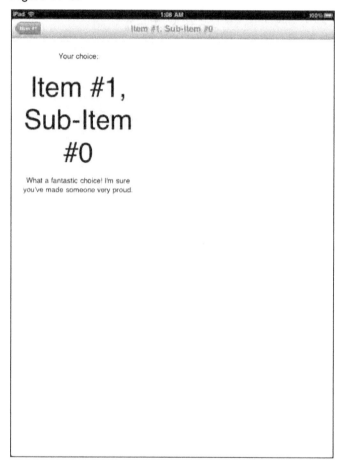

Figure 11–3. *The ChoiceViewController GUI, running on the iPad*

Although this type of upgrade works, it isn't what you really want for an iPad app. The popular iPhone pattern of drilling down into structures, with the entire content of the screen sliding out the side, isn't prevalent on the iPad. In fact, Apple actually recommends against that usage, for a couple of reasons:

- The full-screen wipe in response to simple tap on the screen, which works well enough on a small display such as the iPhone's, begins to feel a little off on a larger screen. The full-screen swish is best reserved for situations where the user actually made a swiping gesture.

- Since the iPad has so much more screen real estate, you can easily show a drill-down navigation view alongside of, or hovering in front of, the main content, by using a split view or a popover view (as you've seen in earlier chapters).

So, let's rethink the NavApp GUI for the iPad version.

Reconsidering iPhone Design ChoicesWhile the navigation views are the first things you see in NavApp, they're actually just stepping-stones leading to the app's main content view, which is handled by the `ChoiceViewController` class.

For the iPad version of this app, let's rework the design so that the final view is now front and center. We'll go about this by reconfiguring some *.xib* files, conditionally changing the behavior of the navigation views in response to user actions, and extending the `ChoiceViewController` class so that it can display something reasonable, even when the user hasn't selected anything yet. The navigation views will end up being displayed in the left-hand side of a split view, or in a floating popover view, depending on whether the iPad is in landscape or portrait mode. This is similar to what we did in the Dudel application earlier in this book, and even goes a step closer to the way that the iPad's built-in Mail application handles drilling down through accounts and folders to reach your messages.

The first step toward making this work will be to redefine what the NavAppAppDelegate class does, both in code and in its related *.xib* files. This class was created automatically when we created the Xcode project, and in its original form, it sets up the navigation interface (since that's the kind of project we created). We're going to add a bit of code that checks at runtime to see if we're running on an iPad, and if so, instead set up a split view interface. The other half of this redesign will be configuring the *MainWindow-iPad.xib* file so that it actually wraps things up in a split view.

Conditional Behavior: Know Your Idioms

Open *NavAppAppDelegate.h*, and add an outlet for a future `UISplitViewController` as shown here:

```
@interface NavAppAppDelegate : NSObject <UIApplicationDelegate> {
  UIWindow *window;
  UINavigationController *navigationController;
  UISplitViewController *splitViewController;
}
@property (nonatomic, retain) IBOutlet UIWindow *window;
@property (nonatomic, retain) IBOutlet UINavigationController *navigationController;
@property (nonatomic, retain) IBOutlet UISplitViewController *splitViewController;
@end
```

> **NOTE:** Throughout this book, we've been creating outlets by putting IBOutlet in front of the instance variable declaration. So why are we suddenly putting it in the property declaration here? The two are equivalent, and the choice of where to put IBOutlet is really a matter of style. In this case, we're working with a class template that was generated by Xcode and contains its IBOutlet markers in the property declarations. Rather than modifying the generated source code to make a change that has no quantifiable effect, we're just following the example of the surrounding code here. When in Rome …

Now switch over to *NavAppAppDelegate.m*, and configure the basics for the new outlet we created by adding this line near the top of the @implementation section:

```
@synthesize splitViewController;
```

Don't forget to free up that new resource as well:

```
- (void)dealloc {
  [splitViewController release];
  [navigationController release];
  [window release];
  [super dealloc];
}
```

Next is the interesting part of this class:

```
- (BOOL)application:(UIApplication *)application
    didFinishLaunchingWithOptions:(NSDictionary *)launchOptions {
  if (UI_USER_INTERFACE_IDIOM() == UIUserInterfaceIdiomPad) {
    [window addSubview:[splitViewController view]];
  } else {
    [window addSubview:[navigationController view]];
  }
  [window makeKeyAndVisible];
  return YES;
}
```

This method uses the UI_USER_INTERFACE_IDIOM function to determine whether the app is running on an iPad. If it is, we'll present a different view than what we show for the iPhone.

This is a pretty subtle shift. Keep in mind that the app delegate class is loaded from the app's main *.xib* file, and once it's loaded and the application has finished launching, this is the method that actually gives the application a view to display. With this small change, we radically alter the entire appearance and flow of the app! Of course, to make that really happen, we'll need to make sure that our new splitViewController outlet is actually pointing at something.

Configuring the Main iPad GUI

It's time to reorganize the main GUI, putting the navigation view inside a split view. Open *MainWindow-iPad.xib* in Interface Builder, and switch the main window to column view, revealing something like Figure 11–4.

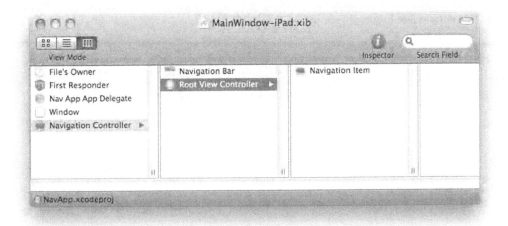

Figure 11–4. *The primary .xib file for the iPad version of our app, before our enhancements*

Here, we've drilled down into the Navigation Controller and Root View Controller objects, revealing the complete structure of the objects in this *.xib* file. If you select the Nav App App Delegate object in this window, and then open the connections inspector, you'll see that it has outlets connected to the window and to the navigation controller—the two objects that are tied together in code when the app launches—by virtue of adding the view controller's view to the window. We're going to add a UISplitViewController to this *.xib* file, and configure it so that the preceding conditional code adds the split view to the window.

Start by finding a UISplitViewController in the Library, and dragging it to the leftmost column of the *.xib* window. Then control-drag from the app delegate to the new split view controller, and hook up the splitViewController outlet.

The split view is meant to display views for two view controllers at once, and by default, the one we created will have a navigation controller and a generic view controller. The navigation controller contains a generic table view controller. We need to modify these objects, making them instances of the real classes we're using in our app.

Drill down into the Navigation Controller object inside the Split View Controller object, and select the Table View Controller object it contains. Open the identity inspector, and change that controller's class to RootViewController. Then switch to the attribute inspector to configure the controller a little more. Set the Title to **Changes**, and the NIB Name to *RootViewController*.

Now backtrack a bit, and select the generic View Controller object inside the Split View Controller object. Once again, bring up the identity inspector, and set this controller's class to `ChoiceViewController`

. Then switch back to the attribute inspector, and set the NIB Name to *ChoiceViewController-iPad*. That's the name of an *.xib* file that doesn't exist yet, but soon will, since we'll create it in the next section. At this point, your *.xib* window should look something like Figure 11–5.

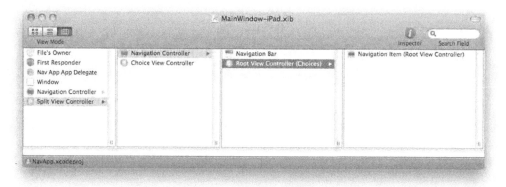

Figure 11–5. *The iPad version of the main .xib file after reconfiguring for iPad navigation*

As you learned in Chapter 8, proper use of a split view requires you to provide the split view controller with a delegate, which plays a role in juggling between a split view and a popover when the iPad is rotated. In this case, we'll connect the split view controller's delegate outlet to the choice view controller, and later we'll implement the delegate code there. Select the Split View Controller item so that you can see its children, control-drag from the Split View Controller object to the Choice View Controller object, and then connect the `delegate` outlet.

The final change for the *MainWindow-iPad.xib* file is to delete the navigation controller that's at the top level of the *.xib* file. The app delegate still has an outlet to it, but that doesn't really matter. When our app runs on an iPad, the iPad-specific *.xib* file is loaded, and the unconnected outlet is ignored.

Creating the Choice View Controller GUI for iPad

Earlier, we configured the `ChoiceViewController` instance in our main iPad GUI to use a special iPad-friendly *.xib* file. Let's create that now. Switch back to Xcode, and use the New File Assistant to create a new View XIB file, located in the iPhone OS / User Interface section. Make sure the product menu is displaying iPad, and click Next. Then name it *ChoiceViewController-iPad.xib* and click Next. You'll see the new file added to your project.

Before editing the new GUI, open *ChoiceViewController.h* and add the following instance variable:

```
IBOutlet UIToolbar *toolbar;
```

This new `toolbar` outlet will point at a toolbar in the iPad version of the GUI, which we'll create soon.

Open both *ChoiceViewController.xib* and *ChoiceViewController-iPad.xib* in Interface Builder. Unlike the original *.xib* file, which was created along with the class, the new one is kind of a blank slate. Select the File's Owner icon, and use the identity inspector to set its class to `ChoiceViewController`. Now switch to *ChoiceViewController.xib*, open its view, select all the GUI objects in there, and press ⌘C to copy them. Then switch back to the new *ChoiceViewController-iPad.xib* file, open its view (which you'll see is iPad-size), and paste in the GUI objects. You'll want to center them in the display, and should probably resize them to fill the width of the display as well—no sense letting all that screen real estate go to waste!

Now use the Library to find a `UIToolbar`, and drag it to the new iPad-ready `ChoiceViewController` view, dropping it at the top of the view so that the toolbar appears up there. The toolbar contains a single default item, which you should go ahead and delete. Finally, connect the outlets from the File's Owner icon to the GUI objects in the *.xib* file: `choiceLabel` to the big label in the middle, `toolbar` to the toolbar you just created, and `view` (which we didn't define in out class, but inherited from `UIViewController`) to the entire containing view.

Implementing the Split View Delegate Methods

Go back to Xcode, and open the *ChoiceViewController.m* file. Add the two required methods for the `UISplitViewController`:

```
- (void)splitViewController:(UISplitViewController*)svc
  willHideViewController:(UIViewController *)aViewController
  withBarButtonItem:(UIBarButtonItem*)barButtonItem
  forPopoverController:(UIPopoverController*)pc {
  // add the new button item to our toolbar
  NSArray *newItems = [toolbar.items arrayByAddingObject:barButtonItem];
  [toolbar setItems:newItems animated:YES];

  // configure the button
  barButtonItem.title = @"Choices";
}
- (void)splitViewController:(UISplitViewController*)svc
  willShowViewController:(UIViewController *)aViewController
  invalidatingBarButtonItem:(UIBarButtonItem *)button {
  // remove the button
  NSMutableArray *newItems = [[toolbar.items mutableCopy] autorelease];
  if ([newItems containsObject:button]) {
    [newItems removeObject:button];
    [toolbar setItems:newItems animated:YES];
  }
}
```

That's all we need to do in order to handle switching between portrait and landscape orientation. The split view controller will call the first method when switching to portrait mode, and the second method when switching to landscape mode.

At this point, you should be able to run the app. You'll see that it works … to some extent. The split view kicks in, displaying itself on the left side in landscape mode, and shrinking down to a button in the toolbar in portrait mode. Rotating from one to another isn't working yet, but we'll get to that a little later.

The problem is in the interaction between the view controllers themselves. All the action—not only the navigation, but also the display of the final selection—is constrained to the navigation view, whether it's appearing in the split view or in a popover view. The big view for displaying the choice just displays the default "dummy" text all the time! Clearly, we need to update our table view controllers so that they do different things in response to the user selecting a row, depending on whether the app is running on an iPhone or iPad.

Tweaking the Navigation Logic

First, we need to make a pair of identical changes for both *RootViewController.m* and *ChoiceViewController.m*, to ensure that the views can rotate properly. In each of those files, uncomment the `shouldAutorotateToInterfaceOrientation:` method, and make it always return YES:

```
- (BOOL)shouldAutorotateToInterfaceOrientation:(UIInterfaceOrientation)o{
  // Return YES for supported orientations.
  return YES;
}
```

Now switch over to *SecondLevelViewController.m*, where we'll make some rather more critical changes. Start by adding this somewhere near the top of the file:

#import "NavAppAppDelegate.h"

Next, uncomment the `shouldAutorotateToInterfaceOrientation:` method, and make it always return YES, as we just did for the `RootViewController` and `ChoiceViewController` classes.

Then, in the `tableView:cellForRowAtIndexPath:` method, add a bit of code so that we don't show the final disclosure indicator (the little right-pointing arrow/chevron that lets the users know that they can keep on digging):

```
  cell.textLabel.text = [NSString stringWithFormat:@"Sub-Item #%d", indexPath.row];
  if (UI_USER_INTERFACE_IDIOM() != UIUserInterfaceIdiomPad) {
    cell.accessoryType = UITableViewCellAccessoryDisclosureIndicator;
  }
```

Then change the behavior of the final selection here, so that instead of creating and pushing another view controller onto the navigation stack, we grab the "global" `ChoiceViewController` and just tell it what the selection is:

```
- (void)tableView:(UITableView *)tableView didSelectRowAtIndexPath:(NSIndexPath
*)indexPath {
```

```
if (UI_USER_INTERFACE_IDIOM() == UIUserInterfaceIdiomPad) {
  NavAppAppDelegate *appDelegate =
    [[UIApplication sharedApplication] delegate];
  UISplitViewController *splitViewController =
    appDelegate.splitViewController;
  ChoiceViewController *detailViewController =
    [splitViewController.viewControllers objectAtIndex:1];
  detailViewController.choice = [NSString stringWithFormat:
  @"%@, Sub-Item #%d", self.choice, indexPath.row];
} else {
  ChoiceViewController *detailViewController = [[ChoiceViewController
    alloc] initWithNibName:@"ChoiceViewController" bundle:nil];
  detailViewController.choice = [NSString stringWithFormat:
    @"%@, Sub-Item #%d", self.choice, indexPath.row];

  // Pass the selected object to the new view controller.
  [self.navigationController pushViewController:detailViewController
    animated:YES];
  [detailViewController release];
}
}
```

Now you should be able to build and run the app, and see something closer to what we're shooting for. You can pick an item and a subitem, and your choice is displayed in the main view (and not inside the navigation view). However, this is still a bit off. That main view is just showing default dummy values (whatever you entered in Interface Builder) until the user selects something, and that's not what we want.

Let's enhance ChoiceViewController a bit, so that we can display something special for the no-selection state, before the user has navigated anywhere.

Enhancing the Main View with a No-Selection State

Basically, the new no-selection state will consist of hiding the labels at the top and bottom, and putting a special text in the large center label.

Start by adding two new outlets to the class definition *ChoiceViewController.h* so that we can access the top and bottom labels:

```
IBOutlet UILabel *topLabel;
IBOutlet UILabel *bottomLabel;
```

Now open *ChoiceViewController-iPad.xib*, and connect each of the new outlets by control-dragging from File's Owner to each of the labels and selecting the proper outlet. Save your changes, and go back to Xcode.

NOTE: If you're worried about the fact that the new outlets won't be used in the non-iPad version of the GUI, don't be! When this code runs on an iPhone and the iPhone version of the GUI is loaded, those unconnected outlets will simply be left as pointers to nil—no harm done.

Open *ChoiceViewController.m* to make a few quick changes. The first changes will be for the `viewWillAppear:` method, to make it display the appropriate content depending on whether or not the `choice` property is populated:

```
- (void)viewWillAppear:(BOOL)animated {
  [super viewWillAppear:animated];
  if (self.choice) {
    self.navigationItem.title = self.choice;
    choiceLabel.text = choice;
    topLabel.hidden = NO;
    bottomLabel.hidden = NO;
  } else {
    choiceLabel.text = @"Make your choice!";
    topLabel.hidden = YES;
    bottomLabel.hidden = YES;
  }
}
```

Next, we're going to implement the `setChoice:` method. So far, we've relied on the `@synthesized` version of this, but now that we need to update the display once the value is set, we should actually do something here.

```
- (void)setChoice:(NSString *)c {
  if (![c isEqual:choice]) {
    [choice release];
    choice = [c copy];
    self.navigationItem.title = self.choice;
    choiceLabel.text = choice;
    topLabel.hidden = NO;
    bottomLabel.hidden = NO;
  }
}
```

Note that we don't need to do anything here to handle the case where the new value for `choice` is `nil` (which would theoretically require us to once again put "Make your choice!" in the main label and hide the other labels), since in practice, this will never occur. The only time that `choice` is set is when the user has just selected something, and in this app, that "something" is never `nil`.

At this point, you should be able to run the app and see it working the way that we intended and that makes the most sense, without any surprises for the users. When you first launch the app, nothing is selected in the navigation view, and the main display reflects this. Once you select something, your selection sticks around in the main view until you navigate to something else. This is pretty much identical to the behavior of other iPad apps such as Mail, so users should feel right at home with another app that works this way.

Thanks to the way we've written the app, it should also continue to work on iPhone just as it used to. To launch your app on the Simulator in iPhone mode, the key is to build the app using the 3.2 target, then switch to the 3.1.3 (or other iPhone OS) target, and select Run ➤ Run from the menu.

Running on Multiple Targets

Earlier in this chapter, when you were first upgrading the NavApp iPhone project to include iPad support, you were given the choice to create a single, universal application or create separate targets for iPad and iPhone. We told you to go the universal route for NavApp, but what about the other option?

There are a number of reasons you may want to have separate iPhone and iPad apps. Maybe your application contains a lot of graphics at different sizes for the iPhone and iPad, and you want to keep the total file size down by eliminating iPhone-specific resources from the iPad version and vice versa. Or maybe you want to have separate products, with the iPad version including additional features and commanding a higher price, while still keeping everything in the same Xcode project.

Fortunately, those needs are easy to accommodate.

If you choose the multiple-target option when upgrading your project in Xcode, it really does most of the heavy lifting for you, and all the code changes you need to make can be done in the same way as you've seen here. In fact, if you were to start over with the original NavApp project, and upgrade it using the multiple-target option, you should be able make the exact same code and GUI changes described in this chapter and achieve the desired result: the ability to build different versions of the app for the iPhone and iPad. The only differences in the process are administrative in nature.

Using the multiple-target option, when creating a new resource such as an *.xib* file, you're prompted to pick which target or targets to include the resource in, so you need to make the appropriate choice there. And instead of just selecting a different Active SDK in the multipurpose pop-up control in Xcode to switch between launching the Simulator in iPad or iPhone mode, you need to select the target (iPhone or iPad) you want to execute. Otherwise, the steps are pretty similar to those described in this chapter. You can do the same sort of conditional coding, using the UI_USER_INTERFACE_IDIOM function to determine whether the app is running on an iPhone or iPad and adjusting accordingly. Sticking with this approach, rather than branching your code into separate projects, also makes things easier if you change your mind later. You can create a universal app without needing to also merge code bases that have diverged.

Juggling iDevices

In this chapter, you created a simple iPhone app from scratch, and then upgraded it to also work well on the iPad by creating some iPad-specific GUIs and using conditional coding to decide at runtime how the app should behave, depending on which platform it's running on. The code shown for tackling this situation is, of course, fitted to match the situation at hand. However, the strategies embodied by the code are general strategies for dealing with combined iPhone/iPad applications. No matter what sort of iPhone app you're dealing with, the lessons you've learned here should help you bring it to the iPad.

Chapter 12

Additional Resources for iPad Development

You've made your way through this book, mastering all of the new iPad features in the iPhone SDK. Are you ready for more? We've got you covered. This chapter points you to resources for additional iPad development assistance, handy programming tips, design aids, and other information.

Here, you'll find our own curated lists of recommended web sites, blogs, community forums, and books. Some of the links lead to commercial products, but most of the listed resources are free. The lists are by no means comprehensive, but they should serve as a helpful starting point for continuing your iPad development journey.

Logging in to the Mother Ship

As you might expect, the center of your iPhone and iPad universe is the Apple Developer Center. Your first stop in acquiring more iPad knowledge should be the vast online archive of developer documentation, sample code, and resources that Apple provides. Much of the primary documentation is available both online and as downloadable PDFs.

If you don't have time to comb through Apple's entire treasure trove of documentation, the essential must-read items for all iPad developers are the *iPad Programming Guide* and the *iPad Human Interface Guidelines*. These outline important tips and rules for creating high-quality iPad applications for the iTunes App Store.

NOTE: Some links may require logging into the iPhone Developer Program for access.

iPad Development

The Apple Developer Center offers the following iPad development documentation:

- *The iPhone OS Reference Library and Sample Code*: Available online at
  http://developer.apple.com/iphone/library/navigation/

- *iPad Programming Guide*: Available online at
  http://developer.apple.com/iphone/library/documentation/General/
  Conceptual/iPadProgrammingGuide/ and downloadable from
  http://developer.apple.com/iphone/library/documentation/General/
  Conceptual/iPadProgrammingGuide/iPadProgrammingGuide.pdf

- *iPad Human Interface Guidelines*: Available online at
  http://developer.apple.com/iphone/library/documentation/General/
  Conceptual/iPadHIG/ and downloadable from
  http://developer.apple.com/iphone/library/documentation/General/
  Conceptual/iPadHIG/iPadHIG.pdf

- *Introduction to Creating Universal Applications:*
  http://devimages.apple.com/iphone/resources/introductiontouniversalapps.
  pdf

Objective-C and Cocoa Touch

The Apple Developer Center offers the following Objective-C and Cocoa Touch
documentation:

- *Objective-C Programming Language Reference*: Available online at
  http://developer.apple.com/iphone/library/documentation/Cocoa/
  Conceptual/ObjectiveC/ and downloadable from
  http://developer.apple.com/iphone/library/documentation/Cocoa/
  Conceptual/ObjectiveC/ObjC.pdf

- *Cocoa Fundamentals Guide*: Available online at
  http://developer.apple.com/iphone/library/documentation/Cocoa/
  Conceptual/CocoaFundamentals/ and downloadable from
  http://developer.apple.com/iphone/library/documentation/Cocoa/
  Conceptual/CocoaFundamentals/CocoaFundamentals.pdf

- *UIKit Framework Reference:* Available online at
  http://developer.apple.com/iphone/library/documentation/UIKit/
  Reference/UIKit_Framework/ and downloadable from
  http://developer.apple.com/iphone/library/documentation/UIKit/
  Reference/UIKit_Framework/UIKit_Framework.pdf

iPad App Deployment

The following are Apple resources for iPad App deployment:

- iPhone Provisioning Portal User Guide for App Testing and Ad-Hoc Distribution: http://developer.apple.com/iphone/manage/overview/index.action

- iTunes Connect Developer Guide: http://itunesconnect.apple.com/docs/iTunesConnect_DeveloperGuide.pdf

- App Store Resource Center: https://developer.apple.com/iphone/appstore/

- News and Announcements for iPhone App Developers: https://developer.apple.com/iphone/news/

Learning from the Experts

Wading through Apple's dense sea of online documentation can sometimes feel like searching for a needle in a haystack. Books provide a more focused, structured approach to learning specific topics. You can also get valuable information from the blogs and web sites of leading app developers.

> **Note:** All of the code examples listed in this book, along with the full source code of the iPad drawing app, Dudel, can be downloaded from
> http://www.apress.com/book/view/9781430230212.

Books

Apress offers many comprehensive books on Objective-C, Cocoa Touch, and iPhone and iPad development, including the following:

- *Beginning iPhone and iPad Development with SDK 4: Exploring the iPhone SDK* by Jack Nutting, Dave Mark, and Jeff LaMarche (http://www.apress.com/book/view/9781430230243)

- *More iPhone and iPad Development: Further Explorations of the iPhone SDK* by Jack Nutting, Dave Mark, and Jeff LaMarche (http://www.apress.com/book/view/9781430232520)

- *The Business of iPhone App Development: Making and Marketing Apps that Succeed* by Dave Wooldridge with Michael Schneider (http://www.apress.com/book/view/9781430227335)

- *Building iPhone OS Accessories: Use the iPhone Accessories API to Control and Monitor Devices* by Ken Maskrey (http://www.apress.com/book/view/9781430229315)

Tutorials and Code Examples

The following are some of our favorite blogs and web sites, which offer helpful tutorials, example projects, and code snippets for iPad apps:

- iCodeBlog app programming tutorials (http://icodeblog.com/)

- Dr. Touch's development blog (http://www.drobnik.com/touch/)

- Games from Within, indie iPhone/iPad game development (http://gamesfromwithin.com/)

- iPhoneDev Central (http://www.iphonedevcentral.com/)

- iPhoneFlow Development Community Links (http://www.iphoneflow.com/)

- iPhone Development Bits (http://iphonedevelopmentbits.com/)

- iPhone Developer Tips (http://iphonedevelopertips.com/)

- iPhone Dev FAQ (http://www.iphonedevfaq.com/)

- iPhone Development Blog (http://iphoneincubator.com/blog/)

- Jeff LaMarche's iPhone development blog (http://iphonedevelopment.blogspot.com/)

- Majic Jungle's development blog (http://majicjungle.com/blog/)

- ManicDev's iPhone and iPad SDK development tutorials and tips (http://maniacdev.com/)

- Mark Johnson's developer blog (http://www.markj.net/)

- Matt Legend Gemmell's blog (http://mattgemmell.com/)

- Ray Wenderlich's developer blog (http://www.raywenderlich.com/)

Designing User Interfaces for iPad Apps

It should go without saying that an attractive, intuitive, easy-to-use interface is a major key to the success of your iPad app. And beyond the importance of usability, the iPad's large screen demands a beautiful, visual experience. To help you in this quest, we've listed links to several time-saving templates, graphics collections, and design tools.

> **NOTE:** If you haven't read Apple's *iPad Human Interface Guidelines* yet, do yourself a favor and check it out. Not only does it offer essential design tips and recommendations for building effective user interfaces, but following Apple's guidelines can also help prevent UI-related rejections when submitting your iPad application to the iTunes App Store.

Paper Prototyping

The following are some paper prototyping products for iPad app design:

- Kapsoft's iPad Stencil (http://www.mobilesketchbook.com/)
- *iPad Application Sketch Book* by Dean Kaplan (http://www.apress.com/book/view/9781430232049)
- *The Developer Sketchbook for iPad Apps* by Dave Wooldridge (http://developersketchbook.com/)
- UI Stencils' iPad Stencil Kit (http://www.uistencils.com/products/ipad-stencil-kit)

Digital Mockups

The following digital templates are available for iPad app design:

- Endloop's iMockups (http://www.imockups.com/)
- Balsamiq Mockups (http://www.balsamiq.com/products/mockups/)
- Briefs, a Cocoa Touch framework for live wireframes (http://giveabrief.com/)
- Teehan+Lax's iPad GUI PSD, for Photoshop (http://www.teehanlax.com/blog/2010/02/01/ipad-gui-psd/)
- Kevin Andersson's iPad editable PSD, for Photoshop (http://blog.kevinandersson.dk/2010/01/29/apple-ipad-fully-editable-psd/)
- RawApps' iPad GUI Kit PSD, for Photoshop (http://www.rawapps.com/849/ipad-gui-kit-in-psd-format-is-here/)
- Iconshock's iPad vector GUI elements, for Illustrator (http://iconlibrary.iconshock.com/icons/ipad-vector-gui-elements-tabs-buttons-menus-icons/)
- Dave Morford's iPhone/iPad stencil, for OmniGraffle (http://www.morford.org/iphoneosdesignstencil/)
- iA's iPad Stencil, for OmniGraffle (http://informationarchitects.jp/ipad-stencil-for-omnigraffle/)

User Interface Icons

Here are some places where you can find icons for iPad apps:

- app-bits iPhone Toolbar Icon Set (http://www.app-bits.com/downloads/iphone-toolbar-icon-set.html)

- Cocoia blog's iPhone/iPad icon PSD, for Photoshop (http://blog.cocoia.com/2010/iphone-ipad-icon-psd-template/)

- Dezinerfolio vector icons (http://www.dezinerfolio.com/freebie/30-free-vector-icons)

- eddit iPhone UI Icon Set (http://eddit.com/shop/iphone_ui_icon_set/)

- Glyphish icons for iPhone and iPad apps (http://glyphish.com/)

- iconSweets Photoshop icons (http://www.iconsweets.com/)

- PixelPressIcon Whitespace Icon Collection (http://www.pixelpressicons.com/?page_id=118)

- RawApps iPad icon set (http://www.rawapps.com/4905/rawapps-com-launches-ipad-icon-set-ver-1-download-it-today/)

- The Working Group's iPhone toolbar icons (http://blog.twg.ca/2009/09/free-iphone-toolbar-icons/)

Design Considerations and Inspirations

Learn more about iPad interface design from these resources:

- Matt Legend Gemmell's observations on iPad application design (http://mattgemmell.com/2010/03/05/ipad-application-design)

- *Smashing Magazine*'s "Useful Design Tips for Your iPad App" (http://www.smashingmagazine.com/2010/04/16/design-tips-for-your-ipad-app/)

- iA's "Designing for iPad: Reality Check" "(http://informationarchitects.jp/designing-for-ipad-reality-check/)

- Landing Pad—A Showcase of Beautiful iPad App Design (http://landingpad.org/)

- iPad Apps That Don't Suck (http://ipadappsthatdontsuck.com/)

- *Touch Gesture Reference Guide* (http://www.lukew.com/touch/)

Finding Answers in Online Forums

What if you need a little one-on-one help? Thankfully, the iPhone and iPad developer community members are very generous and willing to share their wealth of knowledge online for the greater good of the group.

> **NOTE:** What goes around comes around. If people take the time to provide you with assistance, be sure to pay it forward by replying to posted questions if you know the answers.

Here are a few popular web forums worth visiting:

- The Official Book Forum for Beginning iPad Development, and Beginning iPhone Development and More iPhone Development (http://iphonedevbook.com/forum/)

- Apple Developer Forums (https://devforums.apple.com/community/iphone) iPhone Developer Program login required

- iPhone Dev SDK Forum (http://www.iphonedevsdk.com/)

- iDevApps iPhone and iPad Programming Forum (http://www.idevapps.com/forum/)

- iPhone Dev Forums (http://www.iphonedevforums.com/)

- iDevGames iPhone and iPad Game Developers Forum (http://www.idevgames.com/forum/)

- Mac Rumors iPhone/iPad Programming Forum (http://forums.macrumors.com/forumdisplay.php?f=135)

- Stack Overflow, collaborative questions and answers for programmers (http://stackoverflow.com/)

Holding the Future

Congratulations on working your way through each and every chapter as we tackled all of the new iPad features in the iPhone SDK. We certainly covered a lot of ground, so you should now feel confident in creating your own iPad apps. And this is just the beginning. We can't wait to see what cool new features Apple has in store for future versions of its wildly popular iPad tablet. Until then, thanks for reading!

Index

Special Characters

Lines property, UILabel class, 182
#import statement, 107

A

About panels, implementing
   creating Modal Web View Controllers,
      186
   displaying web pages, 187
   integrating with Dudel View Controllers,
      188–189
   overview, 185
actions
   edit menu, 56
   menu, PDF-sending, 210–211
   wiring, 30–31
actionsMenuButton outlet, 211
ActionsMenuController class, 178, 210
activate method, 197
Active SDK, choosing, 226–227
addCurveToPoint method, 42
addGestureRecognizer method, 59, 194
addLineToPoint method, 42
alert sheet, 48
Alm, Daniel, 57
amazonSite button, 186
app delegates, changing, 173–178
app icon images, 64
Apple Developer Center, 240
application:didFinishLaunchingWithOptions:
      method, 217
applications
   designing user interfaces for
      design considerations and
        inspirations, 244
      digital mockups, 243
      overview, 242
      paper prototyping, 243

      user interface icons, 244
   developing
      1Password Pro, 11
      Brushes, 8–11
      ScribattlePad, 14
      Synotes, 12–14
      vs iPhone apps, 7–8
   improving usability with UIKit, 35–37
   iPad, required project images for
      app icon images, 64
      default launch images, 65–66
      document type icon images, 65
   iPhone vs. iPad, 7–8
   optimizing for iPad
      memory, 40–41
      tablets, 39–40
      testing, 41–42
   passing files to
      adding PDF-sending menu action,
        210–211
      invoking Document Interaction
        Controller, 212–213
      overview, 209
      preparing files for sending, 211
   universal
      advantages of, 63
      requirements of, 61–62
applicationWillTerminate: method, 176
apressSite button, 186
architecture, drawing, 74–76
attribute inspector, Interface Builder, 28,
      152, 186
attributedStringFromMarkup: method, 115–
      116
availableModes method, 157

B

beta versions, of SDK, 21–23
Bezier paths, 67–68

247

E

F

Synthesis Lectures on Professionalism and Career Advancement for Scientists and Engineers

Editors

Charles X Ling, University of Western Ontario
Qiang Yang, Hong Kong University of Science and Technology

A Handbook for Analytical Writing: Keys to Strategic Thinking
William E. Winner
2013
A Practical Guide to Gender Diversity for CS Professors
Diana Franklin
2013

A Handbook for Analytical Writing: Keys to Strategic Thinking
William E. Winner

ISBN: 978-3-031-01379-9 print
ISBN: 978-3-031-02507-5 ebook

DOI 10.1007/978-3-031-02507-5

A Publication in the Spinger series
SYNTHESIS LECTURES ON PROFESSIONALISM AND CAREER ADVANCEMENT FOR SCIENTISTS AND ENGINEERS
Lecture #1
Series Editor: Charles X Ling, University of Western Ontario, and Qiang Yang, Hong Kong University of Science and Technology

Series ISSN Pending